Remembering Child Migration

ALSO AVAILABLE FROM BLOOMSBURY

Christianity and the University Experience,
by Mathew Guest, Kristin Aune, Sonya Sharma and Rob Warner

Remembering Child Migration

Faith, Nation-Building and the Wounds of Charity

Gordon Lynch

Bloomsbury Academic
An imprint of Bloomsbury Publishing Plc

B L O O M S B U R Y
LONDON · OXFORD · NEW YORK · NEW DELHI · SYDNEY

Bloomsbury Academic

An imprint of Bloomsbury Publishing Plc

50 Bedford Square
London
WC1B 3DP
UK

1385 Broadway
New York
NY 10018
USA

www.bloomsbury.com

**BLOOMSBURY and the Diana logo are trademarks of
Bloomsbury Publishing Plc**

First published 2016

British Library Cataloguing-in-Publication Data
A catalogue record for this book is available from the British Library.

ISBN: HB: 978-1-4725-9115-9
PB: 978-1-4725-9112-8
ePDF: 978-1-4725-9116-6
ePub: 978-1-4725-9117-3

Library of Congress Cataloging-in-Publication Data
A catalog record for this book is available from the Library of Congress.

Typeset by Newgen Knowledge Works (P) Ltd., Chennai, India
Printed and bound in Great Britain

In memory of Francesca, with love and gratitude

You have homes and schools of training: take these
children from the street;
Show them what God meant they should be; clear a
pathway for their feet.
Make them feel that work is noble; teach them what their
lives may be;
Then we'll give them a hearty welcome to our homes
across the sea.

'Canada's Plea for the "Waifs and Strays"',
poem published in Dr Barnardo's Homes magazine,
Night and Day, June 1884.

CONTENTS

ILLUSTRATIONS

Figures

Tables

ACKNOWLEDGEMENTS

This book has benefitted from conversations with many people to whom I am much indebted. Staff at the Child Migrants Trust were generous with their time and insights, with my particular thanks to Mervyn Humphreys, Ian Thwaites and Pauline Mace. The project was significantly helped by the generosity and hospitality of staff at a number of different institutional archives including the Salvation Army International Heritage Centre, the Together Trust, Barnardo's, the University of Liverpool, CCS (Westminster), the Church of England Record Centre and the Archdiocesan archives at Westminster and Birmingham. Steph Berns and Sarah Hutton both undertook invaluable work in copying archival materials for me at different stages in the project. Steven Spencer and Ruth McDonald at the Salvation Army International Heritage Centre were very helpful in following up on additional archival queries that I had. Martine King at Barnardo's and Liz Sykes at the Together Trust were very generous with their time in talking through the histories of the work in which their organizations had been involved. Rosemary Keenan at CCS (Westminster) helpfully pointed me to additional resources for this project. Stephen Constantine and Roy Parker have been a great help to this project both in sharing their own detailed knowledge of the history of these child migration schemes and thinking about how they might best be evaluated today. Anna Strhan, Mervyn Humphreys and Shai Dromi also generously provided comments on earlier drafts of this work. Any subsequent failings in the book are my sole responsibility as author. It is in the nature of writing on a complex issue such as this that some readers may find my account contentious, sometimes for very different reasons. This book is offered in the spirit of trying to encourage further conversation about how we reflect on the legacy of these migration schemes.

Research for this project was undertaken in conjunction with my role as academic curator for a major exhibition on the British child migration schemes at the V&A Museum of Childhood in London in 2015/16. I'm very grateful to colleagues at the museum, including Rhian Harris, Esther Lutman, Stephen Nicholls, Sophie Sage and Andrea Cunningham for all that I learned from them through this process. Lalle Pursglove at Bloomsbury has been an enthusiastic and patient editor, and I'm also grateful to Anna MacDiarmid and Lucy Carroll for all their help through the production process. As ever Duna and Hani have been wonderfully supportive through this process, and my love and thanks continue to go to them as well, now, as Sami.

Towards the start of this project, a close friend, Francesca Carnevali died after bravely fighting a long illness. She was a profound inspiration and joy to many people and taken far too soon from us. This book is dedicated to her memory and to her conviction that remembering the past well and maintaining concern for justice today are (along with good food and good friendship) among the most important things to which we can give our life.

ABBREVIATIONS OF ARCHIVAL SOURCES

B	Barnardo's archives, Plaistow, London.
BA	Archdiocese of Birmingham archives, Birmingham.
CCS	CCS (Westminster) archives, Ladbroke Grove, London.
CE	Church of England Record Centre, Bermondsey, London.
F	Fairbridge Society archives, University of Liverpool.
MCA	Manchester Central Archives, Manchester.
NA	National Archives, Kew, Surrey.
NY	New York Historical Library, New York.
SA	Salvation Army archives, Salvation Army International Heritage Centre, Denmark Hill, London.
SC	Simmons College library, Boston, Massachusetts.
TT	Together Trust archives, Cheadle/Manchester Central Archives.
W	Archdiocese of Westminster archives, South Kensington, London.

Introduction

In one of Astrid Lindgren's Pippi Longstocking stories, two policemen visit Pippi to tell her that she can no longer live in her house by herself and must come with them to be put in a children's home.[1] After establishing that she would not be able to take her pet horse and monkey with her, Pippi politely informs the policemen that they will have to find other children to put in the children's home because she has no intention of going. The policemen challenge her about the problems she will face in later life if she doesn't go to school to learn about maths and geography. Pippi responds that she has got through her nine years of life without knowing about plutification tables and that if she lies in bed worrying about not knowing what the capital of Portugal is, then, well one has to accept that life is hard. A chase ensues in which the policemen try to catch Pippi, get stuck on Pippi's roof and when she frees them from there they try to carry her off. Their attempt is foiled though as Pippi picks both of them up instead and deposits them on the road outside her front gate. The policemen retreat sheepishly and decide to tell the people of the village that Pippi doesn't need to go into a children's home after all and is managing quite happily as she is.

The appeal of Pippi Longstocking as a character lies in her ability to subvert the expectations and norms of the adult world, a point continually reinforced by the ways in which her unconventional life opens up new pleasures into the domesticized lives of the children living next door to her, Tommy and Annika. The narrative device that enables Pippi to do this is that she is the strongest girl in the world, capable of physically resisting any attempts by adults to control her life – as the two policemen humiliatingly discover.

The whimsy of this imaginative world is precisely that it subverts the reality of children's lives. Children are less physically strong than adults and unable to resist physical restraint or violence.[2] They are largely dependent on adults for both physical and emotional nurture.[3] Consequently their lives are played out in the context of restraints and intentions that adults have for them. As Henry Jenkins has observed, the notion that children exist in a realm of innocence beyond the adult world obscures the ways in which children's lives are always lived out in the context of the various cultural and political projects that adults pursue in relation to them.[4]

This book is concerned with one such adult project for children's lives, the organized migration of children, unaccompanied by parents or adult relatives.[5] Conceived as a way of giving children better futures and making them better people, child migration schemes grew significantly in the United Kingdom and the United States, where more than 300,000 children were re-located away from birth parents and home communities between 1851 and 1970. In the American schemes, children were sent to states across the East, South and mid-West.[6] Most children migrated through the mass UK schemes that began in 1869 were sent to Canada, with several thousand sent to Australia and hundreds also sent to New Zealand and the former Southern Rhodesia.

Child migration schemes are remarkable from a contemporary perspective because the idea of sending children far away from their home communities as a mass form of welfare provision is so alien to current understandings of good standards of child-care.[7] As the chief executive of Barnardos, the charity that sent more children overseas than any other British organization, put it in his evidence to the 1998 UK Parliament Health Select Committee Inquiry, 'it was barbaric; it was dreadful. We look back on it . . . with shock and horror'.[8] The removal of children from their birth family and local community is now only countenanced in cases where authorities consider there to be a compelling justification on grounds of child protection. It is also controversially justified by some people still in the context of trans-national adoption, where communities overseas can still be subject to the same moral assumptions about the benefits of child removal as poor urban communities were in Britain and the United States by child migration organizations.[9] Public memories of these child migration schemes today range from outright censure to accounts of them as flawed projects, justifiable only in terms of the context of welfare provision, social problems and child-care practice of their time.

Child migration schemes constitute a challenge because they are a relatively recent part of the history of child-care. Although the last 'orphan train' party left New York in 1929, the UK child migration schemes persisted well past the Second World War with small numbers of child migrants continuing to be sent to Australia until 1970. The effects of these schemes are still felt not only by an estimated two thousand former child migrants alive today,[10] but in many cases by their original birth families, as well as their spouses, children and grandchildren with whom their relationships have been affected by earlier experiences of trauma. Remembering these child migration schemes is important not only for trying to understand their place in our recent history and their ongoing legacies, but because these schemes form part of a much wider modern history of out-of-home care for children that has become the focus of critical re-assessment, apologies and, in some cases, official redress schemes. Over the last twenty years, there have been major inquiries or truth commissions on the abuse and neglect of children in out-of-home care in Australia, Canada, Ireland, Norway, Sweden, Iceland, Denmark, Germany and the United Kingdom,[11] not including specialist national or institutional inquiries into sexual abuse.[12] Forms of out-of-home care addressed by these reports include foster care and residential homes run by local authorities, industrial and reformatory schools run by religious organizations and forms of fostering, adoption and residential schools developed in the context of assimilationist policies towards minority indigenous groups such as First Nations peoples in Canada and Aboriginal people in Australia. Similar accounts of physical and sexual abuse, humiliation, material and emotional neglect and isolation have been documented in these other forms of out-of-home care as in accounts of some former child migrants' accounts of their experiences.

Against this wider background, this book addresses a specific question. How can we understand the relationship between the moral cultures of these schemes and the suffering that many child migrants experienced through them? Some initial explanation is necessary as to why this question is worth asking.[13]

First, it is important to recognize that the child migration schemes analysed in this book were moral projects as well as practical attempts to help children deemed to be 'deprived of a normal family life'[14] through poverty, parental ill-health or death, or family breakdown. Their pioneers, workers and supporters represented them as ways of removing children from the moral dangers of corrupting family environments, urban slums or life on the streets to place them in new, redemptive environments. Here they would flourish not just emotionally and materially, but in personal, civic and spiritual virtues as well. Public advocacy for these schemes was most commonly made on the basis of moral grounds such as alleviating the suffering of needy children, rescuing them from corruption and building up a better nation or empire. Utilitarian arguments about avoiding the financial and social costs of children liable to fall into criminality or pauperism only tended to be made when appeals to shared religious or humanitarian sentiments appeared to fall on deaf ears. External criticisms were rebutted by arguments about the moral importance of the work and the rectitude of those involved in it. Child migrants, too, generally had a clear understanding of the moral expectations being placed upon them, in terms of deference, hard work and personal piety, regardless of whether they lived up to this or not. There are other important ways in which the child migration schemes can helpfully be thought about beyond these moral dimensions, such as Joy Parr's economic analysis of how child migration from Britain to Canada operated.[15] But any full understanding of these schemes needs to take account of the moral claims, symbolism, emotions and expectations that were woven through their work.

To make this point is to reject the idea that the moral claims and emotions surrounding these schemes were simply an ideological veneer, obscuring the underlying economic interests in those running them in securing a deferential, cheap and productive work-force.[16] To see these schemes simply as an expression of economic interests is far too crude a way to understand the motivations of those involved in them. Some initiatives appear to have been run in order to maximize income from the work.[17] But it was more common for child migration organizations to operate with limited budgets and make little or no profit. In several cases they operated with substantial deficits and sporadic funding crises.[18] Indeed their low level of resources contributed precisely to the poor conditions and overreliance on their labour that many child migrants experienced. Those involved in running these schemes also often invested substantial time and energy undertaking difficult work in managing large groups of children. Moral commitments were of course not the only factor that led people to undertake or support this work. Some were engaged in it because they were placed in this role by an organization, such as a religious order, in which they had little autonomy. Others undertook this work because they had little opportunity in their particular life-circumstances but to accept low-paid positions in organizations who accepted untrained staff, such as cottage-mothers in the Fairbridge farm schools. But many were nevertheless motivated by the sense that they were undertaking morally important work, often understood in terms of following the loving example of Christ or preserving the integrity of the Church. The moral cultures of these schemes shaped the ideas, feelings, relationships and practices of those involved in them as workers or children, and framed the ways in which they were presented to others outside the schemes, whether supporters or critics.

These moral cultures cannot simply be reduced to the 'values' of those who ran or supported these schemes. The notion of 'values' is often taken to mean a moral conviction which determines someone's thoughts or actions in a clear and consistent way.[19] Within some of the historical literature on the child migration schemes this has led, for example, to approaches which focus on the values and beliefs of individual pioneers on the assumption that the working methods of their organizations could be interpreted primarily as the product of their personal beliefs and convictions.[20] In reality, the status of a person or group's moral commitments are far less clear than this. The moral reasons that people give for their choices and actions can be very partial or inaccurate representations of factors that have actually motivated them, which can often be beyond their awareness. Organizational practices also arise out of a more complex range of factors and networks of relationships than just the driving vision of a leader. It may be more useful, then, to think about moral meanings not as inner convictions resting in the individual conscience, but in ways of communicating to ourselves and others about the worlds we live in.[21] These interpret the social world in terms of the good or the bad, or more profoundly between sacred moral realities and the corrupting, polluting evils that threaten to profane them. Thought of as a particular form of social communication, it takes a variety of forms and can be put to different ends. It renders choices, feelings and actions meaningful to ourselves and others by creating a story about how they relate to good or evil. It can be used to defend or legitimize claims or actions that are unusual or open to criticism. It categorizes things and people, establishing what falls within the acceptable moral boundaries of society and what falls beyond. Internalized, it provides a means through which an individual has a sense of themselves as succeeding or failing as a particular kind of ethical person or can develop projects of ethical self-development. Collectively, it can provide a symbolic focus around which a group experiences a strong sense of moral solidarity or generate a sense of a moral ethos in which particular actions appear obvious, reasonable and good. In short, acts of moral communication play a variety of roles in social life, far more complex than simply action-directing convictions. They can be found across all domains of social life, including those where public communication plays a central role such as politics, the media and the representation of public organizations. Thinking in these terms opens up a much wider range of questions about such communication of moral meanings. In what contexts is it used? To what ends is it put? What does it make possible or shut down in terms of people's interactions with themselves and others? What effects does it have? How is good and evil, the sacred and the profane, being imagined? It is these questions about how moral communication works as a particular form of social and cultural activity that underpin the approach this book takes to interpreting the child migration schemes as moral projects.[22]

This book does not simply aim to add to our understanding of how the moral cultures of institutional projects for the care of children operate, but to address the more specific question of how such moral cultures can be implicated in children's suffering. It is important from the outset to say that this question does not imply that all child migration schemes were unequivocally damaging to every child exposed to them, or that children experienced harm in the same ways across all of the schemes. Child migrants' experiences were very different, partly reflecting the variety of ways in which child migration schemes operated. Previous family and social backgrounds, the nature and extent of ongoing contact with family members, the type of household or residential institution in which a child was placed and the kindness, indifference or cruelty of those charged with their care all had significant bearings on the child migrant's experience.[23] The fact that workers who were actively abusive to some child migrants were sometimes regarded with respect or affection by others also makes it more difficult to think about a unified experience among child migrants.[24] While many former child migrants have spoken poignantly about the effects of family separation or loss, neglect, abuse and exploitative institutional regimes on their lives, others have defended their experience of the schemes, claiming that they did offer them better prospects or 'toughened them up' for adult life. When writing about suffering caused by the child migration schemes, my intent is not then to paint a simplistic picture of the child migrant experience or even to attempt the impossible task of quantifying how much good the schemes did relative to their harm.[25] It is simply to recognize that suffering was caused by the schemes in ways that had significant effects on many people's lives, and to ask how this suffering related to the claims of child migration as a moral project of child rescue and redemption. To examine the wounds of charity is not merely of historical interest in relation to these schemes. As will be argued later in the book, these schemes operated through a humanitarian piety which remains a powerful source of motivation and legitimation for charitable and development work today. Attempting to understand the shadow-side of this humanitarian ethos is not a concern that is unique to this book.[26] But given that this ethos remains morally potent in public life today, it is important to understand how moral sentiments that seem so unimpeachable can contribute to suffering while claiming to alleviate it.

The focus of this book is different to that of previous studies of these child migration schemes. Most previous work has been primarily concerned with historical analysis. Several books have been written for a wider readership present historical narratives of child migration organizations and the experiences of child migrants. Academic work has sought to provide more detailed histories of individual schemes and to situate child migration in the wider context of imperial migration, policy and politics, as well as in its broader social and economic setting. This work almost always includes an explicit or implicit evaluation of these schemes, typically adopting a more critical perspective on them than taken by their earlier supporters.

This book's concern with the damaging effects of these schemes is not therefore unusual in the historiography of child migration. By addressing a number of different schemes, however, rather than a single one, it will clarify significant differences between them, not simply in the ways in which they operated, but the ways in which children suffered through them. Previous studies have also done excellent work in clarifying the organizational policies and conditions that were harmful to child migrants, and this book builds on many of those insights. However these critical evaluations of child migration work have not yet addressed the question of how we might understand the relationship between this suffering and the moral claims, assumptions and emotions that suffused this work.[27] Child migration schemes undoubtedly exposed children to some adults who were wilfully abusive to them. But for many, suffering occurred through acts of omission, through the failure of adults to see clearly enough how a moral project to save and improve children's lives could fail them. Such sins of omission are not unique to those who undertook child migration work, but a more common part of the human condition, a risk inherent in any project to do good in the world. If we adopt a critical gaze to the shadow-side of their work, we will learn less of value if we depict the child migration schemes simply as a distant wrong, committed by people less wise or good than ourselves. Doing that might burnish our sense of moral integrity, but provides little insight into our own moral ambiguities. We would do better to ask how we might be repeating their failings in different ways today.

The book begins, in Chapter 1, by situating the emergence of mass child migration work in the broader context of growing interest in the nineteenth century in removing children from social environments deemed to be bad for their physical, social and moral development. It then turns its attention to the development of mass child migration schemes in the East Coast of America, focusing particularly on the practices and moral cultures of the largest scheme of its kind run by the New York Children's Aid Society.

Chapter 2 discusses the rise of British child migration schemes to Canada from 1869, which were directly inspired by the American 'orphan trains'. The schemes are considered against the background of shifting attitudes more generally during the nineteenth century in Britain towards the use of assisted migration as a way of dealing with social problems associated with poverty. The notion that child migration was a widely accepted practice in the late Victorian period is challenged through a discussion of the 1875 Doyle report which made widespread criticisms of early British schemes to Canada, some of which were never adequately addressed in subsequent decades. Charting the proliferation of British child migration schemes to Canada by the 1880s, the chapter considers the varying moral rationales for the work, noting the strong central emphasis on it as a form of humanitarian rescue for children in the context of a failing Poor Law welfare system. It concludes by discussing how child migration to Canada largely came to an end by 1924 following increasing criticism of it in Canada and the UK government's Bondfield report which recommended the end of unaccompanied migration of children under the school-leaving age of 14.

Chapter 3 examines how child migration schemes to Australia grew significantly as schemes to Canada were being wound down. The role of Kingsley Fairbridge is discussed in opening up mass child migration to Australia in the early twentieth century, in the context of growing Australian interest in attracting British immigrants. The paradoxical decisions by the British government to ban child migration to Canada while providing financial support for it to Australia is explained in terms of the relatively weak opposition to child migration within the British government as well as the ability of charities involved in child migration to mobilize establishment support for their work. Again, the notion of child migration as a widely accepted form of child-care in the past is challenged through a discussion of growing criticisms of these schemes after the Second World War. Particular attention is paid here to the 1956 Ross report which provided a clear account of the failings of child migration work to Australia. Internal divisions within the British government, and fear of alienating both the Australian government and the churches and charities involved in this work, meant that no decisive action was taken following the Ross report, with its findings released in such

a way as to minimize any public impact. Chapter 3 concludes by offering
a broader comparison of the British and American schemes considered
in this book. Considerable variations can be found in the experiences of
individual child migrants across this history. But while recognizing these,
the chapter argues that it is possible to see stronger similarities between the
American child emigration programmes and British child migration work
to Canada, than between British schemes to Canada and Australia. There
were some notable differences in working methods between the American
and British schemes to Canada, and comparison of them also shows the
more important role that national government played in the British case
compared to the American one. But there were also substantial similarities
in the moral and religious framing of this work, criticisms made of it from
the 1870s onwards and the strong belief across these schemes in the value
of raising children in private households rather than residential institutions.
By contrast, child migration work to Australia appeared to take little note
of concerns raised in the 1924 Bondfield report, and reversed the previous
emphasis of raising child migrants in family homes by placing them almost
entirely in children's homes in Australia. The greater willingness of some
child migration organizations in the earlier period to maintain contact
between family members was also less evident in several later schemes to
Australia that sought a stronger separation between child migrants and
their surviving family members back in Britain. The notion that child-care
practice is a progressive movement towards ever more enlightened standards
is therefore challenged by the ways in which the practices of much later child
migration work to Australia were in many significant respects less sensitive
to children's emotional lives.

Building on the discussion of these initial chapters, Chapter 4 then
directly addresses the central question of how the moral cultures of these
schemes were implicated in child migrants' suffering. Again, the range of
child migrants' experiences are recognized as is the problem of implicitly
constructing child migrants' lives as being free from suffering before they
were sent overseas. Nevertheless, the chapter argues that in different ways
the American and British child migration schemes caused additional trauma
to already vulnerable children by putting them in contexts where they
lacked strong and supportive social bonds, were exposed to humiliation and
shame and experienced painful basic constraints on their autonomy. While
recognizing the range of factors that gave rise to such suffering, including the
economic basis on which the schemes operated, ineffective supervision and
inadequate selection of staff and placements, the schemes' moral cultures
also helped to create the contexts in which such suffering became possible.
The humanitarian piety on which the schemes were grounded reinforced a
sense of moral certainty around the work for many of those undertaking
it, created wider bonds of trust and legitimacy around it and constructed
relationships between adults and child migrants in particular ways. While
this humanitarian piety had a more ambivalent effect on interactions between

adults and children in these schemes than some contemporary critiques of humanitarian culture might suggest, the desire to alleviate children's suffering in these schemes undoubtedly operated in ways that led to further harm.

In the final chapter, the book considers how the humanitarian sentiments which gave rise to these schemes continue to shape public memories of them today. In the absence of effective criminal and civil prosecutions in cases of the direct abuse of child migrants, public inquiries and apologies have sought to provide a symbolic restitution through public acknowledgement of former child migrants' suffering. While this desire to make this restitution reflects the humanitarian impulse to relieve others' suffering, it can also be problematic if it impedes criminal or civil justice, simplifies complex historical realities or creates an illusory public sense of resolution not shared by former child migrants themselves. Churches and charities involved in child migration work have generally acknowledged problems associated with it. At the same time, some have sought to deal with this legacy in ways that protect public support for their ongoing humanitarian work today by symbolically situating this work in a morally distant past, minimizing problematic aspects of it or claiming it (unjustifiably) as based on standards of child-care appropriate to its time. The book concludes by calling for a more open discussion of the legacy of these schemes, in which the persistence of child migration in the face of criticisms of it may have valuable lessons for us about how the humanitarian desire to relieve suffering may similarly operate in ways that cause harm today.

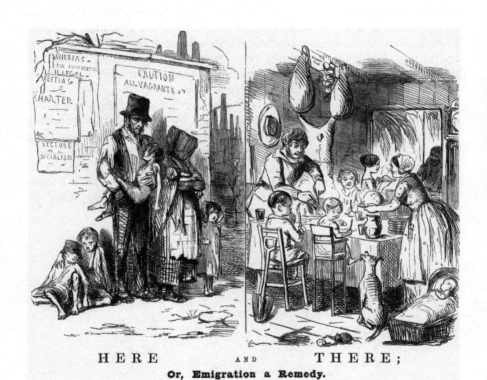

HERE AND THERE;

Or, Emigration a Remedy.

1

'The humane remedy': America and the development of mass child migration[1]

In 1618, the first organized party of a hundred child migrants was sent by the City of London at the request of the Virginia Company, 'for the better supply of the colony'.[2] If these children were seen as much-needed sources of labour in an underpopulated colony, they were equally regarded as a burden by public authorities charged with their care. Fearing that the growing, poor population of London would 'like too much blood, infect the whole city with plague and poverty', the Lord Mayor, Sir George Bolles, readily approved the Virginia Company's request. Until the nineteenth century, however, such child migration parties were sporadic and lacked the sustained organizational structure of the later child migration schemes. Alongside these early forms of officially sanctioned child migration, notorious cases also came to public attention of the abduction of children from Britain who were then put to work in American colonies. Peter Williamson's account of his kidnapping as a child from Aberdeen for sale in Philadelphia in the 1730s was a popular example of this, with his memoirs still being published in their twentieth edition in 1878.[3]

In the nineteenth century, however, child migration began to be seen not simply as a useful means of reducing the financial demands of poor relief or meeting the labour needs of underpopulated colonies but as something that would benefit child migrants themselves. This reflected a growing interest internationally[4] in the idea that relocating poor children to more healthy moral and physical environments could greatly improve their future prospects, both as citizens and workers in this world and their eternal souls in the next. In 1830, the Reformatory School of Prince Carl in Stockholm bought an island in the Stockholm archipelago, whose tenant farmers were then required to accept children from the school in an early form of boarding out.[5] In the same year in Britain, the Children's Friend Society was established which subsequently sent around 660 children to Australia, South Africa and Canada until 1842 when public concerns about the treatment of the child migrants overseas curtailed its work.[6] In 1849, the Ragged School Union received funding from the British Government to send 150 of its children to Australia.[7] At the same time, in Germany, the Christian charity, the Inner Mission, was moving children from poor urban areas into new child-care institutions in more rural areas. These included the Rauhe Haus, outside of Hamburg, which attracted international attention for its pioneering use of smaller 'cottage-style' residential homes for children. The departure of the first New York Children's Aid Society emigration party in 1854 subsequently marked the start of a new phase of mass migration schemes for children. Named by later writers as the 'orphan trains',[8] these schemes used the growing railroad system to re-locate more than 200,000 children from Boston and New York across the United States by 1929.

The ways in which migration was believed to benefit children varied across the organizations carrying out this work. Various claims made in support of it were that migration would remove children from the social and moral privations of poverty, break the bonds of corrupting family ties or the influence of degrading Poor Law institutions, safeguard their Christian faith, and provide them with greater opportunities for building successful, independent lives. They would be taken from the threat of a future of pauperism, criminality or political radicalism and given a new future as productive members of the nation, or in the British case, empire. The principle of using children's labour both as a means of making migration schemes economically viable, and as a source of practical and moral training for the child themselves, was also common to many of these initiatives. This same principle could be seen in operation in Europe as late as the 1960s and 1970s in the use of *Verdingkinder* ('contract children') who were moved across Switzerland by local authorities in a form of out-of-home care that utilized them as farm labourers or domestic helpers.

It is sometimes claimed that the United Kingdom is unique for using child migration as a form of welfare intervention.[9] In reality, though, what distinguished the UK child migration schemes from other European or American initiatives was not so much their underpinning principles or ways of working, but the fact that they sent children across national borders.[10] All of the other migration schemes described above operated as internal schemes within the same national borders. The importance of keeping the child migrant within the same imagined national community was illustrated by a case in 1904 when the New York Foundling Hospital placed a party of child migrants with Mexican households in Arizona. Local white families intervened to remove the children and the incident drew strong comment in national newspapers who censured the New York Foundling Hospital for its careless placement practices.[11] The UK child migration schemes were no different to this. The possibility that child migrants sent from the United

Kingdom to Canada might actually end up being placed, or drifting into, the United States was a ground on which UK child migration organizations faced criticism at home.[12] In the context of building up the nation, the working practices of the UK child migration schemes made sense to their advocates because British colonies were understood as an extension of the borders of a 'Greater Britain'.[13] To move a child from Britain to Canada or Australia was therefore a significant physical journey, but, the child was still seen as residing with the imagined shared space of the British world. As one article in the Dr Barnardo's Homes' magazine, *Night and Day*, put it in 1884, 'the colonies are not merely possessions but part of England . . . we must cease to think that emigrants when they go to the colonies leave England, or are lost to England and . . . contemplate the whole Empire together and call it England.'[14]

This book focuses on child migration schemes operating out of the United Kingdom which sent children mainly to Canada and Australia, with smaller numbers also sent to (the then) Southern Rhodesia and New Zealand, as well as those operating within the United States. With the possible exception of the Swiss *verdingkinder* system,[15] these schemes were the largest and longest-running child migration schemes operating in Europe and North America during the nineteenth and twentieth centuries.

To make broad generalizations even across this limited sample of schemes risks significant problems of oversimplification. They operated over a period that lasted for more than a century in different national and imperial contexts. Over that time, there were significant shifts in the underlying social conditions that gave rise to child migration schemes (such as rapid population growth and mass unemployment), the welfare and policy environments in which they operated, and standards of public health and child mortality rates.[16] New legal standards were established in terms of the amount of education children were expected to receive as well as increasing constraints placed upon the use of their labour.[17] Approaches to child-care informed by new psychological models and the professionalization of social work increasingly displaced approaches premised on notions of religious and moral formation. Public policies towards the British Empire evolved, as did the political relationship between the United Kingdom and British colonies.[18] The world in which child migrants made the first 'orphan train' journeys in the early 1850s – or embarked on steamships to Canada in the 1870s – was very different to that in which the last parties of child migrants flew to Australia a century later.

There were also significant differences in the ways in which various schemes operated. The emigration programme operated by the New York Children's Aid Society was explicitly set up to provide children with placements in private households in preference to keeping them in institutional care. Twentieth-century child migration schemes to Australia strongly favoured keeping child migrants in farm schools and residential homes in preference to fostering them out with families. Some late Victorian organizations sought to ensure that child migrants, in their teenage years, received some wages for their labour. Others did not.[19] Some child migration schemes sought, as much as possible, to break connections between child migrants and their birth parents in the belief that this was an integral part of giving them a fresh start in life. Others sought to maintain contacts between at least some child migrants and their birth families, particularly siblings. Some, notably the New York Foundling Hospital, favoured full adoption for child migrants placed in private households. Others, such as the New York Children's Aid Society and most UK child migration schemes to Canada operated on the basis of children having different forms of contracted service to households as employers, with conditions related to their age. The religious orientation of different schemes varied, from Catholic to liberal Protestant and Evangelical, as did the extent to which they were supported by different forms of statutory funding.

The history of child migration work across the British Empire and the United States is not therefore one of a homogenous movement, operating out of a single set of beliefs or adopting a single approach to its work. Thinking about the history of these schemes requires careful delineations of these differences, on the basis of which both shared patterns and distinctions can then be identified. Such an understanding of these schemes is also a necessary basis for any nuanced account of the relationship between their moral cultures and the harm children experienced through them. For this reason, the focus of the early chapters of this book is on the history, methods and rationales of their work across these different national contexts.

The American 'orphan trains'

What later came to be called the 'orphan trains' developed in the context of pressing social problems in America's major East Coast cities. With urban growth and immigration encouraging the depression of wages and job insecurity, children in poor families were at significant risk from hunger, disease and poor housing. In 1849, the New York's first police chief, George Matsell, estimated that there were 10,000 children living on the streets in Manhattan (although other social reformers suggested that this figure was much higher).[20] Successive studies such as George Foster's (1850) *New York by Gas-Light*, Samuel Halliday's (1861) *The Little Street-Sweeper: Or Life Among the Poor*, and Jacob Riis's later (1890) *How the Other Half Lives* re-iterated bleak pictures of the lives and environments of the poor for their middle- and upper-class readers.[21] Under these conditions, children often subsisted through highly casualized labour, such as selling newspapers or helping with luggage at the docks. They either lived alone or with families who were perpetually vulnerable to the effects of unemployment, illness and parental mortality. Alongside this, there were continued demands for labour in underpopulated states to the West,[22] new possibilities created by an expanding rail network and rail companies keen to encourage their use[23]; and a pervasive cultural assumption which equated the urban environment with disease and dissolution and the country-side as a place of health and renewal in which migrants to America could be effectively assimilated as productive and upright members of society.[24]

These social pressures were exacerbated still further by the effects of the Civil War, as poor families adapted to the challenges of temporarily losing their primary wage-earners to the army, or permanently losing them to injury and death. Middle-class anxiety about the poor and socially displaced – to whom Charles Loring Brace and others referred as the 'dangerous classes' – focused not just on their endemic criminality and pauperism, but on their capacity for violent disorder and political upheaval, fuelled by their resentment at being excluded from the benefits of wage labour. Such anxieties about civil disorder were not merely hypothetical. The Astor Place riot of May 1849 and draft riots of July 1863 had demonstrated the destructive potential of the 'dangerous classes', the latter leaving 105 people dead, black men lynched and the city's Colored Orphan Asylum burnt to the ground.[25]

The first 'orphan train' consisted of thirty children sent by the Boston Children's Mission to the Children of the Destitute in 1850 to be placed out in private households in New England and Vermont.[26] Although in principle a non-denominational organization, the Children's Mission was strongly influenced by Unitarians who saw liberal Christian social mission as being at the core both of Christian faith and any realistic hope for social transformation. Its proactive approach to child-saving work made innovative use of paid agents who would search poor areas of Boston for children whom they considered to be in need of care. The decision to place children out by sending them in train parties to local communities where their placements would be arranged by local clergy or other members of the church was a practical one. Finding individual placements for children in Boston was slow, placed significant demands on the time of Children's Mission officers and blocked places in Children's Mission homes that could be filled by other children. Although the numbers of children sent out in these groups – 1,300 by 1859 – was never as large as subsequent schemes run by other organizations, the Children's Misson was an important source of inspiration. Charles Loring Brace was aware of their work, and the Children's Mission's first president, John Earl Williams, moved to New York in 1851, soon to become the first treasurer of Brace's New York Children's Aid Society.

The largest numbers of children placed out through parties sent out on the railroad were from schemes operating in New York. The New York Children's Aid Society sent out more than 100,000 children from when its first emigration party was sent to Dowagiac, Illinois, on 28 September 1854. In 1865, the Home for Destitute Catholic Children became the first Catholic charity to adopt the emigration party method initially developed by the Children's Mission. As with other Catholic child migration organizations, a central concern was that of safeguarding children's Catholic faith and ensuring that they did not lapse into Protestantism or indifference. As one of its agents commented about visiting Catholic parents sentenced to the Deer Island prison:

> It is most touching to see with what tenacity these people in the midst of all their misery cling to their children. They are perfectly willing that the Home may have them, but the bare idea of some other woman taking them sets them wild. Yet, in the end they prefer this to the thought that their children might lose their faith.[27]

The Catholic New York Foundling Hospital also subsequently used the railroad system to place out tens of thousands of young children whom it usually received into its care from early infancy. Unlike, the Children's Aid Society scheme, however, the Foundling Hospital sent its children to prearranged placements, with number tags tied to them so that their prospective adoptive parents could recognize them on arrival. Railroad emigration parties also continued to be used by other organizations in Boston.

In 1865, another Protestant charity was founded, the New England Home for Little Wanderers, that was to become the largest child migration organization in Boston.[28] Inspired by The Howard Mission in New York, it shared the common child-saving mission for providing welfare interventions for poor children and using railroad emigration parties as a means to achieve this. In its early years, particular emphasis was also given to children in need as a result of the Civil War.[29]

Like other child saving organizations of that period, the New England Home understood its work as both a practical and spiritual mission, one that would yield its supporters a 'rich dividend in Glory' more secure than any 'Mariposa or Colorado' investment schemes.[30] Its emigration programme operated somewhat differently to those of the New York Children's Aid Society and UK child migration schemes to Canada by placing children in private households on terms that were closer to adoption, rather than children being understood more as employees who were given board, keep and schooling (and later wages) for their labour.[31] Its espoused policy was, where possible, to place boys with farming families who had no boys in order to increase the child's prospects of inheriting land to farm themselves in later life – something that happened more rarely with other migration schemes of that period.[32] It shared the wider principle of these schemes, however, that the placement of children in private households was far preferable to keeping a child in institutional care. Residential care provided by the New England Home for Little Wanderers was therefore understood only as a temporary environment in which children taken from the streets could be better prepared for family life.[33] As its published review of its work put it in 1872:

> It is believed to be unsafe to institutionize children . . . As well may we expect to improve the condition of the forest bird by capturing and caging it, as to improve a child out of its natural element. If the bird should be found cold and starving, warm and feed it, and let it fly again to its native woods. So with a child. If left in poverty and wretchedness, let the warm, genial influence of Christian affection be thrown around it till prepared for the home circle, the care of one father and the love of one mother.[34]

The emigration of children to States further West, the organization claimed, provided a supply of private households keen to receive these children, which could not be found in Eastern States. It also allowed the separation of children from home environments considered morally unsuitable as well as the possibility of keeping siblings in placements that were nearer to each other given the greater number of placement opportunities to the West.[35] The presumption remained, it was claimed, to try to maintain family bonds wherever possible. 'It is no part of our work to break up family ties if not absolutely necessary to the salvation of the child.'[36]

The fact that the New England Home for Little Wanderers provided some outdoor relief and temporary residential care to enable some children to remain with their parents in the longer-term suggests that there was no attempt to remove children from poor parents as a matter of course. Where vignettes of children's admission into its residential homes are included in its periodical, *The Little Wanderer's Advocate*, or its annual reports, these typically focus on cases where children are living by themselves on the street, have been abandoned by a parent, or family care cannot be sustained because of parental death or illness.[37] As with other child-saving organizations, though, decisions about whether a child should be given temporary care and returned to a family or permanently separated from them rested on class-inflected moral judgements about the suitability of the parent. As its thirteenth annual report put it, in 1878, 'We also take the children of worthy mothers . . . till the mother recovers and is able to take care of them herself.'[38]

Although this formal policy appeared to give considerable respect to parental wishes, in practice, the degree of control a family could exercise over their child's future was circumscribed. As with other child-saving or public welfare initiatives, poor parents would often try to make such use of them as they could to provide sufficiently for their children but could find themselves with such limited options that signing a child over to a public or voluntary organization became the only realistic option for their care.[39] A parent or guardian's application for their child to be admitted to one of the Little Wanderers' residential institutions usually came with the condition that the charity would then have full control over where the child would be placed without any further parental consent being needed or sought.[40] Any subsequent attempt by a family member to remove a child from their placement would be considered liable to prosecution.[41] The Homes' railroad emigration parties continued until 1906.

The largest and longest-running child emigration programme in the United States was run by the New York Children's Aid Society. It arose in the context of a wider range of philanthropic work directed at urban slum areas of Manhattan, particularly the notorious Five Points district. Charles Loring Brace, a deeply pious liberal Protestant from a well-connected Connecticut family, had undertaken missionary work both in Five Points and New York's dis-spiriting Charity Hospital, public alms-houses and nurseries based on Blackwell and Randall islands. By the time he was offered the opportunity to become the first secretary of the New York Children's Aid Society, this experience had already convinced Brace that missionary work structured around Sunday meetings and occasional pastoral visits could have no spiritual or moral benefit if social problems that undermined the possibility of virtuous life among the poor were not addressed.[42] This view was shared by the Aid Society's Board, many of whom had been involved in running regular Sunday meetings which claimed to reach almost a thousand boys each week but which they saw as having little success in those children's spiritual or moral reform.[43]

The New York Children's Aid Society's emigration programme formed part of a wider range of welfare initiatives undertaken by the organization which included boys' and girls' industrial schools, at which children were able to learn vocational skills, and lodging houses to provide food, accommodation and moral training to children. The Brace Memorial Farm School was also subsequently opened in 1894 to provide farm training for older children prior to them being placed out through the emigration programme.[44] This pattern of provision continued into the twentieth century, although the proportion of children sent out through its emigration programme compared to those trained in its industrial schools fell from around 45 per cent in the early 1860s to less than 5 per cent by the start of the twentieth century.[45] Following the model already established by the Boston Children's Mission, the New York Children's Aid Society employed agents who would actively seek out children in poor neighbourhoods who could be encouraged to attend public schools, its other outreach activities or be considered for migration from the city to the countryside. National publicity for its work generated hundreds of requests from people wishing children to be placed out with them which led initially to a system of individually arranged placements. As the Boston Children's Mission had discovered, however, placing children out through responding to individual requests through the Aid Society's office was time-consuming and costly in terms of administrative resources. Like the Children's Mission, the cost-effective solution to resolve this problem was to send children out in groups on the railroad, where their distribution could then be overseen by local agents.[46] By the time the New York Children's Aid Society sent its last party of child migrants out to Texas on 31 July 1929, it had placed out more than 100,000 children across the United States.[47]

As with many other child-saving organizations of that period in the United States and Britain, the New York Children's Aid Society consistently emphasized the value of raising children within a household rather than a residential institution. While denying that he had an overly idealistic view of life in the rural family, Brace argued that the attention, management and Christian influences a placed-out child would receive within a family home were far more likely to provide a healthy moral formation than life in a large residential institution. In large orphanages or houses of refuge children were inevitably, Brace argued, strangers to the staff. Growing up in the context of rigid institutional regimes, and receiving limited work training, also gave children little useful preparation for adult life – a failing later demonstrated by many residential homes for British child migrants in Australia.[48]

The distribution process operated by the Society giving advance publicity to local communities of when a party of children would arrive for selection. Distribution meetings were held in churches, town-halls or other public meeting places, with those interested in receiving children into their houses invited to make formal applications to members of a locally convened committee. The use of such local committees, it was claimed, would enable an effective vetting process in which children would only be placed out into the homes of people considered reputable in their local communities. The reality was somewhat different. As an independent review of the emigration programme undertaken by Hastings Hart in 1884 concluded that local committees and Society agents could exercise poor judgement in placing children, fail to investigate requests for children properly, and manage the distribution process in a hurried way. The suggestion that local people were best placed to know who was not suitable to receive children was undercut by the fact that local committees were often reluctant to turn down requests for children for fear of alienating people within their communities – a criticism also made of the use of such local references by British child migration schemes to Canada.[49]

The selection meetings could be, in varying degrees, exciting and traumatic for the children involved.[50] Some later recalled them as being like slave auctions, in which they were physically checked over to assess their potential for work. Attractive children were popular, sometimes receiving several applications from prospective carers. Some children sought to draw attention to themselves by performing songs or other acts. Alongside the instrumental inspection of children for their capacities for work, sentimental attachments were also evidently formed between children and adult applicants. In one case a couple who only attended a selection meeting out of curiosity ended up taking a boy home with them after he came up to them and hugged the man's legs.[51] While being the means to new homes, these selection meetings also entailed loss for the children, not just of friends they had made in their group, but of siblings from whom they were separated as they were placed out into different homes. In one case, a child avoided separation from his older brother by clambering on to the knee of the father of the man who had chosen his brother, and pleading with him not to separate them. The father, with tears in his eyes, accepted, and took both boys.[52] This was not the experience of many siblings, however, who were separated because receiving families would often only wish to take one child at a time.[53] The Society's agents often had to content themselves with the knowledge that they placed siblings in homes that were close to one another, though proximity could mean distances of ten or fifteen miles and ongoing contact, occasional meetings at local community gatherings. Those children who were not selected would get back on the train with their agent to move further on to other selection meetings until they were finally all placed. The experience of leaving a selection meeting having not been chosen by the inspecting adults stayed long in the minds of child migrants. This distress did not pass unnoticed by some observers. One newspaper account of children not chosen in a selection meeting commented:

> There is one feature in the distribution of the little waifs in our midst this week that calls for the deepest sympathy. The brightest and handsomest children were in great demand and were given homes in our best families, while a few not so prepossessing or attractive in appearance, nor so bright intellectually, perhaps, as the others, find no one to take them into their homes. Young as they are, these little wanderers recognize this and feel the humiliation, though it is no fault of their own. With eyes dimmed with appealing tears for home and protection they are passed by because of some insignificant physical or mental shortcoming until they feel that nobody cares for them, or entertains the slightest interest in their welfare.[54]

The Society's placements operated on a less regulated basis than those set up by other organizations in that period. In contrast to the New York Foundling Hospital or Dr Barnardo's Homes, for example, the New York Children's Society did not require families taking its children to sign any formal indenture or contract. Families receiving children were given a card, setting out the Society's expectations for the child's board, lodging and schooling (including Sunday schooling). Publicity notices for distribution meetings also made clear the terms on which the Society's children were to be placed out:

> Boys fifteen years old are expected to work till they are eighteen for their board and clothes. At the end of that time they are at liberty to make their own arrangements.

Boys between 12 and 15 years of age are expected to work for their board and clothes till they are 18, but must be sent to school for a part of each year, after that it is expected they will receive wages.

Boys under twelve are expected to remain until they are eighteen, and must be treated by the applicants as one of their own children in matters of schooling, clothing and training.[55]

The child was not formally contracted to stay with the family until adulthood, and either the receiving family or the child could, in principle, terminate the placement at any point with the Society taking responsibility for moving them on elsewhere. The rationale for this was that the placement should proceed on the basis of goodwill between the receiving family and the child rather than the constraint of a contract.[56] In practice, children's experiences of these placements varied – as they did for British child migrants to Canada – depending on whether the receiving family made the child feel welcome as a member of the family or saw them primarily as a source of cheap, domestic labour.[57]

Through its child emigration programme, the New York Children Aid Society was at the vanguard of a new interventionist approach to child-care, in which the separation of a child from its home community or birth family was seen in some cases as being in his or her best interests.[58] This approach cut against previously prevailing emphases on the virtually inalienable rights of parents over their children,[59] as well as objections that interventions to remove such children could reward pauperism and moral irresponsibility by relieving failing parents of their family duties.[60] In the closing decades of the nineteenth century, this new approach found expression both in the creation of Societies for the Prevention of Cruelty to Children in New York in 1874 and in London in 1884, and the development of new child protection legislation.[61] The New York Children Aid Society's emigration programme was, however, one of the first major child welfare programmes to operate on this principle and, as its Secretary, Charles Loring Brace, became one of its leading advocates. Bruce Bellingham has argued that Brace instituted a 'top-down change in the cultural meaning of kinship' in which 'the blood tie was formally and openly rivalled by another, equally valid or even more valid symbolism of loving conduct that might supplant the claims of blood kin who cease to be symbolically "real" for failure to satisfy a code of conduct'.[62] In short, where families were deemed unable to provide proper material and moral nurturance of their children, Brace 'recommended family dissolution as a means of moral reform'.[63]

This approach contrasted with that of the New York Foundling Hospital – which ran the second largest placing-out scheme in New York and re-located children who had already been given up for care or abandoned by parents. Brace's organization used placing out more strategically to break family bonds considered to be an impediment to the child's moral and civic progress. This was not as easily achieved in practice as in principle. For most of the early years of the scheme's operation it was dependent either on parents giving their children over (through their own initiative or persuasion by the Society's agents[64]) or on displaced children, judged to have no contact with their families, consenting to being placed out.[65] But as the Society's emigration work developed into a well-established programme, residential institutions for children in New York began to use it as a way of placing out their residents.[66] As these institutions effectively became the source of consent for these children's placements, parents found that children whom they had placed in residential care during a period of crisis in their families had been placed out without their consent and were prevented from re-establishing contact with them.[67] The process of separating the child from corrupting family influences was thus made easier without direct parental consent.

It has been argued that this practice of placing out was less radical and ran with the grain of poor families' engagement with welfare of that period. This was an era in which the circulation of children beyond the household of their birth family was common-place,[68] and in which the movement of children by charitable organizations represented only a small proportion of the circulation of children that was managed on a more informal basis. Parents might place their children with other family members or neighbours if they themselves lacked the resources to care for them, or might place their children in a residential institution for a period of time until their family situation had improved. Children might also move out of the family home to take up other employment opportunities on shorter- or longer-term basis or because of the family home breaking up for different reasons. The high rates of parental mortality both increased the likelihood that any given household might include children who had lost one or both of their parents and that children would be displaced if they had poor relationships with new step-parents. The circulation of children between and beyond households was therefore a common feature of nineteenth-century family life, particularly among the poorer urban classes who would draw on a patchwork of public and informal support as they negotiated their unstable social world.

In this context, the intention of the emigration programmes to re-locate children to new households might seem to be more in line with wider social practices of that time. While the moral intention of breaking up families to save the child may have been more innovative, Bruce Bellingham has argued that the users of this scheme approached it as just another form of welfare support that they might draw on strategically at points of crisis.[69] The practice of placing children far from their home State was in reality more radical than this, however. While parents who were unable or unwilling to support their child might give their consent to the child being placed out through the emigration programme, this was usually a more permanent break than placements nearer to home. It may have been one option to poor parents, but one that involved a more fundamental loss of their relationship with their children than other possibilities they would normally have sought. Perhaps some parents who felt little bond with their child, or who despaired at their family's prospects, could countenance such a loss. But this was a deeper cut than the normal practices of sending one's child away for a time in the hope of being able to take them back again in better times.

The moral project of child emigration

One reading of the American child emigration programmes is that they were essentially a secular and pragmatic response to the pressing problems of urban deprivation. Brace certainly presented his scheme to potential donors, at times, in terms of the hard-headed realities of cost-effectiveness. Aside from its humanitarian benefits, he observed, the one-off costs of placing out a child through their emigration programme could be one-seventh of the annual costs of keeping a child in an institution.[70] This strategy of using economic arguments where appeals to shared religious or moral sentiment failed was not unique to Brace. The New England Home for Little Wanderers made the same kinds of argument, observing in *The Little Wanderers Advocate* magazine that the costs of running the criminal justice and correctional system in Boston were $500,000 per annum, with recent building costs for jails, court-rooms and police stations more than double that. A better solution, its author argued, was to intervene in the lives of children before their entrenched criminality demanded such an expensive response. 'Enlightened selfishness would therefore dictate, to say nothing of Christian duty, that prevention was a money-saving operation.'[71]

The fact that Brace did not establish an explicit programme of moral reform for placed-out children, and his insistence that the work of the New York Children's Aid Society was non-denominational, despite his own theological training at Yale Divinity School and Union Theological Seminary, has also led some later interpreters to play down the religious emphases in his work. From this perspective, Brace is seen more as a precursor to more professionalized forms of social work in the twentieth century than a Christian missionary.

This is a mis-reading of Brace and his organization, however. Brace's understanding of welfare was inflected with a liberal Protestant philosophy which fused a belief in the unique importance of Christianity as a moral force for Western civilization with a form of social Darwinism that emphasized the individual and collective adaptive benefits of moral virtue.[72] He did not see Christian morality as synonymous with the Church, which he understood as a flawed institution that had often failed to live up to the glories of its moral vision, but as a moral force without which civilization could not progress and individual life would become dissolute. A Christianity that had become becalmed in technical debates over doctrine or dissipated in mere emotional effervescence was, he believed, now being displaced by a more profound Divine movement to build up the Kingdom of God through social compassion and justice.[73] Such sentiments, characteristic of the later Social Gospel movement, were at the same time refracted through Brace's interest in evolutionary progress. The forward movement of society was dependent on the moral inspiration of Christianity, as was the flourishing of its individual members in this world and the next. In his moralized understanding of natural selection, those among the urban poor who were 'vicious and sensual' would inevitably die young, leaving their children free for a better moral formation if there were people charitably disposed to provide this.[74] The process of moral development that Brace sought for vulnerable and displaced children was not that of a highly structured discipline which he believed would create compliance with moral demands in children's behaviour but not in their hearts.[75] Rather Brace hoped to put children in social environments that would nurture their 'sturdy independence' – a quality that defined the races of the American Republic and Western Europe – in ways that would encourage virtuous habits.

In contrast to later schemes that separated children from their parents and sought to mould them through deference to a strict moral regime, Brace claimed to entice children into moral virtue by example and practical incentives. This approach was evident in the operation of his first major welfare initiative, the opening of the News Boys Lodging House on the corner of Fulton and Nassau streets in lower Manhattan in March, 1854. The hostel was set up to support boys who made a subsistence living through selling daily newspapers on the street and provided them with clean overnight accommodation, food and education. Brace was keen not to run this free of charge to its users, however, but wanted to encourage the sense of initiative these boys already brought to their work, treating them as 'independent little dealers' who would get 'nothing without payment, but at the same time to offer them much more for their money than they could get anyplace else'.[76] One practical expression of this moral ethos was the introduction of a 'savings bank' at the hostel – a desk with slots cut into its top into which boys could drop pennies into their personalized savings box – which did not compel the boys to save money, but demonstrated the benefits to them if they did. 'This simple contrivance', wrote Brace, 'has done more to break up the gambling and extravagant habits of the class, than any other influence.'[77] This ethos of encouraging moral virtue through practical methods was infused with a religious sensibility. The vision of God Brace offered to children through his sermons was thus not an authoritarian figure demanding obedience, but a loving Redeemer who had given His own life to save others, the best friend of the lonely and vulnerable child. In response to such Divine love, children were encouraged to think and feel about their lives as an ongoing moral drama, acted out on the stage of eternity, in which the Saviour and Friend with whom they would one day be fully re-united with in heaven longed for them to bend their lives towards goodness.

This represented a very different understanding of children's behaviour – and the process of their moral formation – compared to some later schemes which adopted more overtly coercive means to achieve compliance. As one New York Children's Aid Society publication put it:

He who shall visit the Newsboy's Lodging House expecting to see models of quietness and good behaviour ; boys who would be patterns of correct deportment for school-teachers or Sunday-school superintendents to parade before visitors, will be grievously disappointed; but he who can discern, under a rough and perhaps blunt and uncouth demeanor, the virtues of frankness, generosity, independence and self-reliance, coupled perhaps with some recklessness and swagger, and occasionally a little sauciness, will conclude, after careful observation, that many a boy brought up to the possession of wealth and luxury, and offered every advantage of education, does not play his part in the world so well as some of these poor newsboys.[78]

Such a positive view of children's liveliness remained highly gendered, though. If boys' exuberance and cheek might notionally be welcomed, the moral formation of girls was understood in terms of them turning away from coarseness and bad language to more refined behaviour.[79]

The New York Children's Aid Society claimed that its emigration programme was grounded in four key principles: 'Individual influences and home life as better than institutional life'; 'lessons of industry and self-help better than alms'; 'the implanting of moral and religious truths in union with the supply of bodily wants'; and 'entire change of circumstances as the best cure for the defects of children of the lowest poor'.[80] The practice of placing children out into new homes encapsulated all of these principles. Although enthusiasm for the moral environment of the simple rural home may have taken a rhetorical flourish when presenting the scheme to potential donors, there is no doubt that the home was seen as both a better environment for children's moral formation and a better training ground for the range of domestic and work skills that they would need in their future.[81] By placing them in homes that were far removed from the urban areas in which they had grown up, their attachments to their old lives would be weakened and a genuine opportunity for making a fresh start would be created. By establishing such placements on an informal basis, where there was a verbal or written statement of the principles that should underpin but no formal contract tying the child or receiving adult to it for any fixed period of time, the child's autonomy could remain intact. If unhappy with their placement, the placed child could always contact the Society to find another one, make their own way back to New York or find themselves another home in their new area that suited them better. A significant number of the children placed by the Society did, in fact, do just that.

While the New York Children's Aid Society doubtless saw sound practical benefits to this approach, it was also implicitly structured around an understanding of the moral life. By sending children out into a new environment in which place a 'family name cuts but little figure [and] it's the character of the man that wins recognition',[82] it sought to change the mise-en-scene for the moral drama of their lives. Hopefully, the adults receiving them would provide a good moral example,[83] but even if not, children were still sent out (along with the Bibles given to them before departure) with the knowledge of their own responsibility for their moral fates. To Brace this seemed an obvious approach to the moral formation of a child, with which no morally serious Christian would disagree. But, as the controversy around this emigration programme demonstrated, it was more deeply embedded in Protestant understandings of the moral and religious life than the Society recognized. For Brace, the emigration plan was simply an outworking of core principles of Christian morality with which any Christian familiar with the central tenets of their faith would agree. This espoused non-denominational ethos was shared by other liberal Protestant organizations such as the New England Home for Little Wanderers.[84] For Catholic authorities in New York the Society's work was, however, a clear attempt to proselytize Catholic migrants run by a network of Protestant ministers and lay-workers, leading them to protest that the Aid Society was deceitfully removing children from good Catholic families and stripping them of their faith.[85] Such was the strength of Catholic feeling about this emigration programme, that the New York Catholic Protectory was created in 1863, as a residential alternative for children who could be caught up in the Children's Aid Society's scheme (CAS).[86] By the turn of the century, the Catholic Protectory had become the largest children's residential institution in America, housing 2,500 residents. To Brace, such Catholic opposition to his work was incomprehensible. His assumptions about the formation of the moral and pious individual, free from any obligation to a particular Christian denomination, appeared to him to be an obvious understanding of Christian morality rather than fundamentally Protestant. For his Catholic detractors, Brace could only reserve epithets that were truly damning in the eyes of an educated New England Protestant – they were both ignorant and superstitious.

The moral framework underpinning the emigration programme was evident in the emotional roles that children and their birth parents were intended to act out through it. The role of the child within this process was to embrace happily the new life that was being offered to them. Staff at the Society's offices in New York took particular delight when a child would approach them to ask to be placed out. Accounts by the Society of the placing-out process – both in its organizational records and external publications – consistently emphasized the rescued children's happiness, resolve or enthusiasm.[87] As E. P. Smith wrote in his record of the first migrant party to Dowagiac, the sight of an orchard full of apples from the moving train filled the children he was accompanying with uncontainable excitement at the new world they were entering. 'It was difficult to keep them within doors. Arms stretched out, hats swinging, eyes swimming, mouths watering, and all screaming – "Oh! oh! just look at 'em! Mister, be they any sich in Michigan? Then I'm for that place – three cheers for Michigan!"[88] Children who failed to fulfil this role, through ingratitude or too strong an attachment to their former lives, were regarded with disappointment. As with other child migration schemes, the virtuous child was equated with the deferential and obedient child.[89] In contrast to Brace's espoused belief in respecting the 'sturdy independence' of the child, some former orphan train riders recalled the displeasure that the Society's agents expressed to them when they refused to take up placements that had been offered to them.[90]

The proper role of the parent, within this emotional schema, was to demonstrate fortitude and self-sacrifice in giving up their children for a better life. The New York Children's Aid Society's understanding of parents struggling to raise children in the midst of urban poverty was complex. At times, they would write sympathetically of their struggle to survive in poor housing, through ill-health and little or no employment. But such sympathy was constrained by judgements about race. In contrast to the decent peoples of America and Western Europe, Brace was scathing about the inferior racial stock of immigrants from Southern and Eastern Europe – the 'scum and refuse of ill-formed civilizations' – whose numbers in the urban slums were swelling and from whom nothing good could be expected as parents.[91] But even compassion to the more decent classes of the poor stopped at the point at which parents were perceived to be obstructing charitable efforts to improve the lives of their children. Those who would not give their children up willingly to the emigration programme were considered so 'narrow and pig-headed [that] they can't be talked or driven into saving their own children'.[92] The great obstacle to the emigration programme, complained Brace, was the 'superstitious opposition [of parents, whose] attachment to the city, their ignorance or bigotry, and affection for their children' led them to refuse to give their children up to it.[93] Parents who gave their children up were represented as sensibly welcoming the better life being opened up for them, or bravely handing them over despite the distress this caused. But those who wanted to keep their children were represented as morally culpable for selfishly holding their children back.

These proscribed emotional and moral roles for children and parents reflect the underpinning moral narrative of redeeming the child to a new life with a better family home. Their strong emotional identification with this moral narrative meant that Brace and the Society's other workers appeared only recognize to shortcomings in their work to a limited degree.[94] They knew that sometimes children could be abused in their placements, and acted to remove children from them when they were notified of this. But, in general, the belief that children were being placed in 'good' homes made the monitoring of placements by correspondence from the Society's office seem a reasonable system for many years even when the Society's letters to many placed-out children went repeatedly unanswered.[95] The lack of a formal indenture agreement, while intending to allow children a degree of choice in their placements, also meant that children lacked any legal standing in the homes in which they were placed and could lose out on benefits set out in an indenture, such as the payment of a cash sum to them on its completion. The emphasis on the happy, enthusiastic and brave child appears to have occluded any recognition in the Society's documents of the anxiety, loss and distress that placing out involved for children.[96] The moral insistence that birth parents be prepared to make the necessary sacrifice of letting go of their children – or that children should embrace this as an opportunity for a new life – showed little recognition of the emotional attachments that could still persist even in vulnerable and unstable family environments.

The distinctiveness of the moral project of the emigration programmes is also evident in the significant objections raised to it by other child welfare workers of that era. The Catholic child welfare organizer, Thomas Mulry, supported the work of the New York Catholic Protectory precisely because it was able to return 90 per cent of its children to their birth families as well as maintaining regular contact between them while the child was in residential care. The temporary removal of children from their families might shock parents into reform, Mulry argued. Permanent removal of the child could only lead to parents' demoralization and despair.[97] Homer Folks, who began his child welfare career as Secretary of the Childrens Aid Society of Pennsylvania before becoming Secretary to the New York State Charities Aid Association, raised related concerns about placing out. While Folks shared Brace's conviction about the importance of a good home life for a child's development, he was less convinced that the New York Children's Aid Society's emigration programme was the best way to achieve this. If a child's birth family were unable to keep it because of a temporary crisis of ill-health or unemployment it would be better, Folks argued, not to separate the child from that family permanently but to find some other form of temporary boarding out for the child nearer to home.[98] Placing older children in completely new communities would also give them little opportunity to build up the friendships and social contacts that they would need as they entered adult life. The practice of placing out was also criticized by those who saw it as a means for people 'too mean and penurious to pay for the help they need and want a child to fill a man or woman's place without wages'.[99] Receiving adults might therefore treat the child not with a sense of humanitarian duty, but provide 'poor food, shoddy clothing, work the child beyond its strength, [and] send it to school but a few months, and that irregularly'.[100] In one case, for example, a widow took three successive children, worked them until their clothes were worn out and needed replacing, and then returned them to the placing agency for spurious reasons.[101] The suspicion that placing out functioned less as a charitable exercise than a means of procuring cheap labour led some to question whether placements were being used in some States to make up for labour lost through the emancipation of slaves.[102] In 1858, one newspaper editorial in Illinois went to the length of satirizing abolitionist supporters of the placing-out programme who proclaimed their hatred of slave labour, but were quite prepared to contemplate using child labour instead.[103] There is no reason to imagine that poor parents would not themselves have felt some of these concerns.

The New York Children's Aid Society's emigration programme was never free from controversy. Charged with uprooting and proselytizing Catholic children, it also attracted the same criticisms subsequently levelled at British migration schemes to Canada of using migration as a way of dumping unwanted, morally and physically unfit children onto far-removed communities. As a consequence, it was claimed, these child migrants were now filling the prisons and reformatories of the communities to which they had been sent, or just as bad, roaming uncontrolled having abandoned their placements. Brace responded to the latter charge in the same way that Thomas Barnardo did in Britain, producing his own statistics to show the low failure rate of his organizations' placements and that the level of incarceration of child migrants was at a much lower rate than the average for the communities into which they were sent.[104]

At the start of the twentieth-century the Society was beginning to place less of an emphasis on the work of its emigration programme in comparison to its work with children still living in New York.[105] By 1929, a number of factors had come together to make the emigration programme no longer viable as a part of the organization's work. Welfare payments to mothers improved to some degree, and although eligibility was still judged on grounds of the moral fitness of the parent, the principle became more widely established that a parent should not have to give up their child simply because of poverty.[106] A growing number of States began to pass legislation blocking the placing out of children residing outside the State, reducing the Society's placement options. The development of new legislation restricting child labour also created uncertainties for placements in which the child's labour had been seen as an important return for the cost of their keep. As wider policy and professional developments gave greater emphasis to maintaining the care of the child within the family or their home community, so the American child migration programmes faded from public view until their later rediscovery through fiction, film and renewed efforts to capture the memories of former orphan train riders.[107]

2

'In the children's land of promise': UK child migration schemes to Canada[1]

On 28 October 1869, Maria Rye sailed from Liverpool on the *Hibernian* with her first child emigration party to Canada made up of around seventy girls, all 12 years of age or younger.[2] In fifty-five years following the *Hibernian's* departure, around 90,000 unaccompanied children followed them.[3] Compared to the much smaller earlier schemes previously run by the Children's Friend Society and the Ragged School Union, 1869 marked the emergence of UK child migration schemes as a major form of organized welfare intervention.

Rye's child migration initiative is better understood as a gradual evolution of nineteenth-century emigration policies and practices rather than a radical shift. Emigration from Britain, more generally, rose significantly during the nineteenth century. In the first half of the nineteenth century, an average of 91,000 people per year left Britain for non-European destinations with this rising to an average of 157, 765 British citizens leaving for destinations outside Europe between 1853 and 1869.[4] Closer recording of inward and outward journeys to the United Kingdom after 1870 made it possible to calculate net outward passenger journeys, thus giving a better indication of how many travellers were remaining in destinations outside of Europe. Between 1870 and 1913, net outward journeys from the United Kingdom averaged 140, 911 per year, with these net figures predominantly being accounted for by British nationals travelling overseas and not returning. By 1901, an empire-wide census recorded 2,786,650 'natives of the United Kingdom' living overseas in other parts of the empire.[5] At the start of the nineteenth century, there was still a lingering suspicion that emigration could depopulate, and thus weaken, Britain. By the start of the twentieth century, the emphasis had fundamentally shifted towards the importance of using emigration to strengthen British colonies and developing evermore formalized State mechanisms to support this.

Against this backdrop of a growing population movement from Britain to its overseas colonies, migration was also used more generally as a strategy of ameliorating social problems at home. Growing population rates, recorded every ten years after the first national census in 1801, became an increasing source of public concern. Combined with rapid industrialization and changing approaches to agriculture, population movement to the cities, insecure employment and fluctuating cycles of economic growth and recession, nineteenth-century population growth created a growing class of urban poor.[6] The experience of families struggling with poverty was made harder through the reluctance of Poor Law officials to provide 'outdoor relief' that might keep struggling families together during periods of financial hardship rather than resorting to seeking admission to a workhouse in which husbands, wives and children would be separated from each other. Public responses to such poverty ranged from the perception of it as a moral problem to be tackled through strategies such as the 'workhouse test' of the 1834 Poor Law Amendment Act or the 'scientific philanthropy' exemplified by the Charities Organisation Society to humanitarian initiatives intended to lessen the suffering of the poor.[7] Commonly laced through all of these was also the fear that, unaddressed, a growing class of displaced and underemployed poor would become not just criminalized, but ready recruits for radical political movements.

Between 1815 and 1830 a series of publicly funded initiatives were developed that provided free passages for emigrants wishing to travel to British colonies in North America, Australia and South Africa. Developed, at first, by the British Colonial Office, and then from 1819, in the form of additional schemes authorized by Parliament, these schemes in total supported the emigration of fewer than 10,000 people. These initial experiments in assisted emigration received strong opposition both from those who saw it as a 'pernicious' enterprise of weakening Britain and political radicals who argued that the low wages at home should not be addressed by emigration schemes but better political representation for workers.[8]

As the century progressed, however, emigration came to be used more widely as a means of managing issues of social poverty and change. After 1838, changes to the Poor Law placed the financial responsibility for rural tenants who entered workhouses with the tenant's estate landlord. Government-assisted emigration from Ireland had already been developed in the 1820s as a means of dealing with social unrest arising out of poverty and tenants' loss of leases.[9] Some Irish landlords had also called for further government assistance to fund the emigration of dispossessed tenants to enable the consolidation of small-holdings into larger, more efficient farms.[10] After 1838, Irish landlords increasingly chose to pay the one-off emigration costs of their tenants themselves, rather than having to pay recurrent fees for keeping them in the workhouse. Some landlords conceived of emigration as providing a better future for their tenants than a life of ongoing poverty in Ireland – and some tenants agreed with this. Other landlords saw emigration in more instrumental terms as the most cost-effective way of achieving the desired modernization of their land, with displaced tenants having little choice but to assent to emigration. As a consequence, between 1835 and 1855, it is estimated that around 100,000 tenants emigrated from Ireland to Canada on landlord-assisted passages, with the rate of migration under this provision significantly increasing during the years of the great famine.[11] Similar action was undertaken by landlords in the context of the Highland clearances in Scotland, where tenant farmers were evicted from their land usually to free it for more lucrative use for sheep farming. Some landlords achieved notoriety for the ways in which they enforced their assisted emigration. In 1851, the land-holder John Gordon faced criticism in the press for the manner in which he sent 1,700 impoverished Hebridean islanders to Quebec, with unwilling tenants handcuffed and physically forced on to ships.[12] Such acceptance of the emigration of the poor was also evident in the Poor Law Act of 1850 which provided local Boards of Guardians with the legal authority, subject to the permission of the national Poor Law Board, to arrange for the migration of deserted or orphaned children in their care under the age of 16.[13] This provision appears to have been relatively little used, however, by local Guardians until larger scale, specialist child migration schemes began in 1869.

The use of emigration as a form of social engineering also formed the direct backdrop to Maria Rye's own professional career. Before she left for Canada with her first party of child migrants, she already had seven years' experience of taking migrant parties of women to Australia, New Zealand and Canada. Initially conceiving of her work as providing the means for unmarried middle-class women to find new opportunities in the colonies, Rye quickly became interested in the idea of extending her migration parties to working-class women whose prospects had significantly worsened during the economic downturn caused by the American civil war.[14] By 1867, Rye was proactively recruiting women from workhouses – particularly as the British economy began to improve and women in work were less likely to consider emigration. In doing so, she sought financial arrangements with Boards of Guardians to pay their emigration costs to remove these women as ongoing financial burdens to local rate-payers.[15]

One of the noticeable themes across the history of the American and UK child migration schemes was the commitment of philanthropists and organizations to continuing their emigration work in the face of obstacles and opposition. There was, in many cases, an evident sense of the inherent value of the work that meant that when their work was obstructed in one form or place, it was refocused elsewhere. When individual American

States informally or formally began to reject the idea of receiving placed-out children from other States, the New York Children's Aid Society simply moved its distribution meetings to States that still allowed them. The Catholic Emigration Association in Britain which facilitated the emigration of children to Canada evolved into the Catholic Child Welfare Council which supported the migration of children to Australia after the Canadian schemes had been forced to stop. Dr Barnardo's Homes, the British organization which sent the most child migrants to Canada similarly refocused its child migration work on Australia when opportunities in Canada ended. Maria Rye was no exception to this. Her interest in child migration arose as her migration work with women faced stronger challenges, initially by the cessation of funding for her work by the State Parliament of Victoria in Australia, and then through criticism in the press in both Britain and Canada.[16] In 1868, the serendipitous experience of hearing a talk in London by Reverend W. C. Van Meter, a former New York Children's Aid Society emigration programme agent and founder of the Howard Mission, led Rye to think that child migration might provide a more promising focus for her philanthropic intent.[17]

Rye's child migration scheme developed with some differences to the railroad child emigration programmes in America. Her work had the same basic organizational structure as that of Annie Macpherson, who began to develop child migration work at the same time as Rye, with the former coming to this from a background in child-saving missions in London. Both Macpherson and Rye had their own residential homes in England. By 1869, Macpherson was running three children's home in addition to her 'Home of Industry' in Spitalfields; in 1872, Rye established a children's home in Peckham.[18] These homes provided a supply of displaced and vulnerable children who were then incorporated into their emigration schemes to Canada. Rye also continued to take a proactive approach to soliciting local Boards of Guardians who would pay the emigration costs of children in their care. This coincided with strong pressure from the Local Government Board for local Poor Law Unions not to be too generous in their administration of outdoor relief, thus making the workhouse admission of children more likely.[19] Unlike the New York Children's Aid Society emigration programme which used local meetings to distribute its children, both Rye and Macpherson established distribution homes in Canada – Rye's a former gaol and courthouse in Niagra ('Our Western Home') and Macpherson, Marchmont House in Belleville, Blair Athol in Galt (both in Ontario) and Knowlton in Quebec. Most organizations who subsequently sent child migrants to Canada followed this model, in some cases sharing distribution homes across different schemes or transferring ownership between them. These distribution homes shared some of the same functions as 'orphan train' distribution meetings and local agents, receiving requests for children and references about these potential applicants and taking responsibility for the allocation of children. They also provided a base for the ongoing supervision of placed-out children and for temporarily accommodating children whose placements broke down before they were re-allocated.

Although child migration from the United Kingdom had taken nearly two decades to emulate the model of the America programmes, British initiatives now quickly proliferated. In 1873, the Methodist minister, Thomas Stephenson, impressed by Macpherson's work, opened a distribution home in Hamilton, Ontario, as part of the organization he was soon afterwards to call the National Children's Home. Similarly inspired by Macpherson, William Quarrier began to send children to Canada from his residential homes in Scotland in 1872, using Macpherson's Canadian homes as the distribution points for the children.[20] In Liverpool in 1870, Father James Nugent began the first Catholic child migration scheme to Canada, partly against a background of Catholic concern that children cared for under the Poor Law did not have sufficient opportunities for appropriate Catholic religious instruction and partly out of concern that Catholic children might otherwise be absorbed into the Protestant schemes of Macpherson and Rye.[21] John Middlemore followed this emerging model, setting up children's homes in Birmingham and sending out his first party of child migrants under the organizational name of the Birmingham Emigration Homes in 1873.

By 1875, however, this new work faced a major challenge. Both Maria Rye and Annie Macpherson had received payments from local Boards of Guardians to emigrate children for whom they had financial responsibility and whom were considered to have been 'deserted' by their families.[22] The Local Government Board who provided oversight of Boards of Guardians' work also actively encouraged them to make use of Rye and Macpherson's emigration service for children in its annual report of 1870/71.[23] The fragmented nature of the Poor Law system, however, meant that there was no consensus about the suitability of child migration as a policy and some local Boards who had sent children to Canada with Rye and Macpherson also asked the Local Government Board to conduct a review of how child migrants were faring. When allegations began to be made about the mistreatment and poor placement of child migrants – allegations strongly denied by Rye – the Local Government Board eventually decided in 1874 to send one of its senior inspectors, Andrew Doyle, to undertake a detailed investigation of how the schemes in Canada were working.

Even before going to Canada, Doyle's professional views on child-care were unlikely to make him sympathetic to the way in which the child migration schemes operated. Just before departing for Canada he had made a critical report of the use of placing children out in remote areas in a review of the boarding-out policies of the Swansea Board of Guardians. Such dispersal of children, Doyle argued, made effective supervision of placements far less likely and left children more vulnerable to undetected abuse and neglect.[24] By comparison, keeping children in Poor Law institutions offered children better protection and more consistent standards of care.

When he submitted his report on Rye and Macpherson's child migration work, Doyle did not reject child migration as a policy out of hand. However it was unclear whether his comment that, if managed well, child migration 'might effect infinite good to the Dominion if not to England'[25] was a heartfelt endorsement or sop to make his otherwise extensive criticisms of Rye and Macpherson's work more palatable. Certainly Doyle did offer some praise of individual workers in these schemes that he encountered during his time in Canada.

Doyle's criticisms reflected moral judgements of his time about different classes of children and considerable confidence in the Poor Law system of which he was a part. But they also demonstrated a degree of insight into children's emotional lives that was often lacking in some of the more celebratory literature published by organizations engaged in child migration. His concerns focused on three key areas of Rye's and Macpherson's schemes: the selection and preparation of children for migration, the arrangements for their placements and their post-placement supervision. Concerning the selection of children for migration, Doyle was highly critical of the ways in which these schemes took both children who had several years of education and training in Poor Law institutions as well as 'street arabs' who, until relatively recently, had been living in transient accommodation or on the street.[26] The poor moral traits of the latter had the effect of undermining, by association, the reputation of the Poor Law children among Canadian households: the 'system is becoming discredited through the incapacity, unfitness, and too often the gross misconduct of many of the children who are sent out'.[27] Furthermore, the schemes seemed highly unrealistic in their working assumption that so-called street arabs could be taken from urban life and successfully put in placements in rural Canada on the basis of only a few weeks' preparation in residential homes in Britain or Canada. Doyle also raised concerns about how children not taken from Poor Law institutions were selected for migration. Unlike those taken from Poor Law institutions, it was not clear that the 'waifs and strays' brought to Canada by Rye and Macpherson had either themselves consented to their migration or that appropriate consent for migration had been obtained from their parent or guardian.[28]

Doyle's criticisms became even more trenchant on the placement and supervision of children. The Local Government Board, he noted, had supported Rye's and Macpherson's work on the basis that child migrants would spend sufficient time in training institutions (presumably the distribution homes) to prepare them for their placements.[29] In reality, however, children tended to spend very little time in the distribution homes before being placed out, giving minimal opportunities for staff to get to know a child and to understand what form of placement might suit them. As a consequence, failures in placements were made more likely with not enough acknowledgement given to the demoralizing effect that the breakdown of a placement could have on a child. 'When one thinks of the depressing effect upon a child of being sent back to the "Home" disappointed and discouraged by early failure',[30] Doyle observed, the importance of taking care to get an initial placement right was obvious. But the practice of rapid setting up of placements was so engrained in these schemes that even when a placement broke down and a child was returned, staff in the distribution homes did not take sufficient time to understand properly the causes for its failure before sending the child out on another placement.[31]

Doyle also argued that there were significant problems with the basis on which most placements were established. The majority of requests for children from Canadian households came not from families wishing to adopt a child or raise a child as a member of a family, but from those wanting a child migrant 'on account of the services' that they could bring to the home or farm.[32] This in itself, Doyle noted, should give cause for thinking that strict monitoring of those placements would be necessary. The fact that older child migrants (aged 9 and above) were far less likely to be considered for adoption than younger ones also made the older children less likely to be assimilated into families, leaving them lonely and homesick.[33] While some farm placements provided good opportunities for children to learn relevant skills, the general level of expectation of what children would contribute through their labour was high[34]. Employers were often left frustrated by the failures of poorly prepared children to perform work tasks effectively, but the fact that Rye's and Macpherson's schemes had underestimated the value of the children's labour meant that there remained a very high demand for their services.[35] The process of placement was also, in Doyle's view, highly problematic. Accepting recommendations for households to receive a child from third parties in their local communities was an insufficiently rigorous basis on which to make a placement, and the households in which children were to be placed were rarely visited prior to receiving a child.[36] In some cases, verbal rather than written agreements were made with employers. As children circulated between households when their placements broke down, the terms on which they were placed could become increasingly informal and were not always agreed with the distribution home.[37]

Although Doyle was more positive about Macpherson's approach to post-placement supervision than Rye's, this was the part of the schemes that drew his strongest criticisms. 'The want of sufficient care in selecting homes for the children, though a serious defect in this system of emigration, is far less injurious in its results than is the want of proper supervision of them afterwards.'[38] Macpherson had, at least, initiated a system of supervision visits to children (although Doyle questioned how rigorous these inspections always were), whereas Rye relied more on correspondence with employers or receiving reports when placements had broken down.[39] Neither system was, in his view, adequate to maintaining proper oversight of the conditions in which child migrants were living or working, and in some cases the child migration schemes had already lost track of where the children they had brought to Canada were now living.[40] It would be more appropriate, he argued, to have a similar system for child migrants as used for boarded-out children in Britain where local committees visited children at least every three months. Such frequency of contact could allow trust to develop between the child and the supervising committee, thus giving the child greater confidence to speak out if they were being subjected to any mistreatment. And it would be an obvious principle of good practice, he commented, for these inspections to be carried out by someone independent of the child migration organizations.[41] To suggest that tightly knit local communities would provide an effective informal monitoring of children's placements by reporting any cases of mistreatment was implausible. As Doyle noted from his experience of visiting hundreds of children in placements, it was not uncommon for neighbours to be very reluctant to make such complaints for fear of stirring up bad feeling in their communities.[42]

His concluding point to the report was not one of his weightiest criticisms of the schemes, but an observation that reflected his acute awareness of the isolation and displacement that child migrants felt. 'It is to be regretted,' he commented, 'that some of the Union authorities do not manage to keep up regular communication with their own emigrant children. The teachers would do so I am sure if they could but know what store a child so far away sets by a letter or a word of news "from home". Even the little that I could tell made me a welcome visitor to a few of them of whose schools and teachers I happened to know something. One very bright intelligent child from a London District school, however, did not conceal her disappointment when her mistress called her in to see me. Having heard that an Inspector from England had come out to see her and the other children she had been counting, she told me, upon seeing, not a stranger, but her old friend Mr Tuffnel.'[43]

In the short term, Doyle's report had a significant effect. Despite strong protestations from Rye, numerous public supporters of child migration in Canada and a Canadian Parliamentary select committee,[44] the Local Government Board decided to uphold a moratorium on funding child migration to Canada that it had announced on a temporary basis just before Doyle left Britain to undertake his investigation. In a process remarkably similar to the Australian Government's response to the Ross Fact-Finding Mission in 1956 (discussed in the next chapter), the Canadian Government decided to respond to this by undertaking its own enquiry which exonerated the child migration schemes of any criticism even though it had been unable to trace 31 per cent of the children placed by Rye.[45] The Canadian Government also offered for its immigration officers to visit annually all child migrants sent out by Poor Law institutions. The Local Government

Board invited Doyle to respond to this proposal, to which he replied that it was not an appropriate system as immigration officers had a vested interest in encouraging migration and that regular supervision visits would be better carried out by local school inspectors.[46] The Local Government Board supported Doyle's objections and the moratorium remained in place, although this did not apply to children who were migrated to Canada through private donations or the funds raised by voluntary organizations over which the Board had no control. By 1883, the political climate in Britain was shifting towards stronger support for child migration, and the Local Government Board came under increased lobbying to allow local Boards to fund children's overseas passages again. This was done in 1884, although with approval given only for up to 300 children to be sent from Poor Law institutions and with stricter conditions, including the requirement that children needed to have spent at least six months in a workhouse or district school before being considered for emigration. Failures by the Canadian Government to supply promised copies of reports of supervision visits led to another temporary moratorium in 1886. Again growing public pressure was exerted on the Local Government Board. Samuel Smith, the Liverpool MP who was to play a pivotal role in the development of the first Society for the Prevention of Cruelty to Children in Britain, wrote to *The Times* to complain about the Board's obstructionist approach to child migration schemes that he argued were so evidently beneficial to impoverished children being cared for by the British state. After finally receiving a substantial number of supervision reports on individual child migrants from the Canadian Government in 1887, the Board eventually, and with some misgiving, agreed to allow local Poor Law boards again to pay for the migration of children in their care.

If the Doyle report succeeded in a temporary suspension of child migration – if only for those children whose emigration was funded by local Boards of Guardians – its longer-term legacy was more limited. While Doyle's evidence against the child migration schemes was contested by their supporters, his report had nevertheless established principles against which those schemes could be judged according to what was considered good child-care practice within the Poor Law system of that time. The extent to which Doyle's criticisms were absorbed into child migration schemes' practices were at best mixed, however. The principle that all child migrants should receive regular, annual supervision visits became commonly accepted. Just as the New York Children's Aid Society's early reliance on supervision by correspondence came to be replaced by supervision visits by local agents, so the light-touch approach to supervision adopted by Rye came increasingly to be seen as unacceptable. Even so, the aspiration for annual supervision visits was still not consistently achieved during the period in which the child migration schemes to Canada operated. Children who were sent to rural locations too remote to be feasibly visited by

inspectors were given writing paper or stamped postcards to send back
to their distribution homes if they wanted to raise concerns about their
placement. Although the Ontario Act to Regulate Juvenile Immigration in
1897 sought to introduce a requirement of four supervision visits per year
for each child migrant – the level that Doyle himself had recommended –
it was never fully implemented. When the Bondfield Report presented its
findings on the operation of child migration schemes to Canada in 1924,
it found that even the aspiration of a single supervision visit per year was
still not being fulfilled in the case of all child migrants according to the
Canadian Government's own records.[47]

Some of Doyle's criticisms were more effectively addressed. For the
more established schemes, such as Dr Barnardo's Homes, it became more
common practice for children to be given longer preparation in Britain
before being sent to Canada.[48] Child migration agents in Canada also
became more astute in understanding the economic value of the labour
of the children being placed out. This extended to an appreciation of the
differential rates that older children, who might expect to receive a wage
for their work, might receive depending on the state of the local economy
in which they were placed.[49] Child migration agents also made calculations
as to whether lower wages for a child might be counterbalanced by higher
standards of care,[50] lobbied employers to pay better wages where they
felt this appropriate and would even, in some cases, encourage a child to
move on from a placement if they felt they could receive better terms and
conditions elsewhere.[51] The relationship between child migration agent,
child and receiving household remained, for the duration of the Canadian
migration schemes, predominantly one between that of employment agent,
employee and employer. But, in general, child migration organizations
became more astute in acting in this role than Doyle suggested Rye and
Macpherson's staff had been in 1875.

What was far less well managed were Doyle's fundamental concerns
about a system in which emotionally vulnerable children were placed in
often unstable placements and subjected to expectations on their labour
that they were often unwilling or unable to live up to. Doyle's report
demonstrated a sensitive appreciation of the emotional effects that a series
of broken placements could have on children, as well as the potentially
problematic dynamics of placements in which the expectations of employers
and commitment or skills of children were not well-matched. The Canadian
child migration schemes did not always manage these challenges well and
often showed less sensitivity than Doyle. At their best, they managed to give
some support to the child and address the wishes of the employer despite
their often overstretched resources. More often, though, supervision reports
and correspondence convey a sense of frustration, most often with children
blamed for being unable to keep placements and, more occasionally,
with impatient employers. They continually recycled children into the
system in the hope that one placement would eventually stick with little

obvious appreciation of the emotional effects this would have on the child themselves.

Before the Local Government Board eventually ended its moratorium on allowing funding for the emigration of children cared for within the Poor Law system, a wider range of charities and churches were becoming involved in child migration work. An improving economy in Britain in the latter part of the 1870s had meant that there were more employment opportunities for older children at home and less demand for child migration. By the early 1880s, however, the British economy entered another recession, creating new pressures for the placing out of children in the care of voluntary organizations. In 1882, Thomas Barnardo sent his first party of boys to Canada, followed by his first party of girls.[52] Initially Barnardo's child migrants were placed out through Stephenson's distribution home at Hamilton, but Barnardo quickly established his own distribution homes in Toronto and Peterborough, Ontario.[53] In the same year, the Liverpool Catholic Children's Protection Society began its own emigration work, placing children out through a hostel in Montreal as well as other diocesan contacts in Canada. In 1883, the Manchester and Salford Boys' and Girls' Refuges and Homes began sending its own child migration parties. Their children were placed out from the Marchmont distribution home in Belleville, whose own history of shifting ownership between different agencies demonstrates the degree of interaction between child migration organizations.[54] In 1884, James Fegan began sending parties of child migrants from his residential homes in the Home Counties and around the same time, child migrants began to be sent by the Catholic Archdiocese of Westminster. Catholic child migration work was subsequently overseen by a national body, the Catholic Emigration Association, formed in 1904. Run by Father George Hudson, secretary of the Birmingham Diocesan Rescue Society, the Association established its central distribution home and headquarters in Ottawa. In 1884, the Church of England Waifs and Strays Society (the Church's formal child-care organization) set up a distribution home in Sherbrooke, Quebec, and sent its own first party of child migrants out in the following year. Maria Rye subsequently transferred her homes in London and Canada to the Society in 1896. The remaining organization to play a significant role in undertaking child migration work, the Salvation Army, entered this field relatively late, sending its first party out probably only in 1905 in the context of the Army's interest in the wider use of emigration as a social welfare intervention in General Booth's wider 'Darkest England' scheme[55] (see Table 2.1).

The organizational structures through which child migration from Britain to Canada operated were therefore diffuse, made up of competing and complementary relationships between state welfare providers, philanthropists, civic leaders, donors and churches. Across this diverse provision, however, there were recurrent themes in the public justifications offered for child migration work.

TABLE 2.1 *Canadian government statistics[56] on child migration from United Kingdom to Canada by 1924/25*

Organization	Date range of child migration statistics	Number of children
Annie Macpherson and Louisa Birt	1886–1925	14,327
Maria Rye and Church of England Waifs and Strays Society	1868–1925	3,985
Middlemore Homes	1873–1925	5,079
National Children's Home	1874–1925	3,011
Mrs Biborough-Wallace, Marchmont (including Manchester and Salford Boys' and Girls' Refuges and Homes[57])	1878–1915	5,529
Cardinal Manning (Archdiocese of Westminster)	1880–1888	1,403
Dr Barnardo's Homes	1882–1925	26,447
James Fegan	1884–1925	2,953
William Quarrier	1890–1925	4,185
Catholic Emigration Association and related societies	1897[58]–1925	6,630
Salvation Army	1905–1925	2,281
Dr Cossar, Lower Gagetown, New Brunswick	1910–1925	494
Captain Oliver Hind, Falmouth, Nova Scotia	1913–1925	73
British Immigration Aid and Colonization Association	1923–1925	23
Minor agencies[59]	1897–1925	5,386
TOTAL		82, 026

Notes: Note the incomplete date ranges of statistics for organizations listed means that these are not comprehensive figures for all child migrants sent to Canada between 1869 and 1925 (see note 5 of this chapter). However the figures provide a useful indication of the relevant scale of involvement of different organizations.

Foremost among these was an emphasis on child migration as providing humanitarian relief to vulnerable and suffering children.[60] In published accounts of their work in annual reports and organizational magazines, in line-drawings and photographs, and in the publication of selected letters from child migrants, a recurrent narrative was presented of the saving of the suffering and neglected child. Thomas Barnardo's account of his encounter with a boy in the streets of London in his organization's *Night and Day* magazine is typical of this:

> Harry struggled hard to keep honest, and up to the day I met him been fairly successful; but it was a long continued and stern conflict with starvation, loneliness, cold and wretchedness, in which the poor boy was often sorely pressed to give up and become a thief. The day I met him the weather was bitterly cold, and the clothes he had on were the merest rags, affording but little warmth or shelter . . . I made the fullest inquiry into his story. I traced out every clue I could get as to his relatives, and discovered that the history he gave me was fairly accurate . . . that Harry never had any other dwelling than the common lodging-house, and that during all his life he had been compelled to herd with thieves and persons (male and female) of abandoned character and life. He entered our Home, did fairly well at school, and settled down with great content in our carpenter's shop . . . Grown strong and hearty, Harry's present appearance gives no evidence of his sorrowful past history and in his emigration outfit he really looks a bonnie youth, and better than all, I believe the lad's heart has been truly given in faith and hope to the Saviour. Certainly his life and conduct manifest a great spiritual change.
>
> I am delighted to know that Harry is one of my fellow passengers to the fair Dominion of Canada, and that never again will the cold, bleak streets of London, and the hunger and misery of a neglected and friendless condition be his experience. I think the kind-hearted solicitor who, having heard of Harry's story, at once agreed to pay the amount needed for his emigration must always feel thankful when he reflects from what Harry has been saved, and remembers the bright opening presented through his benevolence to the poor London street boy.[61]

The image of the vulnerable but redeemable child, drawn from a life of loneliness, devoid of family love and subject to the threat of moral pollution, played a central role in the humanitarian sentiments that child rescuers sought to evoke around their work.[62] Often obscuring the more complex social networks and family ties of which children were apart,[63] this humanitarian narrative is one to which our discussion will return later in the book when we consider in more detail the moral cultures of child migration work. Such positive visions of humanitarian rescue were accompanied by deeper anxieties. Just as Charles Loring Brace had feared that unrescued children would go on to swell the ranks of the dangerous classes, creating a disaffected underclass likely to be swayed by demagogues,[64] so British supporters of child migration saw this work as a necessary means of avoiding future social and political problems. Samuel Smith, who made a major donation to Thomas Barnardo on condition that the money only be used to find child migration work, wrote in 1885 that 'the time is approaching when this seething mass of human misery will shake the social fabric unless we grapple more earnestly with it than we have yet done'.[65]

Rather more pragmatic considerations also had a bearing on a number of charities' involvement in child migration. As American charities had discovered, moving children away was an important mechanism for creating space both in their residential homes or run by other organizations who used them as migration agents. During periods of economic recession, rapid population growth and rising unemployment, the demand on charities' services meant that a cost-effective means of moving children on from their own residential care was very welcome.[66] Without the possibility of such an outlet for children in their care, it was argued, residential homes would retain children needlessly who could benefit from a life outside of institutional care and new applicants would be prevented from receiving residential help through lack of spaces. As Dr Barnardo's Homes' *Night and Day* magazine put it: 'If our work was to go on, we must be able to send forth our boys and girls at the end of their stay with us, else we would perish of our own success. Instead of a free health-giving river, our Institutions would be little better than a stagnant lake.'[67] This concern was also reputational. Without such an outlet, Dr Barnardo's Homes would struggle to live up to their public commitment never to turn any child away from their door.

A further rationale given for child migration concerned the wider context of the Poor Law system. Here significant differences arose between those who viewed the problem of poverty from the relative comfort of middle-class or establishment life, and those who had a more sympathetic understanding of what life under the Poor Law was like. The former framed the Poor Law as a problem in relation to child migration because of the financial demands that the care of dependent children placed on tax-payers. Writing in support of emigration as a welfare strategy for the Barnardo's *Night and Day* magazine in 1884, Lord Brabazon observed that the rapidly growing population of Britain created 'a permanent burden to bear in the cost of maintaining, repressing, punishing, and relieving in time of sickness, by means of official and charitable agencies, some two or three million pauperized and degraded people, including in that number the 900,000 persons in receipt of pauper relief'.[68] Child migration was one means by which the pressures of such welfare support on the local rate-payer could be eased.

By contrast, others saw the ethos and operation of the Poor Law system as a problem for which child migration was a necessary remedy. William Quarrier, who himself had some experience of living destitute as a child, wrote critically of parochial welfare provision in Scotland in which a widow with five children might eventually, after much difficulty, secure payments of a shilling a week per child from the parish. 'Mark you, five shillings a week to keep six persons in house, fire, food and clothing! And this is considered a liberal provision.'[69] Even with great frugality, the widow would almost certainly struggle to help the family subsist and would be forced to send one or two of her children out to work, hiding their minimal income from the parish inspector lest the family loses its welfare payments for those children. Such a punitive and ungenerous system, Quarrier argued, had the effect of encouraging dishonesty among the poor and failed to reward their honest work. Child migration thus became a necessary means for dealing with the hardship caused by a flawed welfare system in which poor families struggled to support their own children.

Similar criticisms about the punitive and failing nature of Poor Law provision were also made from within the Salvation Army. Writing in 1896, General William Bramwell Booth was scathing about the lack of wisdom and compassion in the operation of the Poor Law system, in particular how the limited system of outdoor relief and principle of breaking families up on admission to the workhouse was pointlessly cruel:

> The plan of forcing on the sinking poor the alternative of going without help or entering the workhouse is needlessly harsh, and reveals a total want of any sympathy. It is difficult to think with any calmness of the horrible dilemma of the applicant for temporary outdoor relief, who must choose between the starvation he sees slowly marching on and breaking up his little home – the last possession and only happiness left to him in the world. And yet this is the choice that the Poor Law deliberately compels him to make, with the result that large numbers of families who might, with a little timely aid, be able to keep up a home and keep up the strength of the wage earner until better times, are unable to do either, and are positively thrown down by the operation of the very laws which were originally intended to keep them on their feet.[70]

Quarrier's and Booth's empathy for the plight of the poor in a punitive Poor Law system was not universally expressed among child rescue organizations. The notion that such suffering was due to the social and political context of a particular system of welfare was less common in their literature than representations of the poor in terms of bare, human suffering to be relieved by philanthropic intervention.

Such critiques of the Poor Law did not, however, restrict themselves just to their unnecessarily destructive effects on family life, but the morally corrupting effects of Poor Law institutions themselves. Writing in *Night and Day*, Thomas Barnardo railed against the reluctance of Poor Law officials to provide outdoor relief that would enable the poor to continue experience the 'healing preventive influences of which English home life is so fruitful'.[71] Instead, by forcing destitute families into the workhouse, parents and children would be tainted by the vice of other inmates and become more used to relying on the workhouse in future. William Bramwell Booth took a similar view. Quoting from Francis Peek's book, *Social Wreckage*, Booth sought to state 'facts which it is difficult for me to speak of with any sort of calmness':

> Not only is the atmosphere of these workhouse schools pauperising, but the schools are actively educative in a bad way; for very many of the

orphans' school-fellows are the children of thieves, tramps and women of bad character, who enter the workhouse for brief periods, coming from the haunts of vice and crime to which, with their children, they quickly return. Meanwhile, those who have been associated with them can hardly fail to have been infected, not only with opthalmia and other loathsome bodily diseases, but also with loathsome ideas and evil thoughts. Our desolate, destitute orphans having thus been legally trained to live without affection, to accept pauperism as their natural condition and the poor house as their home, having been furnished with precociously wicked companions, well instructed in vice, are at the most critical time of their life, when about thirteen or fourteen years of age, sent out unprotected to fight their way in the world.[72]

The Darkest England scheme, while premised on humanitarian claims to relieve the suffering of the poor, and later to build up the Empire through emigration, also contained a pragmatic intent to provide an alternative welfare system to that of the cruel and corrupting Poor Law. If the Poor Law could not be reformed, the Salvation Army claimed that emigration provided an 'immediate remedy'[73] to the suffering and morally enervating effects of poverty. While presented in morally optimistic terms, the need for political critique was still to some degree acknowledged. In a 1909 review of its emigration policy and methods, it published two letters from leading writers of the day whom it had invited to endorse its work. One, by Rudyard Kipling, gave enthusiastic support for their emigration plans, adding further advice on how emigration and settlement in the colonies might best be managed. The other, by George Bernard Shaw, gave far more lukewarm support – 'emigration is inevitable at present; and its organization is therefore a necessary and useful work which comes well under that general heading of doing good which is the business of the Salvation Army'.[74] But, he added, emigration was only a necessity because the society was in such a poor state and that he regarded the need for emigration as 'a national disgrace, and one that could be easily wiped out by economic reforms at home'.

A final significant rationale for child migration work arose from the sectarian religious environment in which child migration schemes operated.[75] Catholicism had, by the mid-nineteenth century, achieved greater official toleration in Britain and the principle of raising children in the faith of their parents more accepted. From 1869, the Local Government Board established its right to order local Poor Law unions to transfer children from their own institutions to certified Catholic residential homes and schools if this was requested by the child's parent or guardian.[76] For most of the period in which the UK child migration schemes operated, Catholic organizations still functioned with a strong sense of their status as a religious minority as well as a firm belief in the Catholic faith as the only true pathway to salvation. The Catholic sense of religious insecurity in a dominant Protestant culture was by no means without foundation, with anti-Catholic sentiment still able to mobilize political and social elites in the opening decades of the twentieth century.[77] In the context of childcare, this could lead Catholic organizations to adopt a defensive stance towards external authorities deemed unsympathetic to their work.[78] Working agreements were reached with Protestant organizations about not attempting to 'poach' children from the other's respective faith community. But there were recurrent tensions around this and overt anti-Catholic sentiment was evident among some leading Protestant philanthropists, most notably Thomas Barnardo.[79] Catholic suspicion of non-Catholic bodies was clearly reciprocated at times,[80] with, for example, archival records from the early postwar period recording Home Office officials' reservations about the standards of some Catholic religious orders (particularly the Christian Brothers) and the ethos of the British Catholic child-care systems more generally.[81] Just as Catholics had criticized the assimilationist intent and effects of the New York Children's Aid Society's emigration programme, so Catholics in Britain also suspiciously regarded Protestant claims to offer non-denominational welfare assistance to children as implicit attempts to remove them from the sphere of Catholic influence.

Protestant child migration organizations typically spoke of the importance of the religious formation of the child either through an Evangelical emphasis on developing personal faith in Christ or in terms of more general training in piety. Catholic organizations, by contrast, spoke in terms of 'safeguarding faith' from the evils of assimilation into Protestantism or the descent into religious indifference. The importance of safeguarding children's Catholic faith in the period prior to the Second Vatican Council can be illustrated by the policies of the Birmingham Diocesan Rescue Society, one of the sources of Catholic child migrants. The Birmingham Diocesan Rescue Society was not, its terms of reference made clear, intended to intervene in the cases of children who should be assisted by the Poor Law. Instead, the emphasis of its work was focused specifically on (a) the removal of Catholic children who had entered the residential homes of Protestant organizations such as Barnardo's or Middlemore Homes; (b) the removal of Catholic children who had been taken in by Protestant relatives; (c) the removal of children from indifferent (or grossly immoral) Catholic parents; and (d) the removal of children from destitute Catholic parents where their poverty was of a kind as to constitute a danger to the child's faith. As the terms of reference put it, 'the Rescue Society . . . only exists to save the faith of the child'.[82]

In this context of concern for the safeguarding of faith, child migration was presented as an excellent opportunity for relocating children to new environments in which their faith could be nurtured and protected. Writing in 1919, the secretary of the Catholic Emigration Association, George Hudson, commented:

> Many of these rescued children can only be saved to the Church by being permanently removed from their early surroundings. The Bishops and Priests of England turned their eyes of hope to the great Catholic

lands of Canada. They saw there a home for the children, amid Catholic surroundings, denied to them in the Old Country . . . And their hopes have been abundantly and splendidly realised. The work is not run for profit. It is all done for the sake of the child, and in the sacred cause of religion . . . Only those who are of good character and good health are selected. The fair Dominion will only take of our best. And only our best are sent. Above all, they come filled with a love for their holy faith, and ready to take their place in the life of the country of their adoption.[83]

The policy of ensuring that children were placed in good Catholic environments in Canada extended to placing British children in non-English-speaking French households in Quebec.[84] While the challenges were acknowledged of children adjusting to this, placing children in environments where they had contact with families of strong Catholic faith and regular access to the sacraments weighed more heavily than these.[85]

Despite disruption to the schemes because of problems with trans-Atlantic travel during the First World War, many child migration organizations remained committed to their Canadian work in the early 1920s.[86] Political and professional opinion was beginning to turn against it, however. In Canada, as in the United States, social work was becoming more professionalized, with a new generation of leaders within the social work field questioning practices that had been accepted by the previous generation of child rescuers. The practice of migrating children to Canada was increasingly criticized as being out of keeping with contemporary approaches to child-care, with reports of suicides among British child migrants further focusing attention on this issue.[87] In 1924, the director of the Canadian Council for Child Welfare made a speech asking why British child migrants were still being placed out in private households that had not been previously inspected on conditions that would not be accepted for Canadian children. She continued that 'it does not redound to the credit of Canada that in an official publication of the Dominion Government we should speak of getting farm helpers from ten to thirteen years of age. Do not these facts bear out a contention of a cheap labour demand, a cheap labour that approaches perilously near a form of slavery?'[88] Objections to child migration were also raised by child welfare and medical professionals on the basis of a eugenicist concern that British child migrants from poor backgrounds would weaken the physical and mental calibre of the Canadian population.[89]

At the same time, there was growing willingness in some parts of British Government of the need for a review of the Canadian schemes. Since the late 1890s, socialist representatives of local Boards of Guardians had begun to protest at the practice of sending Poor Law children overseas and the trade union movement was conscious of the strong objections by Canadian trade unionists that the cheap labour of child migrants undercut wages of Canadian workers.[90] When the first Labour government in Britain was formed in 1924, it announced that a review of child migration to Canada would be undertaken, led by the Labour MP, Margaret Bondfield.[91] The report offered a mixed analysis of child migration. It noted the good standard of accommodation in distribution homes and observed that most of the children to whom the inspection team had made unannounced visits reported being happy in their placements.[92] A number of suggestions were even made about how child migration organizations might work more efficiently. However, it also reiterated the same criticism made by Andrew Doyle nearly fifty years before that it was unacceptable that children be placed in households that had not had a prior inspection and noted that some children had been placed in households by one child migration organization that had been judged unsuitable to receive children by another. Its crucial concern, though, related to the age at which child migrants were sent to Canada.[93] It concluded that, while the children claimed to be happy, they were undertaking more work than they would be expected to in Britain and that the household demands on their labour meant that their formal schooling was often disrupted. Although it had concerns about only a small proportion of the placements it had visited, it took the view that the migration of children under the school-leaving age of 14 was problematic in principle because younger children were more vulnerable to abuse, to being overworked and to losing out on educational opportunities. In short, younger British child migrants did not 'appear to have gained any appreciable advantage' from their move to Canada.[94] It recommended that child migration for children under school-leaving age be suspended, but allowed to continue for children over 14 for whom migration was conceived of more straightforwardly in terms of providing work and vocational training opportunities. In March 1925, the Dominion Immigration Branch agreed to suspend the acceptance of children under fourteen, unaccompanied by their family. Following further lobbying from within Canada, this ban was made permanent in 1928. Continued organizational enthusiasm, and establishment support, for child migration meant however that the Fairbridge Society was able to lobby successfully for British child migrants to be sent to a Farm School that it opened in Duncan, British Columbia in 1935, despite ongoing opposition from child welfare professionals.[95] In the end, 329 children were sent there until the school closed in 1951. Other reports of British child migrants continuing to be placed out in private households after 1928 suggests that this ban was far from being complete, with the national ban not being consistently enforced at specific ports of arrival. While this adds a degree of uncertainty as to when the last British child migrant was sent to Canada, the end of the 1920s witnessed an end to the Canadian schemes as mass charitable interventions into children's lives.

3

'No placeless waifs but inheritors of sacred duties': UK child migration schemes to Australia

One of the most striking things about the history of the UK child migration schemes is that just as child migration work to Canada was being criticized as a welfare intervention and being formally wound down, child migration schemes to Australia were expanding and would continue to operate for another four decades. This chapter will consider the initial development of child migration to Australia, noting its differences to the Canadian schemes, and examining how it persisted long after it had come to be seen as out-of-keeping with more widely accepted standards of child welfare.

Australia was not the only country to which UK child migrants were sent after the formal ending of Canadian schemes in 1928.[1] Around 300 children were sent to the Fairbridge Memorial College in Rhodesia from 1946 to 1956, in a scheme intended to train middle-class children whose families had fallen on hard times as future leaders of the native population.[2] In 1948, the New Zealand government also began to recruit child migrants, receiving around 550 children until it ended the scheme in 1954.[3] In contrast to Australia, the New Zealand welfare system was already strongly emphasizing care within the family or foster-care in preference to residential care, and child migrants were placed in foster homes with varying consequences for the children. The greater administrative complexity of setting up foster-care placements through government agencies, and desire to encourage child migration in cases where other family members might later follow them to New Zealand, made the scheme slower to operate and contributed to the decision in 1954 to concentrate on older youth emigrants who would not require foster care.[4] There remains less information in the public domain about the Rhodesian and New Zealand schemes, partly because of the destruction of records in the case of Rhodesia[5] and partly because there has been no formal inquiry on the schemes in New Zealand.[6] Despite sharing the ambitions of the Rhodesian and New Zealand programmes to strengthen its white, British population, the scale of child migration to Australia was far greater. More than 3,170 UK child migrants were sent to Australia after the Second World, with an estimated 6,500–7,000 sent between 1912 and the late 1960s.[7] Of these, roughly 2,700 were sent by Dr Barnardo's Homes, 2,300 by the Fairbridge Society, 1,300 by Catholic organizations, 400 by the Church of England and around 100 children each by the Methodist Church, the National Children's Home, the Salvation Army and the Presbyterian Church.[8] Proportionately, though, Catholic organizations contributed more substantially to early postwar child migration. Of the 2,324 child migrants sent to Australia between 1947 and 1955, 912 children were received through the Federal Catholic Immigration Committee of Australia, substantially more than any other child migration agency.[9]

The first child migrants to Australia arrived in June 1834, via the Children's Friend Society, who sent less than a hundred children in migration parties before it ended this work in 1842.[10] The Ragged School Union had, by 1849, begun its own small-scale migration work to Australia sending children from some of its UK schools and providing some of the earliest examples of organizational literature extolling the value of child migration as a welfare policy.[11] Apart from these early initiatives, however, child migration to Australia remained relatively undeveloped during the late Victorian period with most child migration work from Britain concentrated on Canada.

In the early twentieth century, however, a new wave of child migration schemes to Australia began to develop against the backdrop of increasing levels of immigration to Australia more generally.[12] The turn of the twentieth century was marked by stronger calls for the British government to adopt systematic policies to encourage emigration to British dominions, exemplified by the creation of the Royal Colonial Institute's Emigration Committee in 1910, which both co-ordinated the work of voluntary organizations and lobbied central government for greater support for imperial migration[13] Although the Empire was seen positively for different reasons across the aristocratic and professional classes, there was nevertheless widespread support for it among social elites.[14] In 1922, the British government's Empire Settlement Act established a recurrent funding scheme for assisted emigration to British dominions, including the migration of children under the auspices of recognized organizations. The legislation arose both out of British concerns for managing the problems of unemployment at home, a commitment to strengthening 'Greater Britain' and Australian concerns for increasing its population and economic development through the preferred immigration of 'good British stock'. Coinciding with the era of the 'White Australia' immigration policy,[15] such migration was strongly encouraged by

Australian authorities through widespread marketing campaigns. As one 1924 pamphlet aimed at post-school-leaving age, juvenile migrants put it:

> Boys! Australia makes you an attractive offer. She places before you an opportunity of coming to a new land, a rich land and a healthy land; and upon your arrival, of immediately putting you in the way of earning a good living and of soon becoming a prosperous citizen . . . You will learn the business of farming, your wages will increase as you acquire experience, and after some years, provided you have been thrifty, you will be able to take up land of your own and become your own masters.[16]

Against this background, an Oxford Rhodes scholar from Rhodesia, Kingsley Fairbridge, formed an organization that was to play a major role in twentieth-century child migration to Australia. Initially called the Child Emigration Society, it later reverted to the name of its leading founder, becoming known as the Fairbridge Society. Fairbridge, whose great-grandfather had emigrated to the Cape from England and been a committee member of the Children's Friend Society, developed a strong affinity with the idea of the British Empire and colonial citizenship. In his autobiography, he claimed to have had a visionary experience as a teenager in which he came to realize that the emptiness of colonial lands cried out for British settlers to cultivate them.[17] After returning to Rhodesia from his first visit to England in 1903 in which he was exposed to sights of urban poverty in the motherland, Fairbridge's ideas began to focus more clearly on child migration as the means for colonizing and cultivating the open spaces of imperial lands:

> I saw great Colleges of Agriculture (not workhouses) springing up in every man-hungry corner of the Empire. I saw little children shedding the bondage of bitter circumstances, and stretching their legs and minds amid the thousand interests of the farm. I saw waste turned to providence, the waste of unneeded humanity coveted to the husbandry of unpeopled acres.[18]

By 1908, Fairbridge's commitment to this idea led him to write to Earl Grey, the Governor General of Canada, with the outline of a scheme for an agricultural college in Rhodesia.[19] The letter sets out the ethos that was to define the farm schools that he eventually established in Australia. Emulating the migration work of the Salvation Army, Fairbridge intended to take children from workhouse schools, migrate them to Rhodesia, 'bring them up in an atmosphere of energy, endurance and cleanliness' and train them in farming methods. The environment of the college was intended to cultivate both a sense of imperial duty and sense of vigour in them. Describing his scheme as 'a large eugenic concern having certain commercial principles', he claimed that workhouse children, without intervention, would only grow up to produce further generations of 'mental and physical weaklings'. The risk of 'physical degeneration in a land where cheap native labour is available' led him to advocate allowing only white children to undertake farming on the college land. The children's labour should make the college economically self-sufficient, while they received religious and moral instruction that would 'bring furthermore to their notice the acknowledged duty of individuals towards God and Man; the glory of England; the essential unity of the Empire'.

That same year, Fairbridge took up the offer of a Rhodes scholarship at the University of Oxford, and here, in a wider environment of enthusiasm for empire, found the first network of supporters that enabled him to bring these ideas to fruition. Speaking at the University's Colonial Club, he delivered a speech on 19 October 1909, outlining his idea of using child migration as means of colonizing the wider Empire.[20] This advocated the migration of children between the ages of 8–10, 'before they have acquired the vices of "professional pauperism" and before their physique has become lowered by adverse conditions'. Fairbridge argued that this would ease the problem of overpopulation in England as well as the need for increased population in the colonies, 'both for economical reasons and as a safeguard against the possibility of foreign invasion and foreign immigration of low types'. 'To bring the great overseas dominions within the circle of the British Empire was the achievement of the last century', he declared, 'to people them with British stock is the task that faces the race in this.' A motion successfully proposed after the speech that the Colonial Club become the core support for Fairbridge's project created the basis on which the Child Emigration Society could then be formed.

By the time he made this speech, Fairbridge had already learned that his child migration plans to Rhodesia were, in their current form, impractical as the use of white children's manual labour would provoke local opposition and a training college there might only work in the future if aimed at higher-class settlers.[21] Instead, he presented his audience with news of an offer from the Prime Minister of Newfoundland of 50,000 acres of land on which the farm school could be built. This plan also quickly ran into difficulties, however. Fairbridge was advised about the unsuitability of the location and social conditions of Newfoundland. Turning to other senior contacts in the Canadian government, Fairbridge found a cooler response to his plans, with now Earl Grey also advising him to follow the model of other child migration organizations and place his children out with individual households rather than in a training institution.[22] By 1911, the Child Emigration Society had two options for its work – to create its farm school in Newfoundland or to locate it, instead, in Western Australia. In the event, the Premier of Newfoundland was prepared to offer land but no additional financial assistance for child migrants, whereas the Western Australian government was prepared to offer land at a minimal rent, pay the children's shipping costs and provide their compulsory education at no charge. On the strength of this offer, Western Australia was chosen and plans set in place to create a farm school at Pinjarra near Perth. Run by Fairbridge himself and his wife Ruby, this received its first party of children in 1913. The early years of the farm school were made difficult both by the effects of the war in preventing child migrants from being sent out and the problems in securing more direct financial support for the scheme from the Western Australian government. By 1920, protracted negotiations between the Child Emigration Society and the British and Western Australian governments eventually led to a financial agreement to enable the expansion of the Pinjarra farm school to enable it to receive 200 children. The British government contributed capital funding and a one-off capitation payment (making the Fairbridge scheme the first child migration initiative into which it had made a capital investment) and the Western Australian government contributed a recurrent capitation payment.[23] The consolidation of an executive committee in London and a local organizing committee in Western Australia further developed the scheme's administrative structure such that the work was able to continue and expand even after Kingsley Fairbridge's death, at the age of 39, in 1924. The re-named Fairbridge Society subsequently went on to open another farm school at Molong, in New South Wales, in 1938, and a residential home at Tresca House, Exeter in Tasmania, in 1957, in addition to its Prince of Wales farm school in Canada.[24]

Kingsley Fairbridge's work was significant not only for opening up Australia as a point of destination for British child migrants in the twentieth century – with Barnardo's, for example, placing child migrants in Australia through the Fairbridge Society until they had established their own receiving institutions.[25] Fairbridge's commitment to child migration also had noticeably different emphases to those of the earlier generation of child migration philanthropists such as Thomas Barnardo, Annie McPherson and William Quarrier. Reflecting the social and political environment of his time,[26] Fairbridge's work was framed far more explicitly in terms of goals of empire settlement than the late Victorian migration schemes to Canada. The earlier Canadian schemes were primarily conceived by their founders as humanitarian interventions, undertaken within the imagined shared geography of the British Empire, in which migration to British colonies was perceived as an extension to the existing principle of placing children out within Britain itself. Both these earlier philanthropists and Fairbridge shared the notion that child migration was a responsible social intervention because it removed children from areas of overpopulation and underemployment to colonies in which the demand for manual labour was high. But for Fairbridge, this rationale was framed far more explicitly in terms of a sense of the building up of the British Empire as an inherent good and one which, in his writings, appears more strongly emphasized than humanitarian concerns for child welfare. As he put it, in an article on the work of the Child Emigration Society in the Daily Mail in 1914, 'the hope of a splendid and united Empire the sole agent that has brought these little colonists to Australia . . . By degrees, if our driving power holds, they will come to see that they themselves are no placeless waifs but inheritors of sacred duties . . . It is my hope that some day, whether it be under arms or behind the plough, these children may thank Heaven for this chance of fulfilling themselves in the service of their race.'[27]

This shifting emphasis was evident in the kinds of checks made of children before they were sent overseas. As the late Victorian schemes to Canada became well-established, it was common-place for children to be selected for migration only after having passed medical tests. In organizational literature, the rationale for this was focused more around concerns that proper checks were being made on the kinds of children being sent to Canada rather than primarily with the child's own health. The Barnardo's magazine, Night and Day, for example declared that all child migrants to Canada should be 'carefully trained into habits of obedience, cleanliness, honesty, virtue and industry; then carefully selected, with a view to their moral and physical fitness'. In the context of Canadian anxieties about 'the very scum and offscouring of our great cities' being deposited in their country, such checks made it possible to re-assure the Canadian public that children sent as migrants were of the 'right sort', and not liable to be a source of moral or physical contamination for Canadian society.[28] The practice of giving children health checks prior to migration continued on with the twentieth-century schemes to Australia. But by the 1920s, these had been supplemented with newly developed IQ tests to check the child's mental abilities. In 1921, the Australian government made it a condition of funding child migration that children should be given medical and psychological tests at Australia House in London before boarding for Australia.[29] While the Bondfield report had commended the psychological screening of child migrants to test for any 'temperamental unsuitability' to migration, the use of psychological testing in the Australian schemes reflected a eugenic concern to promote the physical and mental strength of the Australian population.[30]

By the end of the 1930s, the Fairbridge migration scheme had been joined by other migration initiatives and receiving institutions. The Salvation Army's Riverview Training Farm opened in 1926. Barnardo's followed suit by opening their first residential institution for child migrants in Australia at Picton in 1929, having previously sent children to the Fairbridge Farm School at Pinjarra. Trustees of the Lady Northcote Emigration Fund also opened a farm school at Bacchus Marsh in Victoria in 1937.

A significant difference between this work and that of the Canadian schemes, though, was that very few child migrants to Australia were placed out in private households. Instead, child migrants to Australia were transferred to residential institutions, either training farms or children's homes, in which it was claimed that if they worked hard they would receive the necessary vocational and educational training, as well as moral and religious formation, to flourish as Australian citizens (see Table 3.1).

TABLE 3.1 *List of residential institutions known to have received child migrants in Australia 1913–1970*[31]

Name of organization	Residential institution (NSW: New South Wales; Q: Queensland; SA: South Australia; T: Tasmania; VA: Victoria; WA: Western Australia)
Barnardo's	Dr Barnardo's Farm School, Picton (NSW) Dr Barnardo's Girls Home, Burwood (NSW) 'Greenwood' Boys' and Girls' Home, Normanhurst (NSW)
Christian Brothers (RC)	St Vincent's Orphanage, Castledare (WA) Clontarf Boys' Town, Perth (WA) St Mary's Agricultural School, Tardun (WA) St Joseph's Farm and Trade School (later known as Bindoon Boys' Town), Bindoon (WA)
Church of England	Swan Homes, Perth (WA) Padbury Boys' Farm School, Stoneville, Perth (WA) Church of England Boys' and Girls' Home, Carlingford (NSW) Burton Hall Training Farm, Tatura (VA) St John's House, Canterbury (VA) Clarendon Home for Children, Kingston, Hobart (Q)
Daughters of Charity (RC)	Murray Dwyer Boys' Orphanage, Newcastle (NSW)
Fairbridge	Fairbridge Farm School, Pinjarra (WA) Fairbridge Farm School, Molong (NSW) Hagley Farm School, Launceston (T) Tresca House, Exeter (T)
Fairbridge/Northcote Trust	Northcote Farm School, Bacchus Marsh (V)
Marist Brothers (RC)	St Vincent Boys' Home, Parramatta (NSW)
Methodist Church	Methodist Girls' Home, Mofflyn, Perth (WA) 'Dalmaar', Methodist Home for Children, Carlingford (NSW) Methodist Home, Cheltenham (V) Methodist Home of Children, Wattle Park, Burwood (V) Methodist Children's Home, Magill (SA)
Poor Sisters of Nazareth (RC)	Nazareth House, Geraldton (WA) Nazareth House, Camberwell (V)
Presbyterian	Burnside Presbyterian Orphan Homes, Parramatta (NSW) Dhurringile Training Farm, Tatura (V)

Table 3.1   Continued

Salesians	St John Bosco Boys' Town, Hobart (T)
Salvation Army	'Seaforth Home', Gosnells (WA)
	Arncliffe Girls' Home, Arncliffe (NSW)
	Boxley Boys' Home, Boxley (NSW)
	Canowindra Girls' Home, Canowindra (NSW)
	Goulburn Boys' Home, Goulburn (NSW)
	Riverview Training Farm, Ipswich (Q)
Sisters of Mercy (RC)	St Joseph's Orphanage, Subiaco, Perth (WA)
	St Vincent's Foundling Home, Subiaco, Perth (WA)
	St Brigid's Orphanage, Ryde (NSW)
	St John's Orphanage, Thurgoona, Albury (NSW)
	St Vincent de Paul's Orphanage, Goodwood, Adelaide (SA)
	St Joseph's Children's Home, Neerkol, Rockhampton (Q)
Sisters of St Joseph (RC)	St Joseph's Home, Kellerberrin (WA)
	St Joseph's Girls' Orphanage, Lane Cove (NSW)
United Protestant Association	'Melrose', United Protestant Association Home, Parramatta (NSW)

In the wake of the passing of the 1922 Empire Settlement Act, the Assembly of the Church of England passed a motion to establish the Church of England Council of Empire Settlement. The objectives of this new organization were both to disseminate information to make people aware in Britain of potential migration opportunities to other imperial territories and to be involved in the selection, support and overseas reception of migrants. Responses to this initiative by King George V and the secretary of state for dominion affairs, Leo Amery, strongly endorsed it, the latter commenting that the 'social and spiritual atmosphere [of Empire settlement] matters no less than the material conditions. In these respects the co-operation of an Empire-wide body like the Church of England ... could only be of incalculable benefit in the success of a policy which aimed not only at helping the individual, but at the healthy up-building of the national life of the Dominions'.[32] By the end of the decade, the Church of England Council of Empire Settlement had arranged the migration of several thousand juvenile migrants, with the economic depression causing both significant problems for these migrants and a major financial challenge for the Council as government funding for migration was suspended until economic conditions improved.[33] In the postwar period the Council, now reformed as Church of England Advisory Council for Empire Settlement, became actively involved in arranging the migration of younger children. In its annual report for 1948, it reported that it had sent twenty-eight children to Anglican residential homes in Australia but with potential capacity to send many more. The demand for child migrants arose from the residential homes themselves, seeking to fill places, with 'requisitions' for nearly 200 children between the ages of 5 and 14 received by the Council from them that same year.[34] The emphasis in its early postwar reports was placed far more on the sense of the Church's duty to continue to nurture the Empire and to consolidate bonds across British territories. Maintaining the viability of Anglican residential institutions in Australia also appears to be a significant motivating factor. A 1954 review of its work noted the 'constant demand from the various Anglican Children's Homes in Australia for Church of England children, which the Church of England is clearly under an obligation to satisfy'.[35]

Alongside this Anglican initiative, Roman Catholic organizations were also proactively seeking to encourage child migration to Australia. In 1927, the Catholic hierarchy in England and Wales supported the creation of the Catholic Emigration Society, a new national organization with a very similar role to the Church of England Council of Empire Settlement to publicize migration opportunities and to facilitate migration to British dominions through financial support available from the provisions of the Empire Settlement Act.[36] The similarity in remit was no coincidence. In its first publicity pamphlet, the Society noted the 'very advantageous State aided schemes which had been introduced' to encourage migration. It lamented the fact, though, that large numbers of Catholics were seeking to make use of non-Catholic emigration societies to access State-assisted migration funding and noted 'how great is the danger in such cases of loss of faith' particularly when non-Catholic organizations placed Catholic migrants in areas remote from Catholic communities.[37] By establishing itself as a specialist migration service for Catholics, the Society thus aimed to provide migration opportunities that would not put the faith of the migrant at risk.[38] A period of conflict arose between the Society and the Catholic Emigration Association over the remit of managing the migration of Catholic children, with this being eventually resolved through the merger of both organizations in 1939 into the Catholic Council for British Overseas Settlement.[39] The complex network of Catholic organizations, which included the formal structures of the Church, child welfare and migration organizations and semi-autonomous religious orders, meant however that Catholic child migration took place without comprehensive oversight or control from any single body.

From 1938, Brother Conlon, a member of the Christian Brothers order, began proactively to approach Catholic organizations in Britain to request that children be sent to Christian Brothers' residential schools in Western Australia.[40] While most children were sent initially through the Catholic Emigration Association and subsequently through the more recently formed Catholic Child Welfare Council, the Catholic hierarchy in Australia and Brother Conlon also by-passed them and continued to make co-ordinated approaches directly to religious orders in Britain after the Second World War to seek the migration of children in their care.[41]

Aspirations of increasing the Catholic population in British dominions, and safeguarding the faith of Catholic children, reflected long-standing concerns that had motivated Catholic child migration work to Canada. What was more evident in the context of postwar Catholic migration was that senior figures in the Anglican Church felt far more threatened by what they perceived as the relative success of Catholic migration services. In the context of Canadian child migration work, Protestant organizations had been far in the ascendancy over their Catholic counterparts in terms of the numbers of migrants sent out. Whether those Protestant organizations harboured antagonistic views towards their Catholic peers or not, the pattern of child migration was resolutely Protestant. In postwar Australia, the sectarian competition was much closer. At times, Church of England bodies wrote in general terms about the importance of maintaining 'religious balance' in Commonwealth countries.[42] At others, it was more explicitly sectarian noting in its annual report for 1955/6 that it was 'very apparent that the Church of England was lagging far behind the highly organised Roman Catholic Church activities in this particular field. The Secretary was informed that the Roman Catholic population had increased by 10% in the last 5 years and, as the number of foreigners (who in the main were Roman Catholics) entering Australia last year exceeded the number of British migrants, it will be realised how important it is that the Church of England should make every effort to sponsor more people from this country.'[43]

The growth of child migration work to Australia from the 1920s onwards raises the question as to why child migration work began to flourish there precisely at the same time when it was being wound down in Canada. It is true that many of the organizations who had previously sent child migrants to Canada continued to do so to Australia. Dr Barnardo's Homes had been critical of the recommendation by the Bondfield Report to suspend the migration of children under 14 to Canada[44] and so it was not surprising that they, along with charities such as the Salvation Army and National Children's Home, continued the practice elsewhere. Indeed the Fairbridge Society was the only major charity that sent children to Australia which did not have prior involvement in child migration work to Canada, with both the Church of England and Catholic Church continuing their earlier child migration work albeit through altered administrative structures.

These organizations were only able to shift their work to Australia, however, because of a supportive environment both in Britain and Australia. Although the Australian Commonwealth government had initially been slow to provide recurrent per capita funding to child migration schemes to Australia, this had shifted to a more supportive approach by the mid-1920s. At the same time, child migration work also had powerful backing in Britain. Some socialists and trade unionists may have been effective in their criticisms of child migration to Canada, but simultaneously, other establishment figures gave their support to the emergent Australian schemes. Barnardo's was, by this time, a well-respected organization with royal patronage since 1902. Kingsley Fairbridge's social connections, helped by his time in Oxford, appears to have been even more successful in embedding support for child migration in sections of the establishment. By 1914, the list of signatories to a letter commending the work of the Child Emigration Society to potential donors included the headmaster of Eton, the president of Magdalen College, Oxford and two Oxford Regius professors, including the professor for Divinity, Henry Scott Holland.[45] Two years after the Bondfield report was produced, the Fairbridge Society was able to have the former governor-general of Australia, Lord Forster, to speak in praise of their work at one of their London luncheon events.[46] Two years further on, it was the Duke of York (the future King George VI) and the secretary of state for the dominions, Leo Amery, who came to give glowing endorsements.[47] The former declared that the Fairbridge scheme 'to my mind has done, is doing and will do in the future untold good in producing the right kind of citizen in Australia'. Amery added that he could think of 'no work of moral regeneration, physical, moral or economic, more effective than was being done at the Fairbridge Farm' and that 'he looked forward to the time when many such institutions would be in existence'. Although the Duke of York's support was to prove important for Fairbridge in the future,[48] Amery's endorsement of the Fairbridge Society demonstrated the complex stance of some public figures towards child migration in that period. It was Amery, as then secretary of state for the colonies who had presented the Bondfield Report to Parliament in December 1924 and had refused to push against its recommendations despite an informal request to do so from Barnardo's. Yet despite this, three years later, Amery was commending Fairbridge's work during a visit to the Pinjarra Farm School, with a photograph appearing in The Times of him talking to boys standing around him in bare feet.[49]

While child migration had its critics in Britain in this period, the broad political consensus of the importance of strengthening the empire meant that child migration could be welcomed as part of the wider process of empire settlement as long as it received no strong resistance from the receiving Dominion. When such resistance arose in Canada there was little political will in Britain to challenge it. In Australia, however, child migration attracted little criticism. Furthermore the Bondfield report had focused its criticisms on the risks of placing children under the age of 14 in private households that had not been subject to prior inspection and in which there was a risk of children being abused, overworked and deprived of educational opportunities they would reasonably expect to have in Britain.[50] For those broadly sympathetic to the value of child migration, such risks might be assumed to be much lower in the case of Australian schemes where children were being sent into the residential care of reputable bodies.

That was to change significantly, however, following the Second World War. In 1945, the Care of Children Committee was set up jointly by the

Home Office and Departments of Health and Education to review current provision for children 'who for whatever cause are deprived of a normal family life with their own parents or relatives' and to investigate what future provision should be established 'to ensure that these children are brought up under conditions best calculated to compensate them for lack of parental care'.[51] Its findings, published in what became known as the Curtis Committee Report, set out key working principles that were to prove definitive for public child-care provision in the postwar period. It recommended the consolidation of child-care responsibilities within local authorities. It strongly endorsed the value of keeping a child in their own home wherever possible, including in cases of illegitimacy.[52] Where this was not possible, adoption of the child was generally commended as the most preferable option, with fostering the next more preferable.[53] Institutional care of children was considered to have some benefits, and to be a necessary form of provision for the foreseeable future given the time it might take for improvements in the welfare system to reduce the number of deprived children. However, the report also noted the tendency even in well-managed institutions towards 'a lack of interest in the child as an individual and to remote and impersonal relations'.[54] A child from a deprived background might, therefore, have a better material environment, food and clothing in institutional care, but keenly felt 'the lack of affection and personal interest', with institutional children's craving for signs of physical affection 'in striking and painful contrast' to the usual behaviour of children kept within the family home.

Given these general principles, it is not surprising that the report's assessment of the child migration schemes was less than enthusiastic. Recognizing that child migration might soon recommence after having been interrupted by the War, the Committee commented:

> We have heard evidence as to the arrangements for selecting children for migration, and it is clear to us that their effect is that this opportunity is given only to children of fine physique and good mental equipment. These are precisely the children for whom satisfactory openings could be found in this country, and in present day conditions this particular method of providing for the deprived child is not one that we specially wish to see extended. On the other hand, a fresh start in a new country may, for children with an unfortunate background, be the foundation of a happy life, and the opportunity should therefore in our view remain open to suitable children who express a desire for it. We should however strongly deprecate their setting out in life under less through care and supervision than they would have at home, and we recommend that it should be a condition of consenting to the emigration of deprived children that the arrangements made by the Government of the receiving country . . . should be comparable to those we have proposed in this report for deprived children remaining in this country.[55]

Although the Report had not called conclusively for an end to child migration, it established principles that were soon to place this work under increasing pressure. On 24 March 1948, the president, chair and secretary of the British Federation of Social Workers had a letter published in The Times that noted that the Children's Bill (soon to become the 1948 Children's Act) still allowed for the emigration of children. Commenting that the 'methods of selection of children, their welfare, training and after-care in the receiving countries are not always of a high standard', they recommended that a special government commission be established to examine the whole system. Such sentiments also found support among Home Office staff keen to pursue the Curtis Committee Report's key principles with a mandate to monitor both child-care provision with local authorities and voluntary organizations. However, while children in local authority care could only be emigrated with the written permission of the Home Secretary, following the 1948 Children's Act, the Act did not provide a clear enough framework for the Home Office to be able to regulate the work of the voluntary organizations undertaking child migration work. Instead, the Home Office sought to apply pressure on the Commonwealth Relations Office, who agreed funding for child migrants under the Empire Settlement Act.[56]

The Home Office's attempts to influence standards applied to child migration in the Commonwealth Relations Office – and through it to the Australian Commonwealth government – began as early as 1947.[57] Progress was slow, however, and in 1949 the Commonwealth Relations Office approved the migration of thirty girls to the Sisters of Mercy's orphanage in Thurgoona, despite the Home Office protesting about the impersonal, poorly resourced home, its remote location and lack of effective after-care provision. In 1950 attempts by the Home Office to establish conditions in residential institutions receiving child migrants in Australia through a questionnaire was rebuffed by the Australian authorities. It then turned its efforts to challenging child migration practices through an interdepartmental review of the renewal of the Empire Settlement Act (including subsidies paid through this child migration organizations). The review deferred to the findings of a report due to be submitted by John Moss, a former member of the Curtis Committee, based on his inspection of residential institutions in Australia. Moss's report was only submitted in July 1952, and while reinforcing basic principles of the Curtis report also, disappointingly for the Home Office, fundamentally endorsed the value of child migration without demanding substantial reforms.[58] The fact that the Empire Settlement Act had only been temporarily renewed in 1952 meant that in 1954 another interdepartmental review was undertaken to decide on its further renewal. The Home Office's objections to child migration were set out very clearly during this process, with it strongly recommending that children should only be sent to Australia in the future if they were placed in adoptive or foster families rather than residential institutions. After some prevarication, it was decided that a final decision on this should be informed by a further review of the Australian institutions to be undertaken by John Ross.

John Ross had, until retiring at the end of 1955, been assistant under-secretary at the Home Office in charge of the Children's Department and had a strong record of advocating for the principles of the Curtis Committee report. Minutes of earlier meetings between him and representatives of Catholic child-care organizations in Britain show him previously to have been blunt in his criticisms of their continued use of large residential homes, the lack of training among their staff and their failures to make more widespread use of foster care.[59] Before undertaking his Fact-Finding Mission to Australia, Ross would also been aware that the Christian Brothers' children's home at St Charles, Brentwood had been threatened with de-certification by the Home Office because of its very poor standards of care.

The verdict of the review team that he led was damning, and was communicated back to the Commonwealth Relations Office in two parts: an official report and a confidential appendix with more detailed comments on individual institutions. The text of the official report contained numerous criticisms of the reception and care of child migrants. Children were often sent with insufficient information about their previous family and social backgrounds in the United Kingdom. The assumption among migration agencies that children who had difficult early lives would benefit from opportunities in a new country neglected the reality that 'it was precisely such children, already rejected and insecure; who might often be ill-equipped to cope with the added strain of migration'.[60] The review team noted with concern stories of siblings who had been separated on arrival in Australia, sometimes to institutions far removed from each other, and recommended that children should not be migrated unless they could subsequently be ensured regular contact with each other. Warm assurances by receiving institutions that children generally settled down quickly on arrival were treated with scepticism in the Report, with it being noted that child migrants had themselves spoken to the review team about their distress at separation from their families. While there were exceptions, the care in most receiving homes took an institutional form, lacking privacy or a homely atmosphere and in some cases often poor standards of accommodation. Staff were in many cases well intentioned, but the lack of specialist training in child-care work meant that they did not necessarily understand the needs of the children with whom they were working. The remoteness of many of the receiving institutions meant that child migrants often had little opportunity to assimilate with wider society before leaving the institution. While adults in Australia might be used to travelling considerable distances to undertake social activities, children in receiving institutions were dependent on them making external activities available to them and those arrangements were not always adequate. Even receiving homes in or near towns did not always do enough to ensure that their children had opportunities to engage in wider social interactions beyond the institution. As a result, children often left with inadequate training in everyday life skills and insufficiently familiar with the social environments they were now expected to live in.

The Report's recommendations, while allowing that child migration could continue and that residential care might still be needed until fostering became the established means of care for child migrants, were nevertheless a substantial challenge to existing practice. Migration of all children, not just those in local authority care, should now be subject to the permission of the Home Secretary. Sending agencies should provide full information of children's backgrounds to receiving institutions. Staff in residential homes should have relevant understanding of child-care methods. Children should be given greater opportunities for assimilation into Australian life. Foster care should become the preferred method of care for child migrants. Most ominously of all, for the child migration agencies, was the recommendation that the list of establishments approved to receive child migrants should be now reviewed with these basic standards in mind.

Alongside the text of the report, Ross also submitted a series of brief confidential reports about each of the institutions that they had visited which were even more frank about their shortcomings. From these twenty-six individual reports, it was clear that the problems described in the main text of the report were widespread. Only five of the institutions visited by Ross's team received an entirely positive review from him: the Clarendon Church of England Home for Children, Barnardo's Farm School at Picton, the Hagley Farm School, the Methodist Home at Burwood and Burton Hall Training Farm.[61] For the rest, the reports present a litany of failings. The standard of accommodation in some homes was of poor quality and created a dis-spiriting environment for children.[62] Staffing in many places was insufficient, too dominated by men or involved individuals in key positions who lacked training and insight into children's needs.[63]

Ross reserved some of his strongest language for the failings of staff in this regard. The attitude of committee members of the Dhurringile Training Farm towards boys in their care was 'deplorable' and Ross made a point of contrasting the bleak, exploitative and uncaring environment with a British publicity brochure for the Farm which stated that 'boys are given a splendid opportunity at Dhurringile under ideal conditions under trained experts in social work'.[64] The practice of transferring boys aged 6 or 7 from St Joseph's, Leederville to St Vincent's, Castledare, where they would be almost entirely under the care of men was 'to be entirely deprecated'.[65] The views of key staff were reported where these demonstrated an obvious lack of insight into children's emotional lives or a lack of understanding of more broadly accepted principles of child-care. In some cases, staff opposition to fostering children out was noted. A staff member at the Fairbridge Farm School at Pinjarra, for example, declared himself to be against giving the children anything more than very short-term experiences of foster-care as children tended to find their exposure to life in a family home 'upsetting' when they returned to the Farm School.[66] At Clontarf Boys' Town, the principal said that 'he had no information about the boy's previous background or previous history, and did not consider there would be any advantage in having such information. He did not think that the boys themselves would ever worry about their parentage.'[67] He also expressed the view that enuresis was sufficient grounds for refusing children to have temporary placements in foster homes during the summer holidays, meaning that children who wet the bed would have to stay living at the institution during their breaks.[68] Noting again the lack of information about boys' previous backgrounds, the principal of St Vincent's, Castledare said that 'he thought none of them had any relatives. He said that they settled quickly and without difficulty, and that, in his opinion, children did not think about what was happening to them and were not disturbed by moves.'[69] Lack of knowledge about children's previous home backgrounds, as a result of little or no information having been passed on by sending organizations, was a source of complaint from staff in a number of residential homes, suggested that particular sending agencies may have had an effective policy of withholding this in the belief that it would give children a clean break from their pasts and the opportunity for them of a fresh start. This problem was repeatedly noted by Ross in relation to children sent by Roman Catholic organizations and the Church of England Council for Commonwealth and Empire Settlement.[70]

The isolated and institutional nature of many of the residential homes noted in the main report was described in more detail in the Confidential Appendix.[71] In contrast to homes dealing with smaller groups of children, many remained large-scale, impersonal institutions. In a number of cases, children were reported as sleeping in dormitories accommodating twenty children or more – in some instances up to fifty children.[72] These were predominantly institutions run by Catholic religious orders. Staff at St Joseph's Children's Home at Neerkol told the Ross review team that 'there had never been any need to provide lockers for the boys [in the home], as they did not acquire possessions of their own.'[73] Toys displayed at Nazareth House, East Camberwell were so pristine and tidily ordered that it seemed unlikely they had ever been played with.[74] Children were subject to rigid institutional regimes and given limited opportunities for social interaction beyond their institution, with some homes allowing trips outside of the home only in organized groups.[75] The principal at St John Bosco Boys' Town told the review team that it was necessary to keep their boys under 'constant supervision to guard against corruption'. The amount of work children were expected to do at the Fairbridge Farm Schools at Pinjarra and Molong, as well as institutions such as St Joseph's, Bindoon and the Dhurringile Training Farm, was contrasted very unfavourably with the Hagley Farm School where children's manual work contributing to the running and maintenance of the school was said to be only around two hours a week. As a consequence, children produced by these impersonal, highly structured, work-dominated environments tended to have 'little opportunity for independent thought or action'[76] and as such, poorly prepared for life beyond the institution.

There were inevitable shortcomings in Ross's confidential assessments of these institutions given the brevity of his visits to each one. His report on the Fairbridge Farm School at Molong, for example, describes its principal, Frederick Woods, as 'a man of good personality, kindly and interested in the children'.[77] While some children at Molong did indeed have positive, or at least mixed experiences of Woods, Ross's assessment of Woods's leadership was made in ignorance of the fact Woods had already been investigated twice in relation to allegations of sexual and physical abuse of children and that his practice of punishing children by beating them with a broken hockey stick had led, in one case, to a child's back being broken.[78] Ross's acknowledgement in the main report of the complaint by many homes of the intellectually or physically 'sub-standard' children they received could also have been more insightful. While many homes did indeed complain to the review team about children being 'dull' or 'backward', it is notable that in almost all cases these complaints came from impersonal and highly regimented homes run by staff lacking insight into children's emotional needs.[79] There was no recognition that children's withdrawn behaviour or educational underperformance may have been related to their experience of separation and their ongoing lack of emotional nurture. By contrast, homes that provided better environments had no complaints about the children they were receiving.[80] Nevertheless, despite its flaws, Ross's Fact-Finding Mission report, and the accompanying confidential appendix, constituted a more substantial challenge to the system of child migration to Australia than anything to have previously been produced within the British government.

This challenge was quickly recognized when Ross submitted his draft report and confidential appendix to the Commonwealth Relations Office. In a confidential letter to the Secretary of State for Commonwealth Relations on 28 March 1956, attached to his draft report, Ross noted the sensitivities of this issue with regard to relationships with the Australian authorities. He proposed that while residential institutions be allowed to keep child migrants already resident with them, periodic reviews every three years should now be established to ensure appropriate standards were maintained. Permission for receipt of new child migrants should now, he suggested, be put on a more rigorous footing with no further children to be sent to institutions that were large and impersonal or in remote areas.[81] In particular, Ross suggested that no further children be sent to five specific institutions: the Salvation Army Training Farm, Riverview; the Dhurringile Rural Training Farm; St John Bosco Boys' Town; Methodist Children's Home, Magill, and St Joseph's Farm School, Bindoon. The Home Office later queried why Ross hadn't included at least another five institutions on this 'black-list', though also recognized that the royal and political patronage enjoyed by the Fairbridge Society put black-listing their schools at Pinjarra and Molong 'beyond the sphere of practical politics'.[82] In reality, though, Ross's suggestion of no longer sending children to large or remote residential institutions would have had the effect of extending this ban far beyond his five highlighted organizations, including these Fairbridge institutions.

Shortly after this, the Office of the High Commisioner for the United Kingdom in Canberra, who had made the practical arrangements for the Ross mission's visit, contacted the Commonwealth Relations Office with its own comments.[83] Had it not been, they noted, for the presence of a member of the mission known to be sympathetic to child migration, the report would doubtless have been even more critical than it was.[84] Although its criticisms were a compromise, they would nevertheless come as a strong disappointment to the voluntary societies running the schemes and it was lamented that Ross had not taken up their suggestions to give a warmer account 'of the many kindnesses shown to the children and the money raised in this country'. A discussion then began within the Commonwealth Relations Office, including the secretary of state, the future prime minister, Alec Douglas-Home, as to whether the Ross report should be published or not.[85] The main argument against publication was that the report 'contained a number of observations that will be unwelcome to the child migration societies and to the Australian Governments, both Commonwealth and State'.[86] In favour of publication was the sheer fact that the review had taken place at all. Both the voluntary organizations and Australian authorities were obviously aware that it had taken place, and the Fairbridge Society had already by 19 April made several enquiries about its contents. Any attempt not to publish was likely to lead to inevitable demands for its release and any attempt to formulate policy on the basis of the report would also require its publication. On 27 April, at a meeting with the secretary of state, it was agreed that the report should be published as a guidance paper, not yet accepted by the government, in early June after the Australian authorities and voluntary organizations had been notified of its contents.[87] Showing copies of a government report to the voluntary organizations before it had formally been presented to the Parliament was not common practice, but the House of Commons publications office agreed to this given the 'rather unusual' nature of the circumstances.[88]

After the contents of the report became known to the Australian government, its publication was managed in such a way as to soften its impact as much as possible.[89] By 25 May, the Commonwealth Relations Office sent a telegram to the Office of the UK High Commissioner asking them to inform the Australian authorities that the Fact-Finding Mission's report would now be delayed until mid-July.[90] This would coincide with the publication of comments on the report by the Overseas Migration Board, an advisory panel to the Commonwealth Relations Office which had been strongly supportive of child migration schemes (and who on hearing the outcome of the Fact-Finding Mission had expressed strong regret that the report had ever been commissioned in the first place[91]). On 6 June, this was followed up with a further telegram in which the Commonwealth Relations Office encouraged the UK High Commissioner's Office to liaise with the

Australian authorities to set up some form of review that could be referred to when the Ross report was finally published to re-assure public opinion that any problems were in hand.[92] Privately, officials in the Commonwealth Relations Office now expressed concern that simply publishing the Ross report alongside critical comments on it from the Overseas Migration Board would not be enough to mitigate its criticisms.[93] The Overseas Migration Board were not experts in child-care after all and they had no direct evidence themselves of conditions in the residential institutions. If publication of the Ross report were not managed more effectively, the criticisms would rebound on to organizations running the schemes and probably effect public donations to them. The revised mid-July publication date would still be before the start of the Parliamentary summer recess, and could lead to demands for a Parliamentary debate on child migration. Unresolved questions would then continue to be picked up by the press during the 'silly season' of the Parliamentary summer recess with the government poorly placed to respond to these.[94] These problems clearly continued to concern officials in the Commonwealth Relations Office. An appeal from Sir Colin Anderson, a member of the Overseas Migration Board and director of the company that ran the Orient Line shipping service to Australia, not to publish the report at all was given serious consideration.[95] But this course of action still seemed impractical given that the report would inevitably have to be published given that the review was known to have taken place. After further discussion with the Overseas Migration Board's chairman,[96] it notified the UK High Commissioner's Office on 12 June that the Ross report would now be published in mid-August during the Parliamentary recess to prevent calls for a Parliamentary debate in late July when the government was already managing a very busy Parliamentary schedule. This delay, the Commonwealth Relations Office argued, made it even more urgent that the Australian authorities be seen to be making a start on 'securing improvement of such arrangements as they agree need improvement' before publication of the report.[97] Prior to the report's eventual publication on 14 August, the media strategy was being internally discussed in which the report was to be released with 'the briefest possible announcement and no explanation' in the hope that it would attract as little attention as possible.[98] By the time of its publication, John Ross had left Britain on a long trip to Scandinavia, unavailable for public comment, and fully aware by then that his hopes that it could affect child migration policy would almost certainly not be realized.[99]

Meanwhile, discussions were underway between the Commonwealth Relations Office and the Home Office about how to proceed with future applications for the migration of children. The Commonwealth Relations Office did not send the confidential reports on individual residential institutions to the Home Office until 9 June.[100] Within a week of receiving these, the Home Office suggested that the best option would be to have a temporary suspension of all applications for child migration until either a more thorough review had been undertaken or a decision taken which would render further reviews unnecessary (i.e. cease approval for child migration as a matter of general policy). To continue to send children to institutions known to be problematic was recognized as not being in the best interests of the child. To try to make approvals only to selective institutions would require making decisions in some cases based on limited evidence and would also have the inadvertent effect of drawing the voluntary societies' attention to the fact that a secret black-list existed. In a tone characteristic of interactions in the coming months, however, the Home Office showed no great inclination to express an authoritative view or to take responsibility for any decision in the face of opposition from the Australian authorities and voluntary organizations. While recommending temporary suspension of all child migration applications, it was made clear that 'we do not feel that we are in a position to advise you definitely in favour of it, and if on grounds of expediency, you preferred to adopt the first course [i.e. continue to approve applications], we could not dissent'.[101]

Any intention on the Commonwealth Relations Office to follow this suggestion quickly evaporated,[102] both through pressure from Australia and from British organizations undertaking child migration work. By the end of June, the Commonwealth Relations Office had begun to share content from the confidential appendices with the Australian Commonwealth government. John Ross, when made aware of this, expressed considerable disquiet. Ross argued that the release of this information would make it possible for the report to be marginalized by disputing facts about individual institutions and that a focus on the five 'black-listed' institutions would obscure the 'ignorance of child care considerations, and the complacency' that the review team had found in many of the institutions.[103] His objections were to no avail, but proved prescient given the events that were to take place later that summer.

On receipt of the confidential appendices, the Australian government's response was to argue that the main criticisms within them concerned staffing and accommodation and that these required more time and investment (as well as an ongoing commitment from the British government to child migration) to be addressed. Its suggestion was to set up its own review, focusing on three of the five black-listed institutions (St John's Bosco Boys' Town, St Joseph's Bindoon and Dhurringile Rural Training Farm) as the other two were no longer intending to receive child migrants.[104] The Commonwealth Relations Office commended this plan – ever conscious of the need for something to be seen to be taking place by the time of the publication of the Ross report[105] – and suggested that more institutions be visited in this review to avoid drawing attention just to the black-listed ones. It also suggested attaching an observer, Anthony Rouse, from the UK High Commissioner's Office to the Australian team.[106] The date of 11 July was set for the Australian review team to begin its visits to selected institutions. The desire of the Commonwealth Relations Office to ensure that this process went smoothly, went so far as a telegrammed enquiry to the Office of the UK

High Commissioner to check that the Australian authorities understood that they would need to share the findings of their inspections with the British government and that the content of their reports could have a significant bearing on whether child migration schemes were able to continue or not. 'Have the Australians,' it asked, 'considered this implication, which would need to be borne in mind in preparing reports?'[107] As the planned review quickly took shape, the Home Office began to sense that its fight was nearly lost. In a letter to the Commonwealth Relations Office, it expressed the hope that a constructive discussion could take place with the Australian authorities on the standards of child-care by which they would assess residential institutions to which child migrants were sent and regretted that this had not happened before the Australian review had begun.[108] By this stage, however, this was little more than aspiration and lament.

At the same time as the Australian 'solution' to the Ross report began to take shape, so the British government was coming under increasing pressure to approve more child migration applications. On 3 July, the Commonwealth Relations Office notified the Office of the UK High Commissioner in Canberra that the Fairbridge Society and Northcote Trust were pressing for approval of another sixteen and three child migrants respectively to be sent to Australia.[109] Feeling unable to resist this pressure, it agreed to approve these applications but notified Fairbridge and Northcote that any future approvals would need to be considered in the light of the Fact-Finding Mission's report and any subsequent consultations on it.

The Fairbridge Society was clearly unhappy at this prospect. On 13 July, the home secretary, Gwilym Lloyd-George, was forced to offer a bland holding statement about future policy decisions on child migration after Douglas Dodds-Parker, MP, under-secretary of state for foreign affairs had met him on their behalf.[110] Dodds-Parker claimed that there were 'rumours' that it would be compulsory in future for the Home Office to approve applications for the migration of all children and not just those in local authority care. The fact that this was indeed one of Ross's recommendations strongly suggested that the contents of the report had already been leaked in some form to Fairbridge.[111] Any such recommendation, Dodds-Parker argued, would effectively kill off child migration work given that any consultation that the Home Office had with local authorities would lead to individual applications being blocked because of the latter's ignorance of the benefits of these schemes. Sounding a clear note against the move towards greater local authority powers over child-care under the previous Labour government, Dodds-Parker noted that 'we hope that a Conservative Government will encourage voluntary child welfare organisations'.[112]

In the event, the Australian review team did extend its inspections to more institutions than the three that were originally proposed. From Rouse's private notes,[113] later sent to the Commonwealth Relations Office, it appears that at least eight institutional visits were made. Some of these were evidently fairly peremptory, with the Australia review managing to visit three separate institutions in Western Australia in a single day. Rouse's

observations accorded to a great extent with those expressed in the Ross
confidential appendices. He endorsed the review team's positive assessments
of the Clarendon Church of England Home, the Burton Hill Farm School,
Tatura, the Methodist Home at Burwood, and noted that some improvements
had been made at Castledare and Swan Homes, Midland Junction, since the
Ross team had made their visits. The Fact-Finding Mission's less positive
assessments of the other institutions that Rouse visited were also endorsed
in the case of Nazareth House, East Camberwell. For other institutions,
Rouse added his own criticisms. The 'worst feature' of the Fairbridge Farm
School at Pinjarra, he commented, 'was the refusal to allow adoption or
the boys to go to foster homes'. Despite the State Child Welfare Officer for
Western Australia, Mr McColl, having frequent arguments with the school's
principal about this, it was a 'rule laid down by the Fairbridge Society in
the United Kingdom and evidently nothing can be done about it locally'.[114]
At Clontarf, he discovered that Mr McColl was hardly on speaking terms
with the principal any more after he had reprimanded the principal 'for
beating one of the boys unnecessarily severely'.[115] At Pinjarra, Castledare
and Clontarf, Rouse was shocked that the children wore no shoes. This, he
noted, 'must be cold for them in the winter'.[116]

When the Australian review submitted copies of its reports to the Office
of the UK High Commissioner on 10 September, its comments were much
fuller than Rouse's, but reports were only presented for the three institutions
that it visited which Ross had proposed for black-listing.[117] The report on
St John's Bosco Boys' Town focused mainly on the physical environment
of the school which it found entirely suitable. It also addressed what
had evidently been a primary concern of the Fact-Finding Mission in its
confidential comments on the school – that it was a highly regimented
institution run on the basis of constant surveillance almost entirely by men
with little effective arrangements for pastoral care. Discussion of this took
place in a pre-arranged meeting with the school's principal and the Catholic
Archbishop of Hobart, Guilford Young, prior to the inspection of the school.
Here, the principal, Fr Cole, defended the ethos of the school vigorously:

> He challenged us to name a better school of this kind in Australia or in the
> world. He also defends very stoutly the system of 'prevention' on which
> the school is run. With the operation of such a system boys are prevented
> from sinning or getting into trouble, thus 'prevention is better than cure'.
> The Archbishop and Father Cole pointed out that this 'preventative
> system' operates in all Silesian homes throughout the world and both,
> particularly Father Cole, were amazed that it should be questioned at
> Bosco's.[118]

Lack of effective female presence on the staff was not considered to be a
concern because the youngest boy at the school at present was aged 13.
While apparently intending to report these as robust defences of the school's

ethos in response to the criticisms of the Fact-Finding Mission, some unease seems to have persisted for the Australian reviewers. They noted that the boys seen were poorly dressed, with Fr Cole apologizing that if he had not been off-sick recently he would have ensured that the boys were much better turned out for the inspection. Their conclusion that the school required no further improvements to be considered suitable for receiving more child migrants was also qualified by their recommendation that its future in-take be restricted to children 'already familiar with the "Silesian Order" and not be aged under 10 or 11.

Dhurringile Rural Training Farm and St Joseph's, Bindoon were given similarly (guardedly) positive reviews by the Australian team though some minor improvements to their accommodation were identified that should be completed by the institutions within a period of three months. Dhurringile was required to improve its ground-floor bathrooms used by the boys and put floor coverings and curtains in their bedrooms.[119] At St Joseph's, Bindoon, their report went into some detail with a recommendation for a wooden frame for hanging towels on to be built in the boys' shower room. It was also recommended that younger children no longer sleep on a veranda but in one of the main dormitories inside the building and that mats be placed on the bare concrete floors in the bedrooms. Again, while strongly recommending that the school continue to receive further child migrants subject to these improvements being carried out within three months, there was also some evidence of unease. It was questioned whether the principal, who was clear that his background was only in teaching, was necessarily the most suited person to hold this role and noted that the Archbishop of Perth had also asked the review team in a prior meeting whether they thought that the principal was 'the right man for the job'.[120]

The contrast between Rouses's private comments on each of these institutions and the final reports submitted by the Australian inspectors was stark. Rouse found the material conditions at Dhurringile to be generally poor and was not particularly reassured by the promises of improvements made by the head of the Presbyterian Church's Social Services Department for Victoria. The dairy was, he noted, in a better condition than the boys' bathrooms, probably because it was inspected more often. The boys complained of not having sufficient packed lunches, being cold at Dhurringile, not getting hot drinks before tea if they were delayed coming back from school and travelling to school in a truck that was cold, draughty and insufficiently water-proofed. The elderly management committee seemed more interested in the farm than the school itself and had no understanding of current principles of child-care.[121] At St John Bosco Boys' Town, Rouse records a series of arguments with the principal, who seemed almost entirely unreceptive to any suggestions made by the inspection team. At one point, the principal objected to the discussion of having a stronger female staff presence in the school by saying that 'he would not tolerate a woman on the staff "interfering with the whole organization"'. The staff, Rouse, concluded had little understanding of general child welfare and the ethos of the school was 'austere and severe'.[122] At St Joseph's, Bindoon, where the Australian inspectors had been particularly exercised by the problems of damp towels, Rouse was at his most damning. The bathrooms were in a disgusting state – including one toilet for use at night which had no seat – and had left Mr Wheeler, the lead Australian inspector, feeling nauseous. Most beds were without sheets, and where sheets were in evidence they were dirty and in poor condition. Children who wet the bed slept on a veranda where there was no protection against the elements. Amidst the spartan accommodation for the boys, the principal proudly displayed the painted pillars (made to look like marble) in the school dining room which he claimed were designed 'to give the boys "spiritual uplift as they would not have seen anything like this from where they came"'. 'If this remark had not been made in all seriousness', commented Rouse, 'it would have been laughable.' The boys had obviously been 'spruced up' for the visit and were wearing their best clothes, including shoes. From footmarks around the institution, though, it was clear that they normally went around in bare feet. The boys themselves told the inspection team that they had been put to work to clean the place up prior to their visit. Rouse expressed amazement that such poor conditions had been allowed to persist for such a long time, something for which the state director of Child Welfare made an apology to the rest of the reviewers. Despite these obvious shortcomings, 'the Principal appeared to think that there was nothing wrong with the establishment'. 'He struck me,' Rouse noted, 'as being utterly callous and lacking in all understanding of child welfare'.[123]

The Australian government's view of this review process was clear, however. It had considered conditions at institutions that wished to continue to receive child migrants but had been identified by Ross as not being up to standard (limiting its definition of that to institutions that Ross had explicitly proposed for black-listing). With the exception of remedial work on some parts of their accommodation, these institutions had been found to be suitable for this purpose. As no other institutions had been explicitly identified as unsuitable to receive further child migrants, the government's conclusion was that 'there is no justification for your [the British] government to take any action to cause even the temporary deferment of child migration to Australia'.[124]

The British response was one of resignation, rather than attempting to press for any more substantive changes. The Office of the UK High Commissioner in Canberra forwarded the official Australian reports alongside Rouse's private notes to the Commonwealth Relations Office, noting the obvious disagreements between them and questioning the credibility of the Australian position. There was evidently no will to challenge this, however, and an initial response of the High Commissioner's Office was to ensure that its staff would no longer be implicated in inspection visits by Australian authorities, claiming that they no longer had sufficient staffing or budget to support this.[125] By late autumn, the Commonwealth Relations Office recognized that its strategy of slowing down approval of applications for migration of children through 'administrative delay' could no longer be sustained. After forwarding the Australian reports and Rouse's notes to the Home Office in early November, it again contacted the Home Office on 23 November to ask if in the light of these documents the Home Office had any objections to approval being given to these applications. These included requests to send children to Dhurringile, Castledare and the Fairbridge Farm School at Molong.[126] The Home Office's response was that the documents from Australian 'confirm only too clearly the Mission's view that the Australian authorities have no real appreciation of what a good institution of that sort should be like'.[127] Its suggested solution was again a temporary holding measure. With the Empire Settlement Act, and terms of assisted passages, coming up for renewal, it was proposed that the Commonwealth Relations Office informed voluntary organizations that no further assisted passages for child migrants would be agreed for a further six months. This could seem a reasonable delay, particularly as the Suez crisis was likely to hold up migration journeys during that period as well. Despite having little optimism that it could achieve even this delay, given that 'the C. R. O. have consistently ignored our advice on this subject', this suggestion was made in a meeting with Commonwealth Relations Office who responded that this would not be 'politically practicable'.[128] The Home Office conceded that 'political considerations, which were the province of C. R. O., might well override merits and, if that were so, we should not wish to press our objections.'[129] No written response was ever given to the Commonwealth Relations Office's letter of 23 November. The applications for child migration were approved. The Home Office adopted an unofficial policy of trying to not to approve applications from local authorities to send children to institutions criticized by the Fact-Finding Mission (which were, in any case, few and far between given the strong opposition to child migration generally felt in local authorities). The Commonwealth Relations Office subsequently began to emphasize standards of good practice to voluntary organizations who sent and received child migrants.[130] Foster-care was to be used rather than institutional care, and where children were kept in institutions there should be sufficient opportunities for them to integrate into local communities. Information on staffing and educational provision was also to be regularly provided, and UK government representatives were to be involved with any interviews with prospective British child migrants. The extent to which these expectations were enforced was, however, uneven with children continuing to be sent to the large residential institutions that Ross's Fact-Finding Mission had criticized.

There were some changes in the working methods of some child migration organizations after 1956. Recognizing the decreasing number of child migrants available to them, given local authority opposition to their work, the Fairbridge Society initiated its One Parent scheme in 1957, where single parents in the United Kingdom would send their children to Fairbridge institutions in Australia on the basis that they would also emigrate at a later date, at which point their children would be returned to them once settled.[131] The annual report of the Church of England Council for Commonwealth and Empire for 1957/58, reported that it welcomed what it claimed was a new policy by the Australian government that child migrants with a surviving parent would only be accepted if the parent was also accepted for immigration and would follow on in due course.[132] The Council commented that this was an idea that it had long supported.[133] The lack of any mention of this in its previous reports and the fact that the Ross inspection team found that many children had been sent to Australia by the Council with minimal information on their backgrounds despite having been taken from family homes suggested, however, that this might not have been the case. In its 1960 annual report, Dr Barnardo's Homes similarly reported a series of gradual changes that it had made to its work in the spirit of the Curtis Committee report. In Australia, larger residential accommodation at the Picton Farm School and parts of the Normanhurst Home had been sold to fund the purchase of smaller family group Homes and a boarding-out officer had now been employed to assist in fostering out child migrants.

Alongside these new developments, however, child migrants continued to be sent to Australia unaccompanied by parents. In several cases they were sent to institutions that had been criticized by the Ross Fact-Finding Mission. As the 1960s progressed, child migration schemes began to wind down not through decisive government action in Britain and Australia but because vulnerable children were increasingly coming into the care of local authorities who wanted to keep them in Britain. Receiving organizations in Australia, recognizing that child migration work was becoming economically unviable for them, sold their residential institutions or changed them into colleges, boarding schools or other kinds of use. Until they became the focus of renewed critical attention in the late 1980s, the schemes faded from public view, absorbed into the institutional histories of organizations that remain some of the most important providers of children's services in Britain today.

Comparing British and American child migration schemes

Considering the American and British schemes in relation to each other provides greater historical perspective on them. Taken together, they suggest a clear periodization of child migration in which the American 'orphan trains' and the British schemes to Canada shared much more in common with each other than the latter did with the twentieth-century British schemes to Australia. As has already been noted, early schemes to Canada were directly inspired by the 'orphan trains', and both were undertaken as humanitarian interventions intended to address the perceived problems of the growing numbers of poor families and children in the context of social and economic instability and failing welfare systems. The ways in which children's old lives in urban slums and their lives in new rural environments were imagined across these American and earlier British schemes shared much in common, as did the justifications provided for the migration work. The schemes also operated in the context of similar debates about the relative merits of placing children out compared to institutional care, with their advocates strongly favouring the former.

There were also obvious differences between the American and Canadian schemes, for example in the former's use of short-term distribution meetings and the latter's use of more stable distribution homes.[134] The American model worked if local communities proved trustworthy in identifying suitable placements for children and monitoring any subsequent problems, which was not always the case. The Canadian model worked well if distribution homes established suitable placements and were able to maintain effective post-placement supervision, which again was not consistently the case. Certainly the processing of applications through a stable distribution home in Canada did at least spare most children the ordeal of being selected through public distribution meetings as happened in America. Canadian distribution homes became important sources of emotional and practical support for many child migrants. In America, where local community support failed, the reference point was the offices of the sending organization in Boston or New York, which may not have seemed quite so far removed as British homes did to children who migrated to Canada.

Comparing the American and Canadian contexts also indicates the relative lack of Federal intervention in the American case. In the case of the British schemes to Canada, central government played an important role both through funding for child migration allowed by the Local Government Board and the reviews undertaken in the Doyle and Bondfield reports. By contrast, in the United States, the main policy interventions that influenced child migration work were undertaken at state level, either through policy changes that increased the numbers of child migrants through preventing their extended stay in orphanages or that blocked the schemes in receiving states by banning out-of-state placements.[135] This contrast could be overstated. While funding for child migration was allowed by the Local Government Board, decisions as to whether to spend money in this was made at the level of local Boards of Guardians and so local variations in state funding for child migration persisted in the United Kingdom. But the Doyle report, and subsequent suspension of funding by the Local Government Board, demonstrated that national structures operated in relation to the British child migration schemes that were largely absent in America.

Despite these differences, the broad practice in both the American and Canadian schemes of placing children with individual households contrasted strongly with the widespread practice of placing children in institutions in the British schemes to Australia. As will be discussed more in the next chapter, these differences had a profound effect on the nature of child migrants' experiences of those respective schemes. That is not to suggest that children necessarily fared better in schemes where they were placed in households, as some of those proved to be as abusive and exploitative as any residential children's home could be. The fact that 'orphan train' riders and 'British home children' were not always accepted as family members in the households in which they were placed and were seen with a stigma in their local communities made assimilation into their new lives difficult. But child migrants placed in Australian children's homes often had additional problems caused by being raised in rigid institutional environments that provided little adequate preparation for adult life. This difference is all the more striking in that early advocates of child migration such as Charles Loring Brace and Thomas Barnardo explicitly argued that a significant advantage of their work was that it prevented children from being raised in soul-less, unloving residential homes that would 'institutionize' children rather than enable them to develop as autonomous and productive members of society. While flawed, the American and Canadian schemes increasingly operated on the basis of a regular inspection system intended to check on children's welfare. In the case of the Australian schemes, apparent trust in the organizations receiving child migrants meant that while some general contacts took place between Australian child welfare departments and institutions housing child migrants, no meaningful external supervision of individual children took place.[136] Organizations sending British child migrants to Canada often tried to maintain family bonds, particularly between siblings. In some later schemes to Australia, the breaking of bonds with parents appears to have operated as a more general principle, perceived as being in the best interests of the child by giving them a fresh start overseas, unencumbered by their family history.

These later failings demonstrate that the modern history of child-care cannot be optimistically read as a progressive narrative of ever-improving insight and standards of care. Andrew Doyle's awareness of children's emotional experiences of migration in 1875 were far more perceptive than the principals of Castledare and Clontarf who respectively claimed, in 1956, that children were not disturbed by moves and that they were unlikely to worry about who their parents were. While it is possible to understand why, in the social and political context of the 1920s, child migration to Australia grew after it had been banned to Canada, it is less easy to understand why specific criticisms of the Canadian work did not inform later work to Australia. Given the Bondfield report's observation that young children were particularly unsuited to migration, it is striking that so many child migrants to Australia after 1945 were aged under 10. If it is reasonable to think in terms of a broad periodization that distinguishes between the earlier phase of the 'orphan trains' and British schemes to Canada and the later phase of British schemes to Australia, it is clear that the latter were not simply increasingly problematic in terms of standards of child-care of their day. They also, in many instances, represented a step backwards from principles of good practice in child migration work that had been established in the late Victorian period.

While helpful in certain respects, thinking in terms of these earlier and later phases of child migration work also needs to be qualified by the recognition that these schemes also varied significantly depending on the cultures and working practices of the organizations running them. As noted before, American schemes varied between using prearranged placements or public distribution meetings, arrangements similar to formal adoption or very loose placement contracts. In Canada, British child migrants sent by Catholic organizations were more likely to be sent to French-speaking families in Quebec than if sent by other organizations, because the Quebecois were seen as more likely to instil a proper Catholic faith in the child. In Australia, a British child migrant's experience varied significantly depending on whether they grew up in a Fairbridge cottage home (and on what their cottage mothers were like), in a large Catholic children's home or a smaller children's home. Growing up in large, remote, regimented institutions far from an Australian town was different to growing up in a smaller home in a residential suburb where greater integration with the local community was encouraged. Different admission routes or staff changes meant that former child migrants could emerge with strongly contrasting accounts of the same organization.[137] All of these variations at the level of organizational culture and practice had a significant effect on child migrants' experiences.

A final point to be made on the basis of a comparison of the American and British schemes is that there was no consistent factor that determined this approach to the care of children. It would be wrong to portray the history of these schemes in a way that implies a strong homogeneity across them. There was no single idea of why child migration was a commendable practice that persisted across the whole of this history, nor was there a single model by which this work was conducted. While religious motivations remained an important factor, these did not determine the schemes in any straightforward way. Catholic support for child migration in Britain, for example, contrasted strongly with Catholic opposition to the principle of child migration in New York where it was argued that the New York Catholic Protectory did valuable work precisely because it kept open the possibility of children returning to their families if family circumstances improved.[138] Similarly while the rise of secular child-welfare professionals and agencies became associated with greater opposition to child migration schemes in Britain and America, this was not the case with the secular child welfare departments in postwar Australia who continued to support them. The political motivations of Charles Loring Brace, who had some sympathies with radical groups in Europe, contrasted with the political conservatism of many supporters of the Fairbridge Society. The history of the American and

British child migration schemes was not therefore one shaped by a single religious or political ideology. It was a form of practice, shared across many different organizations, which made sense to its advocates in the context of different assumptions and aspirations about what it would mean to build a better society and to improve children's lives. These assumptions and aspirations varied across time and place, as did the social, political and technological structures through which the schemes operated. Across these differences, though, there was a common emphasis on child migration as a humane intervention that was in the best interests of the child. The implications of this broadly shared humanitarian impulse for children's experience of this work is the focus of the next chapter.

Left behind!

HIS friends have gone; will YOU help him to join them? It costs £30.

This appeal is made through the generosity of
a friend to extend the work of the Society.

THE FAIRBRIDGE SOCIETY

President :
H.R.H. THE DUKE OF GLOUCESTER, K.G., K.T., K.P.
Director : W. R. Vaughan, O.B.E.
38, Holland Villas Road, Kensington, London, W.14.   Tel. : Park 6822

4

'I love both my mummies': Moral meanings and the wounds of charity

In March 1951, a series of newspaper articles were published about a young British child migrant to Australia.[1] The story concerned a young girl, Marcelle O'Brien, who had become the focus of a very public attempt to get her returned from the Fairbridge Farm School at Pinjarra. Marcelle had come under the care of the Fairbridge Society at the age of 2 after her mother had died and was placed with a foster mother with the intention that she then be sent to Australia after a further two years. The foster mother, Mrs Chapman, built a strong bond with Marcelle and was distraught when she was removed for emigration. Her sense of loss became even more acute when her own daughter died at the age of 9, leaving Mrs Chapman to feel even more strongly that she would like to have Marcelle back in Britain and that Marcelle would do better in her care.

Fairbridge had a well-established record of refusing or obstructing as much as possible the return of their child migrants to families back in Britain. What made Mrs Chapman's case unusual, though, was that she was able to raise the funds to pay for Marcelle's passage home. This requirement usually presented an insurmountable barrier for parents on low incomes trying to get their children back from Australia.[2] But Mrs Chapman had been able to raise the funds to meet these costs through the financial support of people in her local village of Lingfield in Sussex. Her second, unusual step for someone in her situation was to write directly to the Queen and the Duke of Gloucester to appeal for them to intervene on her behalf in this case. The third, very unusual feature of this case was that this appeal for Royal intervention and the support of her local community led to this family drama being played out through the gaze of the national press.

On 10 March, the *Argus* newspaper in Melbourne printed a front-page article with the headline 'The Drama of a Child in Australia – the Queen intervenes',[3] explaining that Mrs Chapman's appeal had been met with a flurry of royal responses. Queen Elizabeth, the mother of Queen Elizabeth II, initially wrote expressing deep sympathy for her and saying that she would see what could possibly be done in this case. The next day, the Duke of Gloucester wrote to say that while sympathizing, he felt that Mrs Chapman should reflect and not pursue her request for Marcelle to be returned. Would it not be better, he asked, to leave Marcelle in the warmth of the Australian sun and to grow up with all the wonderful opportunities that her new life there offered? The day after, a letter arrived from the Queen, via her lady-in-waiting, saying that there were insurmountable legal difficulties in returning Marcelle and that regardless of this, it probably was in her best interests not to be disturbed again by moving back to Britain.

Shortly after this another front-page article appeared in the *Argus*, in which a picture of a smiling Marcelle with a doll appeared with the caption, '"I love both my mummies", says Marcelle'.[4] The story emphasized how happy Marcelle was in Australia, how much love and affection were being showered on her at the Fairbridge school, and how she now loved her new Australia 'mother' even more than Mrs Chapman. The process by which this story appeared in the press, following the earlier sympathetic coverage of Mrs Chapman's appeal for Marcelle's return, is not difficult to imagine.

Marcelle O'Brien never recalls saying the things that were reported in that article, nor was she aware at the time of the public interest in her fate. Her experience of Pinjarra was far more bleak than the article suggested. One of her memories of her time there was of being told 'You belong in the gutter, you are nothing, you have nobody'.[5] On leaving her unhappy time at the farm school, she was sent to work on a family farm where, unprotected, she was subject to physical and sexual abuse from other members of the local community. It was not until she was 50 years old that she learned that 'Mummy Chapman' had tried to bring her back from Australia. Mrs Chapman died before they met again, having kept a keep-sake of Marcelle's for all of her life. When Marcelle was eventually able to trace her birth mother, she found she had dementia and they only had three weeks before the dementia went into an advanced stage.

Marcelle O'Brien's case, while not unique among child migrants, demonstrates in a particularly acute way harm that could be caused by moral projects of child rescue. There was no practical reason why she could not have been returned to Britain. Her fare would have been paid. Legal transfer of guardianship would not have been impossible. Marcelle could even have returned to Mrs Chapman under the legal guardianship of the Fairbridge Society as she had been when she first lived with Mrs Chapman. Child migration organizations at that time often sought to break the bonds between parents and child migrants, and to obstruct their renewal, in cases where the parent was considered unsuitable. But this could hardly have applied in Mrs Chapman's case given that Fairbridge themselves had used her as a foster parent. The only thing that ultimately prevented Marcelle

O'Brien's return to Britain was the moral conviction that she was in a better place from which it was in her own best interests not to be disturbed. She was the recipient of good work and that work was not to be undone.

How then might we understand this relationship between the moral cultures of child migration work and harm experienced by those it claimed to help? To begin, it is important to understand the nature of harm experienced by child migrants across the long and complex history charted so far in this book. As noted earlier in the Introduction, it is not possible to reduce child migrants' experiences simply in terms of harm. It is clear that across the schemes discussed in this book there were some children who found a degree of family care overseas that had not been available to them in their home communities.[6] Although only a very small proportion of British child migrants to Canada were fully adopted,[7] some households who received children as workers appear to have treated them with affection and as a member of the family.[8] In some instances, placing organizations regarded such affection with concern, seeing it as potentially 'spoiling' the child. As one supervision report on a girl from the Manchester and Salford Boys and Girls Refuges and Homes put it, 'she is in a good home where she is the only girl, so that she receives rather more attention than is good for her. Her grandma and grandpa fairly idolize the child and think there is no other girl in the world to compare with "Dot"'.[9] In a similar vein, some former orphan train riders interviewed for a PBS documentary spoke positively about the care and generosity of families who took them in.[10] Often, the succession of placements that many child migrants in Canada or the United States had would expose them to both caring and exploitative households. Even some former child migrants sent to residential institutions in Australia have spoken of positive aspects of their experiences in care, although these might be phrased in terms of being 'toughened up', being provided with three meals a day or the experience of friendship with other children.[11]

Thinking in terms of the harm of child migration can also risk creating an implicit impression that children's lives were devoid of harm prior to migration and that migration was the primary source of harm in their lives. As will be discussed shortly, there are strong grounds for arguing that child migration schemes did expose many children to a form of social trauma that exceeded previous suffering to which they had been exposed. To claim this is not to suggest that their lives were necessarily devoid of any suffering prior to migration, however.

The causes of suffering for children in their home environments, prior to migration, were complex, and both structural and interpersonal. In both Britain and America, a major impetus for the development of the mass child migration schemes was the social effects of poverty exacerbated by population growth, insecure employment, economic fluctuations, and (in the case of New York and Boston) very high levels of immigration. The failure of welfare systems to provide financial support to enable families to maintain care of their children within the home, along with legislative failures on slum housing, created social conditions that drew humanitarian laments and philanthropic action.[12] These structural pressures placed severe strains on interpersonal relations as well. Overcrowded housing, unemployment and the struggle for financial survival made the care of children much harder. Alcoholism, domestic violence and neglect arising from either the illness, depression or death of a parent all affected children's lives as well.

While these structural pressures and interpersonal strains weakened the bonds of care around some children's lives, in many cases parental attachment to a child remained strong.[13] The lack of welfare provision to reinforce such attachment with practical resources of housing, food or income meant, however, that many poor parents faced the prospect of having to give their children over to workhouse schools or charitable homes as a last resort. While such attachments could sometimes be viewed impatiently by charity workers keen to improve children's lives without such family 'interference', it was also recorded with a sense of deep pathos by others. In a description of a public procession of child migrants leaving for Canada, an early annual report of Quarriers' Homes gave the following account:

> The emigration procession is led by the biggest boys and brought up at the rear by some 'toddlin wee things' . . . The children received at our Homes are chiefly orphans, or friendless waifs, and a very few had parents looking out for them.
>
> Amongst the crowd, however, stood a poor, but decent looking couple, eagerly scanning the faces of the little ones as they came up in procession. The man was a shattered paralytic . . . and clung to his wife for support. Both looked very sorrowful, and when a sharp fine little fellow halted a moment in front of them and clasped a hand of each, the man broke down and wept bitterly. He was the boy's father. The child was too young to work for his own support, and the bread winner had become a helpless paralytic . . . The mother tried bravely to keep up at parting with her boy, and it was touching to see how she tried to smile down the tears that welled up from her heavy heart.
>
> Near this group, leaning on a staff, was a feeble-looking man, who was hardly able to stand on his legs. He too, was eagerly watching the departing emigrants. His little son was amongst them, eight years old . . . But the boy's mother was dead, and he (the father) had fallen into bad health, and was not able to work . . . When Charlie came up, it was pitiful to see the lingering clasp of the dying father as his dim eyes fondly rested on the boy. Doubtless he felt it was the last time he would ever look on his face in this world. It is to be hoped that they will meet again under happier circumstances.[14]

While the socioeconomic pressures of poverty and an inadequate welfare system were particularly acute in the late nineteenth and early twentieth centuries, they still provided the backdrop against which many children entered the later twentieth-century schemes to Australia.[15] Many parents regretfully gave their children over for migration in the hope of better lives for them overseas, a process facilitated at times by solicitous charity workers keen to persuade them that they should not deprive their children of all the benefits that migration would give them.[16] In other cases, children were taken from stable foster-care arrangements, in which the foster carers were distraught at having to give them over for migration, but where they had little or no power to prevent this.[17] As these structural pressures weakened, however, so the numbers of child migrants fell. In postwar Britain, as welfare provision for families improved and a stronger framework for child welfare under the management of local authorities developed, the numbers of children who became available for migration decreased. Those children who were migrated in the 1950s and 1960s were primarily those who had been placed (whether temporarily or permanently) in voluntary organizations' and religious orders' children's homes by unmarried mothers, from struggling families were persuaded of the benefits of migration, or who were going overseas through schemes in which one or both parents would later be following them.[18]

Many children who entered migration schemes had therefore had previous experience of the difficulties of poverty, social approbation (of children born outside of marriage), family disruption and institutionalization. While some have memories of positive early relationships with parents, carers or siblings, others have no little or no memories at all or predominantly memories of hardship.[19] Migration introduced some to positive new environments, and many to lives in which they were able to find moments of reprieve from the routines of domestic work or institutional life.[20] There were also successful outcomes for some child migrants, for example including British children sent to Canada who went on to save enough money from their placements eventually to buy their own land. These were arguably less frequent than glowing testimonials published by child migration organizations suggested, with only a small minority of child migrants going on to run their own farms.[21] But alongside positive outcomes, where they did happen, migration also introduced new forms of suffering into children's lives.

To understand the nature of this suffering across such a broad period of time raises wider questions about what constitutes human well-being. As the anthropologist, Michael Jackson, has argued, notions of well-being are always to some degree culturally specific and shift over time.[22] In his repeated fieldwork visits to Sierra Leone he noticed, for example, that people's sense of deprivation has now extended to their sense of being excluded from new technologies of digital communication. Before mobile phones existed, such a sense of relative deprivation made no sense. But as this technology becomes more available across Africa, so the inability to access it for financial or infrastructural reasons is increasingly experienced as a painful constraint. The content of what people take to be well-being therefore constantly evolves as societies themselves develop.[23] As Jackson puts it, more generally, well-being is therefore always just beyond human reach. However much we progress towards it, new elements of well-being always come into view that are not yet in our possession.

Although our notions of well-being may be like never reachable horizons and change across different times and places, Jackson nevertheless argues that there are certain existential traits that tend to define people's sense of a better or worse life across cultures. These are, fundamentally, that we experience a need to belong in meaningful social relationships, that we feel that we stand in a positive relationship to things considered worthy of honour and respect, and that we have a sense of a degree of control over our lives. Many child migrants experienced traumatic disruptions of at least one of these three basic existential conditions that caused not simply childhood pain but affected their capacity to maintain a sense of self-worth or close relationships long into their adult lives.

Again, the nature of this harm cannot be generalized across all child migrants, particularly given the variety of forms of child-care to which they were exposed. Life in a small family group home was not like life in a large, older-style orphanage or a large farm school – three different types of institution that all operated in the postwar period in New South Wales. Life in these institutions was not like the household placements of 'orphan train' riders or child migrants to Canada. Nor was the experience of being adopted by a family the same as being in a contracted placement in which the child might move between several different households before reaching adulthood. The various forms of abuse and neglect that child migrants experienced across these different forms of child-care were also not unique, but shared with other children who had traumatic experiences of life in foster-care or residential institutions in many different countries.[24] Nevertheless, despite the diversity of experiences of children within these child migration schemes, there were particular patterns of existential wound that occurred across them.

One of these was that basic social bonds were broken and in many cases children found themselves in relationships with other adults that were precarious, lacked love or empathy,[25] and were instrumentalized or abusive. For many children, migration constituted a painful loss of relationships with family and friends, or a wider sense of belonging associated with their home community. Child migrants to Canada, for example, often wrote to their distribution homes or sending organizations expressing a sense of loneliness and asking for any news of their families. 'I was waiting till my brothers wrote to me but they have not wrote yet. Dear Mrs Wallace I wanted to ask you please did you send my letters to them yet for I feel so unhappy not hearing where they are no hearing from them.'[26] 'Do you know where my little brother Harry is or do you know where my mother is? I often get lonesome for them.'[27] For these children, relationships with staff in distribution homes and sending organizations back in Britain took on particular importance for them as an alternative source of attachment. Matrons in children's homes were frequently referred to as 'mother' in child migrant's letters, and news and letters from these staff obviously had great emotional significance for many child migrants. As one put it, 'I could do with asking you to write every day if it be possible. But please do observe it I have kept that letter and read it over and over again and it seems sweeter every time. I was washing my dress and it was in the pocket and it got wet but I dried it. But it is getting old but I mean to keep it until it is done for.'[28]

The sense of loss of former relationships was accentuated by the physical distance (including sea journeys lasting several weeks) that migration put between child migrants and their former lives. In the case of the American 'orphan trains', it was not unknown for children to leave their placements and make their own way back to Boston or New York to renew contact with family members.[29] For British child migrants, trans-national travel was not something they could attempt independently and the realization that life in their new country meant permanent separation from home was painful. For some this loss was crystallized in particular moments or interactions that remained traumatic memories into adult life:

On 28th August, my father's sister came to visit me. She had brought my two cousins [and] my younger sister was there . . . We sat in a room talking. A nun then came into the room and said 'Time to go.' I grabbed [my younger's sister's] hand thinking that I was going home and that I needed to go the other way out of the building with my family but they walked out of the front door and I was put with the other girls that were being sent to Australia. That was very sad. I thought I was going home . . . When we got off the bus [in Australia] I went to grab my sister. I got boxed across the ears by [Sister x] and my sister was sent the other way. We were separated. I never saw my sister again while I was at the orphanage . . . After about six months [in the Australian orphanage] a nun told one of the girls who was crying that she would never be returning home and that none of us would ever be returning to our homeland. Prior to that we had all thought that we would be going home at some stage.[30]

I can't remember exactly what he told me, but [before I got on the train] my biological father gave me a pink envelope with his address on it and asked me to be sure to let him know when we got to our destination. I took the envelope my father had given me and put it in my inside coat pocket trying to be very protective of it. And that night, like all kids, we went to sleep. The next morning I woke up and the first thing I thought about was that pink envelope and I reached inside my coat pocket and it was gone. And I was heart-broken, and I asked Leo to get down on the floor and help me look for it. We were looking for it when one of the care-takers came by and asked us what we were doing. I told her that we were looking for the envelope. I was afraid to tell her anything else as the punishment sometimes was a little severe. And she told me to get up and get on my seat. Where I was going I would not need that envelope.[31]

This sense of loss and isolation could be a commonly acknowledged experience between child migrants themselves. As a former resident of the Fairbridge farm school at Molong recalled, displays of distress were rarely treated sympathetically by other children, with the exception of children crying because they felt homesick. This was such a basic part of their shared experience that it was beyond reproach or mockery among their peers.[32]

This sense of loss of key relationships with people and place was often compounded by child migrants' experience of relationships that were lacking in nurture. A common reflection that many had of their receiving families or institutions was of the lack of affection or encouragement they received from them. As one former orphan train rider commented about the family he was placed with, 'they never touched me or said they loved me and they didn't want me to call them Mom and Dad. Think what that does to you. They weren't mean, they were cold . . . When I was fifteen or sixteen I decided I'd live in a garbage can before I'd stay there any longer.'[33] While some child migrants were reported to be treated like members of the family, others experienced various forms of exclusion that reminded them of their liminal status in the home. The Bondfield report, for example, noted the case of a Canadian household where the young son of the family was allowed to play the family piano, but the child migrant living with them was not.[34] In residential institutions in Australia, the lack of nurture was in part a facet of low staff–child ratios (with some larger institutions having only one member of staff for every twenty or thirty children), and in part the result of staff who either didn't understand or were not committed to the notion that their role included providing emotional support to children. As the Ross report demonstrated, these failings became increasingly stark as they contrasted with what was increasingly understood as appropriate empathic approaches to child-care.

Many child migrants also experienced a lack of stability in their new relationships. Although some 'orphan train' riders and child migrants to Canada were fortunate to remain with a single, supportive household until they entered adulthood, it was common for many to go through several placements. The loose contractual basis on placements set up by the New York Children's Aid Society was intended to allow children and employers to end them easily if either found them unsatisfactory. As a consequence, children moved between placements, with the Society sometimes losing track of where they had moved on to. In Australia, children moved between institutions run by the Christian Brothers depending on their age, apparently reflecting the assumption that these institutions functioned primarily as schools than stable homes for vulnerable children. In Canada, many child migrants had at least three or four placements, some eight, nine or more.

In part, this reflected the fact that as they got older, boys were able to command higher wages as the value of their labour increased and so moved (or were encouraged to move by distribution homes), so as to increase their income. However, a common source of precariousness in children's placements was employers' dis-satisfaction with children sent to them, with many children being returned to distribution homes for impertinence, dirty habits (sometimes a euphemism for bed-wetting) or failure in their work.[35] Employers' expectations of the contribution that a child migrant would make to the work of the home or farm were often disappointed. As one complained, when returning a child placed with her:

> She did not have any zeal in her work and had no desire to learn and was most disobedient. She made up her mind before coming out she would not go on a farm – had been led to think she could choose the sort of place she fancied . . . She evidently expected everything would be made thoroughly pleasant and easy for her here and thought it very hard to get up at half past five, requiring to be called and recalled again and again. She could not sew so I had to do what mending she wanted, tried to teach her to darn but she would sit and sulk and do nothing . . . A most trying state of affairs when I had so much work to do . . . Certainly if she wishes to get on in Canada she will have to learn *to work* and not expect others to pay her wages and do her work. I did my best for her.[36]

Many child migrants, in return, recalled being expected to undertake excessive physical tasks or work very long hours which limited their wider social contact and for which they were sometimes unpaid or underpaid.[37] One, after being returned for a second time to Dr Barnardo's Homes' distribution home at Hazelbrae having struggled with the workloads in her placements, wondered if people in Canada expected more than they would in Britain. She remembers staff telling her in reply, 'Now you are in Canada and you must learn to do what Canadians do.'[38]

At times, this gap between the child's contribution to the household and the employer's expectation of them were not simply to do with the child's motivation or previous training, but their physical suitability for the work.[39] Letters and child record books note cases where employers returned children for being 'too small'. As one put it, 'A. is a very good girl for his [*sic*] age, but I would like a larger one if I can get one. I will keep this one until you can find me a larger one if you would *do that*.'[40] Such attitudes reflected an instrumental view of children as labourers, with employers making decisions on whether child migrants remained in their homes not on the basis of what was in the best emotional interests of the child but on whether their labour was worth the expense of boarding, clothing and wages.[41] As one child's placement notes lamented, 'Mr V. says he is returning J. on the 13th December and that J. has some habits that he does not like, but I fear it is largely because the winter is here and he is not as useful as in the summer.'[42] It is striking that while some child migrants accepted that these transient placements were the terms on which their lives were now based, others sought as much stability as they could. One Canadian employer who had returned a young boy because he was too small, regularly wet the bed and had an eye infection, said that he was sorry to hear that the boy was so desperate to return to their home.[43] In other cases, child migrants refused attempts by distribution homes to move them on to other placements where they would be better paid because they valued what form of family life they felt themselves to have in their current placements.[44] Such stability eluded many, though.

For some child migrants, these problems of uncaring, precarious or instrumentalized relationships with adults were further compounded by active exploitation or abuse. In a few cases, the abuse and neglect of child migrants came to public attention. In 1924, a Canadian newspaper reported that a farmer, George Ford, had been acquitted for the manslaughter of a child migrant, John Bayns, who had died in his care.[45] While censuring the neglect and lack of medical treatment for Bayns (who had received no medical help while suffering from the double pneumonia from which he eventually died), the judge ruled that the farmer had no legal responsibility to provide such medical care. The case had echoes of the acquittal in 1895 of Helen Findlay for the manslaughter of George Green, a 'Barnardo's boy' in her care.[46] Witnesses testified that she had regularly kicked and beaten him and sent him to sleep in the pig's sty as a punishment. When Green's body was recovered from her house, it was found that he was in a state of extreme malnutrition and had died in a filthy room, curled up in a hole in the middle of his badly soiled straw mattress. Following conflicting medical evidence, Findlay was eventually acquitted on the grounds that Green's death was the result of preexisting medical conditions. Public criticism turned more against Dr Barnardo's Homes for allegedly sending such physically ill-suited children, rather than any suggestion that this was a miscarriage of justice.[47]

For cases of such abuse to come to public attention was relatively rare, however.[48] For the most part, child migrants who experienced emotional, physical or sexual mistreatment suffered in silence. Some ran away, if they could. A few boys, as they grew older, managed to deter their abusers by physically threatening them in return.[49] In some cases, such as those of John Bayns and George Green, this ill-treatment proved fatal, and it was not unknown for some child migrants to commit suicide as a result of it.[50] More commonly, though, ill-treatment came at the cost of children's sense of well-being than their lives. As Andrew Doyle recorded in his 1875 report:

Although I did not hear of any cases of gross cruelty, I did hear of many cases of ill-treatment and hardship. A girl complained to me that 'for temper' she had been sent to bed on Saturday afternoon and kept there without food till Sunday evening: a mistress told me that she had kept a girl on bread and water for three days for refusing to admit that she had stolen five cents: a master I ascertained had horse-whipped a girl of 13: I found the marks of a flogging on a boy's shoulders, the flogging having been inflicted a fortnight before: in reply to my question, 'Why did you leave your former place?' the answer would very often be to the effect . . . 'I couldn't manage to please them; they were always scolding me; they used to beat me; I was very unhappy'.[51]

Although sending organizations did remove children whom they knew to have received physical punishment that exceeded accepted standards of corporal discipline for that time,[52] children were also at times judged culpable to some degree for their harsh treatment. As one visitors' note recorded, 'J. complained of harsh treatment, but has no doubt given great provocation for the whipping she has received. Is very dirty in many of her habits. I left her with the understanding that she is not to be whipped again!'[53] While employers were discouraged from using excessive physical punishments, sympathy for their disciplinary role sometimes meant that children's complaints about this did not always lead to them being removed from placements.[54] For example, E. A. was described as 'slow, disobedient' and 'rather dull and heavy' by her visiting agent, who went on to comment that she 'appears to be kindly treated though sometimes had to be whipped'. At a later inspection, E. A. complained to this visitor that she had been horse-whipped, but in the face of a denial of this from the employer and a promise not to inflict beatings, E. A. was kept in the placement.[55]

In Australia, child migrants experienced physical and sexual abuse in a number of institutions in which they were placed. Rather than controlled and moderated forms of corporal punishment that would still have been considered acceptable in the early postwar period, later child migrants to Australia have many memories of violence from staff that was spontaneous, excessive and intended to create an atmosphere of fear:[56]

> During my time in the home there were a lot of public floggings. The nuns used canes that had been soaked in water to beat the girls. Girls could be flogged for talking to boys or getting our period . . . These floggings were often out of control not stopping until the nun in question had drawn blood from the girl being punished.[57]

> Our cottage mother was the most wicked person I've ever come across. She used to belt us with a riding crop. A little boy like [R. H.], he used to get flogged terribly here. Forty times – because he ran away after arrived. He was only four. After he arrived he ran away up the back paddock and she brought him back and flogged him. She used to boast about it.[58]

Such punishment formed part of wider physical mistreatment of children within some institutions. One former resident at Tardun recalled a collective punishment after one boy's misdemeanour that involved all the boys in their group sitting in 105 degrees heat for two hours, without any protection from the sun.[59] Another recalled that when staff at Castledare learned he couldn't swim, he was thrown into the water, leaving other boys to pull him out.[60] Other painful or humiliating forms of non-physical punishment were also remembered long afterwards by former child migrants. One recalled being disciplined several times for minor offences by being made to attend film nights at his children's home with his back turned to the screen for the whole film while other children sat laughing at it.[61]

Both boys and girls were subject to sexual abuse from staff and visitors to the residential institutions in which they lived, and girls experienced sexual abuse and exploitation in the placements to which they were sent.[62] In some cases, this abuse was sustained over a number of years. It is clear that in some institutions, the sexual abuse of children by staff was not simply committed by isolated individuals, and that a wider culture of abuse operated.[63] The Child Migrants Trust has argued that there is now sufficient evidence to indicate that there were networks of sexual abusers of children between some sending and receiving institutions.[64] In both the American and British schemes, girls were also vulnerable when placed out in households and many suffered sexual coercion, assault and rape.[65]

The loss of contact with family and homeland – and exposure to relationships that were far from nurturing – left former child migrants emotionally wounded at a formative period in their lives. Some stories former child migrants tell of their lives tend to minimize this, emphasizing more their resilience or sense of achievement at having gone on from difficult early lives to have had productive working careers and families of their own. Other narratives give greater voice to this sense of loss, recognizing with sadness the ways in which these harmful relationships with replacement carers have left them struggling with intimacy and the expression of affection:

> I find it difficult to show emotion, even with my current wife . . . My abusive background had a devastating effect on my ability to show love and affection and it is still a problem today and demonstrated by my poor relationship with two of my sons. The pain and isolation of my childhood goes on and affects the next generation.[66]

> I have lived a solitary life. I like the open space of the country and my independence. I have worked hard and I own my own home . . . The thing that hurts most is the lack of family. I was deprived of knowing my family. I never married but I had friends who married and had children and I know what a family should be.[67]

This sense of loss is felt even more poignantly by those for whom the migration schemes operated in such a way as to deprive them of knowledge of their original family or make it difficult to renew contact with them:

> People say that 'you are lucky you are here' and to some extent I am, but I feel hurt at being taken away from my family and what I have missed

out on, being told that I was an orphan, my mother being told that I had been adopted out, having my name and date of birth changed so that she would have no way of tracing me. I missed out on 50 years of special moments that only a family can provide. I was taken away from my mother and family as a child and that loss cannot be filled.[68]

The harm caused by this feeling of being displaced from meaningful relationships – symbolized for many in later life by not receiving cards on their birthdays – was added to by the difficulties that some former British child migrants had in gaining citizenship in their new countries through lack of adequate record-keeping of their original migration.[69] For them, displacement from a sense of home nation was layered onto the sense of displacement from family creating an even more profound sense of lack of identity. Children who were meant to have been the building blocks of the empire were deprived of this most basic recognition from their new adoptive country. Such loss and displacement from key relationships left many former child migrants without a strong sense of belonging in the social worlds they inhabited. As one put it, in later life, 'I still feel that I don't belong anywhere and that I don't belong to anyone. My time in care has always made me feel throughout life as if I am on the outside looking in.'[70] Another, noting the superficiality of judging whether child migration improved children's material circumstances, commented, 'I deem myself to be one of those successful people but I would forego the total success I have had for another ten minutes with my mother'.[71]

A common aspiration of the child migration schemes was to take children from situations in which they were perceived to have little hope and to place them in new relationships and roles where they could live with a new sense of purpose. This purpose could range from the more everyday civic vision of becoming a productive worker or home-builder, to grander visions of spiritual redemption or, in Kingsley Fairbridge's words, the realization of one's contribution to nation, empire and race. That migration should give children's lives a greater sense of value and purpose, there was no doubt. In reality, though, for many children, migration entailed not a greater sense of moving towards something meaningful and honourable, but an experience of shame. If one understands shame as a sense of an inherent failing or tainting of one's self,[72] then there were a number of ways in child migrants came to feel that there was something inherently wrong about themselves.

In part, such shame arose through public representation of child migrants in the communities to which they were sent in newspaper articles, public speeches and local gossip. Many 'orphan train' riders and British child migrants to Canada found themselves suspected in their receiving communities of bringing the worst moral and physical diseases of city slums with them.[73] Allegations that child migrants brought criminality with them were at times inflected with the assumption that such bad traits were an

effect of their heredity from pauperized and dissolute parents. The East
Coast accents of 'orphan train' riders marked them out as different in the
mid-West communities to which thousands were sent. In Canada, the term
'British home child' was a stigmatized one, with some former child migrants
never telling their spouses or children about their early lives for fear of the
shame that this entailed.[74] The sense of being marked out meant that when
child migrants did encounter children in the local communities to which they
were sent, they did not always mix successfully with them. As Rouse noted
in his private comments on Dhurringile Rural Training Farm, although the
boys attended a local secondary school, they did not mix with other children
there, conscious of the differences symbolized in the better packed lunches
of the local children.[75]

Child migrants also had experiences that they felt marked them out
as different, and inferior, to people around them. For some 'orphan train
riders', this was the lasting memory of not having been chosen at a public
distribution meeting, or having been exposed so vulnerably to such a
process of public appraisal even if they were selected. For some British
child migrants to Canada, as Andrew Doyle discerned, it came through the
experience of repeated failures and rejections in placements. For others, it
came in memorable statements from those now responsible for their care
that they were worthless and not worthy of love:

> From Nazareth House in Victoria my sisters were later separately placed
> with adoptive families but I was left behind in Camberwell. I was fifteen
> years old when this happened. I remember crying and feeling distressed
> when they left and wondering why I could not go with them or why I
> could not also be adopted by another family. I was told by the nuns that
> I was too stupid and that 'nobody would want to take such a fat lazy
> cow'.[76]

> As soon as I turned sixteen I was told by the Brothers that I had to leave
> the home . . . The Brothers arranged for me to work on a farm in New
> Norcia run by the Benedictine monks. Brother x told me on the day I
> left the home that I would never make anything of myself and that I was
> not welcome back at Clontarf. I felt lonely and at times suicidal working
> there.[77]

Public beatings – often administered in uncontrolled bursts of violence –
were deeply shaming to those exposed to them:

> Brother Keaney belted me over the head with his walking stick. In front
> of all the boys, he stripped my clothes off. Brother Keaney beat me with
> his fists and stick, leaving me bleeding on the floor and in pain. He nearly
> flogged me to death. I was only 12. I was terrified . . . Nobody came to my
> aid. I received no medical attention. This assault stands out for me, above
> all others. I am now left with a stutter, which I still have today, and which

has caused me so much suffering, so much bullying and humiliation over the years. Medical advice has told me that Brother Keaney's assault is the reason for my stutter.[78]

Intentional forms of shaming were also used as a disciplinary measure in some residential institutions in Australia. Those children who wet the bed were particularly subject to public humiliation:

I was very anxious as a child and I continued to wet the bed until I was fifteen years old. I was cold at night and had only one thin blanket and a flat pillow. The children who wet the bed were humiliated and treated badly. I recall being left to stand at the end of my bed for an hour or more with the urine soaked sheet over my head.[79]

Humiliation did not simply occur through such intentional actions, but through experiences that reflected the environments of neglect in which some child migrants grew up. As one former child migrant to Australia commented to Margaret Humphreys of the Child Migrants Trust, one of his most humiliating memories at the generally abusive institution at which he grew up was foraging for food in the bins of another local school because he was so hungry.[80]

Former child migrants also carried a sense of shame into adult life through feeling less well prepared for successful adult life than others. This was ironic, given that migration was meant to improve children's opportunities in life, albeit that many British schemes assumed that working-class children would primarily have a future of manual or agricultural work.[81] For many the classed expectations of what a working-class child could hope to be, together with the economic dependence on their labour for Canadian placements and Australian institutions to be viable, meant that their educational opportunities were limited. Despite the contractual agreement for children under 14 to receive schooling as well as board and clothing that many organizations had with Canadian employers, these agreements were not always upheld in practice when households and farms needed the child's labour.[82] The fact that children were then expected to work full-time after reaching the age of 14 meant that those who wished to develop their education further had little opportunity to do so, unless they did it later in their adult lives. Child migrants in some Australian residential institutions suffered either because the standard of in-house education was poor or because, in the case of Fairbridge farm schools, child migrants in their mid-teenage years were generally needed as full-time workers on the school land and so discouraged from taking higher exams.[83] This sense of educational dis-advantage, and lack of wider training in life-skills and sexual education, left former child migrants feeling ill-equipped for adult life. Some continued to be aware of how lack of early educational development, and lack of confidence arising from this, meant that they never developed in their own careers as much as they would have hoped. Many former child migrants demonstrated considerable resilience, building families, work and social respectability out of difficult early lives.[84] For others, the dream of a transformed life overseas continually repeated through publicity materials for child migration schemes remained unrealized and was internalized through a sense of personal failure and shame.

Children negotiate their lives in relation to a series of constraints placed on them by adults. In this sense, child migration schemes were no different to families or other child-care structures in setting limits on children's actions and ability to make decisions for their lives. But many former child migrants recognized in their experience a degree of constraint that was a lasting source of pain for them. As has been noted before, the ways in which different schemes operated placed different kinds and degrees of constraint on children. The informal nature of the New York Children's Aid Society's placements meant, for example, that while children notionally lacked the protection that a more formal contract might have given, they also in principle had the freedom to leave placements with which they were unhappy. This might, in practice, have been a choice exercised only by older children, and individual agents working for the Aid Society may have been for less sympathetic to children who left placements.[85] But this allowed a degree of choice for children to leave placements in which they were unhappy that other child migrants never experienced. In Canada, while child migrants did sometimes take the initiative to leave employers,[86] the sheer remoteness of some placements made this very difficult. Supervision records and employers' letters for child migrants to Canada also suggest that their lives were sometimes very carefully managed, either to ensure their productivity or their safety from perceived moral harm.[87] A supervision report on a child migrant in her late teens similarly reported that 'A. is doing fairly well and Mrs P says trying to improve. Her weak point is love of dress. Mrs P tries to check it as much as possible. A. is allowed to get one good book from the library once a week.'[88]

At times these constraints doubtless reflected wider assumptions about the limits that should be put on children's lives, particularly girls, in the periods in which the American and Canadian migration schemes operated.[89] The fact that these child migrants did not always have effective advocates meant, however, that constraints on their lives could operate with particular harshness if employers saw a child as something to be managed and used as effectively as possible rather than a person to be nurtured. A different form of institutional constraint was exercised over the lives of many child migrants who grew up in children's homes in Australia. Here, low proportions of staff to children, the practical demands of clothing, bathing and feeding large numbers of children, and a belief in the value of institutional discipline all played a part in sustaining rigid institutional environments. As a consequence, the moral and practical demands of the institution was given greater priority than children's opportunities to experience freedom or choice in their lives. As noted in the previous chapter, the confidential appendices to the Ross Fact-Finding Mission's report recorded a number of examples of such institutional constraints. These included children's days being highly structured around a rigidly enforced timetable, contacts with the wider community being limited to organized group activities and a lack of regular pocket money (which might encourage a sense of personal independence). The ability of children to create a personalized environment for themselves in these institutions was undermined by large group dormitories, in which there was often no space to keep personal objects, or the expectation in some institutions that children would have few or no personal possessions. At its most extreme, suspicion of children's innate proclivity to sin created the institutional environment noted at St John Bosco Boys' Town in which the boys were meant never to be left without adult scrutiny to prevent their moral fall. The strong and often arbitrary reinforcement of these institutional regimes through physical punishment or the withholding of the few 'privileges' open to them, meant that while children did still try to find ways of resisting, such resistance was limited and could be laden with fear.[90]

Such stifling experiences of institutional life were shared with other children who grew up in large residential institutions. But many former child migrants also recognized a lack of choice that was distinctive to their experience – a fundamental lack of choice in the decision over migration. Organizational records suggest that there were children who actively chose the possibility of trying their luck overseas. The fact that child migrants paid to go to Canada by local Poor Law unions also had to give their consent to their migration in front of a magistrate – and that some children refused to give this when presented – also indicates a degree of choice for some. But others recalled that the decision to remove them from family contacts and home communities and to move them to new lives far away was something done to them, without any meaningful consent on their part:

> I just finished eating and this matron came by and tapped some of us on the head. 'You're going to Texas', 'You're going to Texas'. Well, some of the kids clapped and laughed. She came up to me. I looked up and I said, 'I can't go, I'm not an orphan – my mother's still living. She's in a hospital right here in New York'. 'You're going to Texas'. No use arguing.[91]

> I recall someone, I think it was Brother Conlon, coming in to a room and calling out my name. I cannot recall ever being asked whether I wanted to go to Australia, but the next thing I knew there were eight of us from the home chosen to go to Australia.[92]

> I recall two Christian Brothers coming to Nazareth Lodge from Bindoon to speak to us about Australia. I think they had Australian accents. They asked who wanted to go and I put my hand up as did another fourteen boys. We had no idea where Australia was and I thought it was a picnic spot somewhere in Belfast.[93]

The decision to migrate a child always had a profound effect on their lives. For children who experienced little meaningful say in this process, or who came to see the process as one in which their parents and families had not consented either, this decision could become one of the most fundamental sources of regret for their lives.[94] For those who experienced unhappy relationships, abuse, humiliation and exploitation in the new environments to which they moved, this regret had even deeper resonances.

There was no single, typical biography of the child migrants who lived through the schemes discussed in this book. The lives they went on to lead were complex conjunctions of the people and institutions they were fortunate or unfortunate to encounter, the social and economic conditions of their time and the organizational policies and structures through which their lives as child migrants were lived. Their experience of child migration marked them in different ways, with their remaining lives woven through their choices, relationships and chance. Nevertheless, in the midst of such varied lives, it is possible to see these basic existential wounds of severed relationships, loss of belonging, relational meaning and identity, shame and lack of choice running through many of them. How people lived with, and made sense of, those wounds again varied, but they remained wounds from charitable interventions that were believed to be in their best interests.

To observe that the effects of child migration schemes fell short of their moral aspirations is hardly surprising. It is a common-place of social life that organizational policies are rarely entirely successful in achieving their aims. The complexity of society, and the laws of unintended consequences for institutional actions, inevitably create gaps between intentions and outcomes. The point of this chapter is not simply, though, to make an obvious point about the gap between aspiration and reality in these child migration schemes, but to think about the ways in which moral meanings were implicated directly or indirectly in the suffering that many children experienced through them.

The causes of the suffering already discussed here were not simply the result of the moral framework of the schemes. At the level of individual relationships, children suffered considerably when in the care of adults who used their power over them abusively, exploitatively or insensitively. Suffering was caused not simply by abusive or uncaring individuals, though, but through various systemic problems in the way in which the schemes operated. The economic basis on which the schemes operated meant that they were inevitably premised on children's labour either as an incentive for households to take a child migrant on placement or a means of reducing running costs of residential institutions.[95] This was not true in all cases, such as households who took children to extend their families or residential homes sufficiently well funded not to rely significantly on children's labour, but these were exceptions rather than the norm. Such reliance on children's labour led to the instrumentalized relationships and closely controlled childhoods already discussed here. Failures in systems of supervision also led both to a lack of knowledge about some child migrants' distress or interventions to address this.[96] As has been previously discussed, problems with the monitoring of placements had been noted by critics of the 'orphan trains' and the child migration schemes to Canada from an early stage in their operation. While some improvements were made to the supervision systems of these schemes as they developed, their coverage of placed-out child migrants remained incomplete. Andrew Doyle's question as to whether it was appropriate for the supervision of child migrants to be left in the hands of those delivering the schemes, or colonial government departments with a vested interest in encouraging immigration remained unaddressed. In the case of the schemes to Australia, few former child migrants recalled any meaningful supervision contacts with children's officers from the state welfare departments legally responsible for their care. The frank admission of negligent supervision by the children's welfare officer for Western Australia, recorded in Anthony Rouse's private notes on his visit to Bindoon with the Australian review team, further indicates a system failing to protect children.[97] Allied with flawed systems of supervision was the fact that schemes often operated in ways that showed insufficient discrimination about the people into whose care child migrants were passed. As noted in previous chapters, both the New York Children's Aid Society and child migration schemes to Canada were criticized for relying on local references about receiving households rather than direct visits to them – a point the Bondfield report repeated in 1924. In the case of the Australian schemes, the lack of training and careful selection of staff led to vulnerable child migrants being placed in the care of adults with little interest or understanding of their emotional lives. The gap between the quality of staff provision and expectations about appropriate standards of child-care in Britain became, as noted in the previous chapter, even starker after 1945.

Such systemic problems played an important role in the suffering of child migrants. Migration would never have been an easy experience for vulnerable children, but was doubtless made worse by unsuitable staff and placements, the expectations on children as manual workers and failures in their supervision. The schemes persisted, however, because those delivering, funding and supporting them believed this to be good work and in the best interests of the child.

The unintended harm of humanitarian piety

As has been clear from the previous chapters, child migration schemes were motivated by a range of factors including the aspiration to strengthen the British empire and growing colonies, the desire to reduce public welfare costs and sectarian religious rivalries. Through much of their work, however, ran a more common thread of humanitarian piety.[98] Although its cultural roots were older than this, the nineteenth-century saw the consolidation of a humanitarian ethos concerned with the relief of human suffering as a sacred moral commitment. While humanitarianism has arguably been extended much further as a defining ethos of public life in more recent times,[99] the nineteenth century gave rise to an important early wave of organizations from the International Committee of the Red Cross to the wider child-saving movement of which child migration schemes were a part.

This humanitarian piety was grounded in the cultivation of a particular form of moral life – to become a person who would not turn away from other's suffering. Various publications on the child migration schemes continually celebrated those who exemplified this moral virtue. One way of doing this was through focusing on the work of founding figures of charitable organizations, represented as giving themselves tirelessly to the relief of other's pain. 'Men who befriended children' ran the simple caption to a series of photographs of leading figures in the New York Children's Aid Society that introduced a seventy-five-year review of its work.[100] One biographer likened William Quarrier to one of Christ's disciples who 'kept with Him day by day, week after week, and year after year, in His work among the poor, and in His ministration to the sick'.[101] The life story of Kingsley Fairbridge similarly drew praise for his 'unquestioning, selfless devotion to an idea' which 'lifted him entirely above the common run, one of those "warriors of the sighting brain" whose lives are a song and star to lead their generation.'[102] The role of leading figures in producing copy for their own organizational publications also reinforced this sense of moral pioneers struggling to relieve the suffering of vulnerable children, even though Thomas Barnardo's more self-publicizing stories of his adventures in child rescue contrasted with William Quarrier's perpetual self-critique as being an imperfect channel for the greater work of God. Alongside these pioneers, donors were also held up as exemplars of humanitarian piety,[103] in particular children who gave to ease the suffering of children less fortunate than themselves. Such examples of childlike moral generosity were praised not simply to evoke sympathetic reactions among other young readers, but to make the point to adult donors that children were not so burdened with cynicism or indifference as to allow their humanitarian moral impulses to be stifled. One such story has the generous child singing a hymn to remind themselves of these moral truths: 'Not more than others I deserve/ Yet God has given me more/ For I have food, while others starve/Or beg from door to door.'[104]

Most important of all moral exemplars, however, was the divine source of all compassion. Coming to the aid of vulnerable children was seen as both a reflection of God's love for them and a means of paying service due to God through the figure of the lonely, cold and hungry child. 'Our Divine Lord gave Himself for every outcast child. What ought we not to give for them, for in giving to them we give to Him', declared an annual report for the Crusade of Rescue.[105] The Little Wanderers' Advocate similarly observed that:

> The Saviour is no longer upon the earth as he once was; we cannot receive him as did the sisters of Bethany . . . Sight is given place to faith; but the blessing is no less real, the promise no less sure . . . Would we realize the Saviour's promise? Would we receive him ourselves? Then, listen to his own words, 'Whoso shall receive one such little child in my name, receiveth me.' Just *one*, not ten or twenty or a hundred. We may receive him into our homes, at our firesides, into our hearts, with all his blessedness and with all his reward, by receiving one such little child in his name.[106]

Alongside these models of moral generosity, publications by organizations undertaking child migration work directly challenged readers to follow these examples and censured those who did not through self-interest or indifference.[107] To fail to give was seen as not only selfish, but unwise (given the potential risks of children turning to pauperism and criminality) and a breach of one's fundamental duty to God and humanity.

Within this broader humanitarian ethos, churches and charities cultivated the sense of child migration work as a moral necessity. A range of media was used to do this. Annual reports and periodicals carried case studies of the suffering of poor children as well as letters and testimonials from child migrants, their employers and placement agents telling the ways in which children's lives had been changed for the better:

> Ethel, 1896. 'E. was out when I called came in looking very bright and happy, she is in an excellent place, chiefly looks after the children. Her mistress says, "Ethel is a good girl, and she could not do without her now. She has plenty of nice clothes and is saving money."'[108]

> James N., a little boy nine years old, found a most excellent home with Mrs H. She says: 'I had expected to take Frank P., who had been represented to me as a fine-looking boy. I saw this little fellow coming up the path in front of the house. He was a little midget of a thing . . . I confess I felt a little disappointed when they told me he was not Frank P., but I seemed to have a strong affection for him in a moment, and couldn't let him go. I thought perhaps God has sent this little fellow here, and he may need a home more than Frank, and so I determined at once to keep him. He said . . . "May I call you, ma?" I didn't intend to have him do so, but couldn't refuse his request . . . We didn't quite like the name of Jimmy N., and so we call him Burt, H. He is a good boy, and we wouldn't part with him now upon any account.'[109]

> Dear Rev. Father, I am writing to tell you I arrived out here safely. I am very happy in my new home, and I am not very lonesome. Please will

you tell me where my two other brothers are? Their names are Willie and Bobby. I have fine times here . . . My boss has three horses, eight calves, and twenty-nine cows . . . I can drive a horse very well now. I help to feed the calves. There are two little babies. I get enough to eat. We have very hot weather here. My brother is not very far from me; my boss and I are going to drive down to him some day. I am getting to know all the people about here.[110]

Alongside the narratives of individual transformation presented by such case studies and letters, visual representations of this transformation also played an important focus for moral sentiment. The relative significance of these images in organizational publications grew with greater use of photography. Until the early twentieth century, line drawings accompanied lengthy text in annual reports and periodicals. From the 1920s, these publications gave more space to photographs that were allowed to convey their message of transformed lives with shorter interpretative text. Some forms of content and composition were used repetitively. Late Victorian periodicals and annual reports frequently provided sentimentalized line drawings or – in the case of Dr Barnardo's Homes' *Young Helpers League* magazine – colour illustrations depicting poor, destitute waifs with downcast expressions and ragged and dirty clothes. Sometimes, these objects of compassion were depicted standing alone, sometimes begging or sometimes looking longingly through the windows of middle- and upper-class homes, gazing at the domestic comforts unavailable to them.[111] Before and after images – used controversially by Thomas Barnardo – contrasted the hungry, ragged child prior to rescue with the child migrant in their new home, well-fed and clothed.[112] With the shift to photography, the professional photographers who produced publicity images for the child migration schemes also used certain repetitive compositional styles.[113] The physical structures of ships, such as stairways and upper decks were used to pose groups of smiling children, arms raised aloft in celebration of their impending new lives. Another common compositional approach was to have a line of child migrants walking confidently towards the camera, cases in hand, implying that they were moving purposefully towards the new futures being offered to them.

Text and images were not the only media created to evoke a sense of moral identification with child migration work. For some organizations, the singing of hymns and institutional songs also played an important role in the shared construction of narratives that framed child migration in a feeling of greater moral and spiritual significance. Hymns became a way of connecting organizations and their supporters in a shared moral and religious ethos, either when printed in organizational publications or performed at fund-raising events.[114] When taught to children, they became a means through which children could learn to experience their lives against the background of a wider spiritual drama. One recurring theme across these hymns is an understanding of the child migrant's life as a pilgrimage both to new life in their new homes and, more broadly, as a transient journey towards to the true and final spiritual home in paradise.

An account of a departing party of child migrants in a Quarrier's annual report illustrates this:

> Meanwhile a large company had gathered on the quay side, including the boys ... not in the emigrant list. These were ranged immediately in front of the ship, and as the sailors were making ready to clear away, they sung a parting hymn to their young comrades on deck –
>
> *Whither, pilgrims, are you going,*
> *Going each with staff in hand?*
>
> Then the young emigrants joined in –
>
> *We are going on a journey,*
> *Going at our King's command,*
> *Over hills and plains, and valleys:*
> *We are going to his palace –*
> *Going to the Better Land.*[115]

These various textual, visual and auditory media all sought to evoke an emotional sense of the moral value of child migration work. How could one object to the stories child migrants told about their new lives? How could one deny children the opportunity that had been extended to these child migrants, staring into the camera with excited expressions? Child migration was thus surrounded by its supporters with an aura of moral obligation. It was an irresistible moral transaction in which those supporting these schemes found assurance that they were acting in accordance with the 'deepest springs of life and character'[116] by providing suffering children with an unquestionable means of help and transformation. Such support constituted a fulfilment of duty to society, to the vulnerable child and to God.

The moral meanings woven through the stories, images and emotions had the effect not only of cultivating a humanitarian piety among advocates and supporters of child migration schemes, but also helped to shape the ways in which these schemes operated and were publicly perceived. This had a direct bearing on the kinds of harm that many children experienced through these schemes, either through weakening people's ability to think and act against this harm or by shaping relationships in ways that made harm more possible.

One effect of the circulation of moral stories, images and sentiments around child migration work was that it created a sense of moral certainty about the value of this work. The moral commitment to intervene to give hope and new life to suffering children seemed such an obvious expression of humane moral sentiment as to be a self-evidently right thing to do. By constructing child migration as a natural expression of this principle of humane concern, the work itself acquired a moral obviousness that made it harder for its advocates and supporters to perceive any serious failings in it. As has been noted in previous chapters, one of the striking features of these child migration schemes is how committed its supporters were regardless of any evidence of its failings. British and Australian management committees for the Fairbridge child migration schemes were, for example, clearly aware from the mid-1940s, about the failures of the Fairbridge farm schools to provide adequate educational training.[117] These concerns, however, were only ever shared internally within Fairbridge circles and, to a limited degree, with local state educational authorities. They never dampened the positive claims made in Fairbridge's organizational publicity about the positive educational and developmental opportunities that migration through them would offer children.[118]

It could be argued that withholding knowledge of problematic aspects of the schemes from a wider public gaze is merely an act of institutional self-interest. While this clearly can sometimes involve conscious judgements about what actions should be best undertaken in the interests of the organization and its work, to see this in a reductionist sense of merely protecting interests fails to recognize the role that moral claims about charitable work play. It was precisely the moral assumption that child migrants' lives were made better through their time at Fairbridge that made it seem appropriate to continue to produce promotional materials extolling its value at the same time as knowing that there were fundamental problems with the work. The point here is that the moral commitment to the work, sustained by all the relationships, media and ways of working together that circulated these moral convictions, had a strong claim on how supporters of the schemes interpreted this work. As a consequence, claims about harmful effects of the schemes were often seen by their leading supporters as impugning their moral value and typically evoked defiant rebuttals rather than any serious self-critical reflection. Such processes were evident, for example, in Maria Rye's public refutation of the Doyle report or Charles Loring Brace's firm rejection of criticisms of the practices of the New York Children's Aid Society's emigration programme. They could still be seen a century later, in claims made to a UK Parliamentary Health Select Committee review, in which the then chairman of the Catholic Child Welfare Council declared that most Catholic child migrants to Australia had benefitted from the experience and the then director of the Fairbridge Society suggested that concerns about child migrant abuse in Australia were simply the result of sensationalized media coverage.[119] Moral certainty about the value of the work meant that uncomfortable evidence of its shortcomings were more likely to be denied, minimized or rationalized away.

The moral ambition of the child migration schemes also gave them, for some wider audiences, an unquestionable aura of legitimacy and respectability. This is exemplified by some of the adverse responses to the comments of the Ross Fact-Finding Mission from civil servants in the Commonwealth Relations Office, shocked that the moral rectitude of organizations undertaking child migration work was being called into question. As one departmental note on the Ross report prepared within the Commonwealth Relations Office put it:

> The Fairbridge Society is a name known throughout the world, known in particular to the public; and most important, well-known to influential members of Parliament in this country. The criticism in the report [of the assumption that children should be primarily trained for manual work on the farm schools] would . . . be regarded by the public and those concerned with child migration as a quite gratuitous and uncalled for comment about the work of the Fairbridge Society. The Society runs farm schools, and it is obviously necessary and right that a child going to a farm school should co-operate in making the farm a success. Many children at school in this country who live their young lives in towns and after school start work in office or factory [sic] would regard the opportunity of working on a farm school as of immense psychological and spiritual value. It is this kind of criticism in the report that makes one doubt whether it would be wise for the Government to appear, still less to go on record, in unqualified support of it.[120]

The tone of moral indignation in this note is strikingly different to the pragmatism of Home Office memos noting that powerful support for the Fairbridge Society made black-listing its institutions impossible in terms of 'practical politics'. It demonstrates deference not simply to Fairbridge's political capital, but more strongly to the inherent moral authority of its work. The self-evident legitimacy of the moral ambition of transforming children's lives in a healthy colonial environment made any criticism, and critic, of that work morally illegitimate, such that any responsible government would have to distance itself from it. The role of moral communication in creating such feelings of respectability around child migration schemes played an important role in other contexts as well. When the Doyle report was discussed in the Canadian Parliament, a number of people rose in indignant defence of the moral rectitude not only of the schemes run by Maria Rye and Annie Macpherson's but the Canadian households who took British child migrants in. As one put it, even if occasionally a child was unwittingly placed in a bad home, 'Canadian social habits are such as to make it morally certain that some neighbour or other, if not the whole neighbourhood, will protect any child from wrong'.[121] Wider public support for child migration work could therefore assume that it was motivated by the best of intentions and delivered by morally respectable people. Moral confidence in this work made it easier to believe that children's best interests were being protected through it. Sadly, while it is convincing to these supporters, such confidence was not always well-placed and created environments in which it was harder to think publicly about the scheme's shortcomings or to act in a concerted way to address these.

The moral cultures of the schemes did not, however, simply shape the ways in which their advocates and wider public supporters thought and felt about them. They also shaped the ways in which relationships within these schemes operated. An important consequence of the moral conviction that migration was in the best interests of the child, undertaken by people who shared a common commitment to easing children's suffering, was to create bonds of trust between those involved in delivering these schemes.[122] One of the striking features of their work was the sheer physical distances that networks of supporters, sending agencies, distribution points and receiving households and residential institutions covered. These charitable initiatives depended on bonds of trust between people who could never meet face-to-face or have much personal knowledge of each other. Child migrants were placed in households in America and Canada that had never been visited by placing agencies, based on references provided by local people most of whom, again, were personally unknown to those agencies. While degrees of contact varied between voluntary organizations sending child migrants to Australia and those receiving them, a high degree of trust again made it possible for people in Britain to assume that children sent several thousand miles away were being cared for. Some charities, such as the Fairbridge Society and Dr Barnardo's Homes had affiliated local branches in Australia with whom they worked, but in which significant trust needed to be shown for these relationships to work over a great distance.[123] Such trust was even more striking between different Catholic religious orders, or the Church of England Council for Commonwealth and Empire Settlement and Anglican children's homes, who transferred children between them with no formal arrangements for ongoing monitoring of their welfare by the sending organization. While some child migrants did receive some form of regular supervision, for the most part child migration schemes operated on the assumption that those receiving children into their care were motivated by the best intentions and would do their best to bring them up as good and productive people. Trust in the moral value of the work, and of the character of those undertaking it, also spread out into wider public networks of supporters. This is illustrated in a local public official's praise for the Christian Brothers at an annual meeting at the Tardun farm school for their success in the 'sacred duty to train up and support potential good citizens'.[124] Such public expressions of confidence made it easier for many residential institutions to continue their work in Australia with relatively little external scrutiny of their day-to-day work.

These networks of trust significantly extended not only between human actors but also drew in the divine. Children were sent overseas in the belief that they would not only be cared for in households and residential institutions, but that God's loving presence would also welcome them in their new lands. Shared faith between those sending and receiving children supported the sense of a common purpose rooted in faithful relationship to God. As an early Quarriers' annual report put it:

> It was very hard to part from the dear boys and girls, towards whom our love has gone out so strongly during the last few months, whose very slippings and stumblings seem to have made them dearer to us; but we were cheered with the hope that the Lord has made some of them his own children, through faith in Jesus; and that He is leading them to Christian homes, where they will be cared for and loved for Jesus' sake.[125]

A hymn sung to departing Quarriers' emigrants by other children in the orphan homes included the lines, 'Don't forget the Orphan Homes of Scotland/ Don't forget the dear friends here/ Don't forget that Jesus Christ your Saviour/ Goes with thee to Canada.'[126]

Underneath such sentiments it is possible to detect an understandable anxiety on the part of those sending children overseas about how they would fare in their new lives. Such anxiety was never voiced explicitly in promotional literature for these schemes, although was implicit in the reassurances that they gave readers about the suitability of the environments to which children were being sent. Trust in God became an important means of containing such anxiety and providing sending organizations with a sense of continuity of care. If receiving communities were motivated by the same devotion to God as those undertaking the migration work, then fears for children's futures would be eased. Some children might well have hard times in their new placements. But then, ultimately, they could always rely on God's own care for them if their faith could be nurtured to make them attentive to His love for them.[127] Such an emphasis on divine love was by no means the only way in which those undertaking child migration understood their work in religious terms, nor the only form of faith that they sought to cultivate in children. The duties of faith and the elimination of vice were given much stronger emphasis by some than assurances of God's personal love for children.[128] But the importance of the ways that adults and children imagined their relationships to God should not be underestimated in the cultivation of trust in the networks of relationships through which child migration schemes operated.

The moral project of redeeming children from suffering and threats of moral corruption also shaped relationships between children and adults within these schemes. Children's deference to adults would have been expected for most of the period in which the schemes operated. But within this moral frame of humanitarian piety, child migrants were expected to become certain kinds of people in order to demonstrate that the redemptive work had indeed taken place. These expectations are, for example, woven through the evaluative comments made about children in supervision records and progress notes in annual reports. Children were expected not only to be deferential, but physically wholesome, grateful, productive and (hopefully) pious. Children were aware of these expectations, sometimes apologizing in their letters to distribution homes about their failures and promising to 'do better', or sometimes telling the reader things that they knew would be treated as good news such as having found personal faith in Christ. Equally, children were aware of these expectations when they resisted them by arguing back or disobeying rules, knowing the sanctions that could fall on them as a result. While, in some respects, providing an ideal to which children could strive, and which some might feel pride in achieving, these expectations also discouraged children's autonomy or engendered an ongoing sense of failure in those judged not to have lived up to them. In the context of those residential institutions in Australia characterized by rigid institutional governance such an ideal could become the basis of harsh forms of discipline, in which children faced painful or humiliating punishments when judged to have fallen short of it either by some perceived slight against institutional authority or wetting their beds. Becoming the desired result of humanitarian intervention was not always easy, then, for children on the path to redemption.

This discussion has focused on the ways in which the humanitarian piety of these child migration schemes had unintended consequences, contributing to children's harm through the blind-spots, uncritical moral confidence and unwarranted trust that it helped to create. The significance of this is not limited to these child migration schemes, however. The humanitarianism of which Victorian organizations such as the New York Children's Aid Society and Dr Barnardo's Homes were early organizational examples, has grown into a global moral culture shaping the work of an extensive network of international NGOs and charities. Worked out both through religious organizations, who understand their traditions increasingly in terms of non-sectarian humanitarian mission, and secular forms in which humanitarian sentiment becomes the touchstone for moral life, it has become a dominant form of the sacred in modern times.

The rise of this humanitarian moral culture has been subject to critique. The anthropologist Didier Fassin has argued that humanitarianism can be understood as an illusory pursuit of social solidarity in the face of intractable and extreme social inequalities.[129] It is illusory, he argues, both because it often contains hidden judgements about what kinds of life are more valuable than others (e.g. based on a person's nationality or ethnicity) and because its focus on the immediate suffering of the 'victim' usually ignores the historical and political causes of that suffering. Humanitarian sentiment is concerned primarily with the 'obligation of the giver' than the 'rights of the receiver', with the life of the 'victim' reduced to a performance of suffering that fails to recognize a person beyond that victim-role.

While Fassin's argument about the increasing cultural and political influence of humanitarianism is hard to disagree with, the discussion of the moral cultures of child migration schemes in this chapter challenges his critique to some extent. Fassin's claim that the appeal of humanitarianism lies in its promise of moral coherence in the face of deep social injustices rings true to some extent for the early history of these child migration schemes. Late nineteenth-century British and American societies were characterized by very stark contrasts of wealth and absolute poverty that were not only visible to city-dwellers, but agonized over in philanthropic literature and were even a source of grim fascination to middle-class parties who would undertake tours of slum areas.[130] Humanitarian responses to this poverty offered a way of maintaining a sense of moral decency in the face of such blatant inequalities and suffering. They were, as Fassin also argues, characterized by an operation of power in which acts of compassion were undertaken by those with more social resources to change the lives of those with less, with little sense of this being a collaborative endeavour.

But these responses cannot be reduced to mere moral self-justification or the exercise of social control. They involved a measure of empathy with others' pain and the hope that this could be relieved – a more positive impulse than the 'scientific philanthropy' of that period that parsed which kinds of suffering should be given some limited relief and which left unaided as a moral lesson. They were also not devoid of political critique. Charles Loring Brace may have spoken less about his enthusiasm for political radicalism as his career in leading a major philanthropic organization developed. But as we have noted before, William Quarrier and William Bramwell Booth all undertook their child migration work alongside a critique of the Poor Law system. Their response was not insensitive to the political context of poverty, but undertaken in the belief that the needs of the destitute demanded urgent action in the face of failing public welfare provision. Perhaps their time would have been better spent campaigning for political reform, but their judgement was that such reform was not a likely prospect and extreme social conditions demanded a more immediate response. The promotional literature of the child migration schemes, and child rescue organizations more generally, did tend to represent the children of the poor as the passive recipients of others' generosity. But despite the asymmetries of relationships between adults and children, it is still possible to detect in some of the correspondence between staff in sending organizations and distribution homes and child migrants a genuine and mutual affection. Alongside the humanitarian impulse to ease others' suffering, more complex forms of political awareness and mutual relationships with others can also potentially be maintained.

Where the humanitarian piety of these schemes failed children, however, was at the point in which human relationships were interpreted too uncritically in its moral terms. The conviction that child migration was good work, that those receiving children were trustworthy or that children should show the marks of redemption in their new lives all worked against an empathy for the ways in which the schemes added new pain to children's lives. Ironically, then, the empathic attentiveness to suffering that motivated humanitarian interventions was often lost when the moral claims of those interventions were worked out in people's lives. The lesson of the child migration schemes is not therefore that humanitarian sympathy should be treated with inherent suspicion. Rather it is that it is wrong to assume that the out-working of humanitarian sentiment, however deeply felt, necessarily produces positive effects in the lives of those it claims to help. When the moral certainties of humanitarian action dull sensitivity to the experiences of those believed to be its beneficiaries, then humanitarianism is as capable of causing harm as any another other sacred tradition.

5

Remembering child migration today

Far from being a spent force, the humanitarian piety in which child migration schemes were grounded continues to shape the ways in which this work is remembered today. Over the past two decades, a growing number of public inquiries and truth and reconciliation commissions across the world have addressed issues of historic child abuse and neglect.[1] These have focused public attention on experiences of trauma resulting from the institutional policies of governments and other organizations, as well as from the cruelty or negligence of specific individuals. Trauma – particularly the traumatic experiences of children – has become an object of cultural fascination, a sacred touchstone around which the moral sentiments of humanitarian concern are evoked.[2] Addressing past traumas can be understood in terms of the wider political and legal movement for transitional justice, in which 'fixing the past' has become an increasingly important concern in many countries.[3]

Such collective remembering of past trauma has become particularly important in cases where direct criminal prosecution of those who caused harm has not happened whether because of lack of willingness on the part of prosecutors or difficulty in securing evidence given the length of time elapsed since the original offence.[4] In place of such prosecutions, public acts have arisen – primarily focused around reports and apologies – which respond to historic trauma by trying to guide public memory of it. Reports catalogue historic wrongs, censure those responsible and seek to give public recognition to those who have experienced trauma. Public apologies again give due recognition to past suffering, usually acknowledge some form of collective responsibility for this and assert the need for transformed attitudes in the future.[5] These processes of symbolic restitution do not happen as a matter of social inevitability, as a spontaneous gesture flowing from the humanitarian values around which many modern societies claim to be based. They are social and political processes, made possible in specific situations where powerful social actors who control media of public memory accede to moral and political pressures placed on them by past sufferers and their advocates.

There have been no such moves towards public inquiries or apologies in relation to child migration work in Canada or the United States, where public memories of the latter have, in particular, been relatively benign.[6] However, there have been significant attempts to transform public memory of the UK child migration schemes since the late 1980s. Public knowledge of child migration was already beginning to fade in Britain by the late 1950s, as the numbers of children being sent to Australia decreased. By the 1970s, the work had entirely dropped from public view. It is symptomatic of this loss of public memory that when the Nottingham-based social worker, Margaret Humphreys, first discovered stories of former British child migrants in 1986, her initial reaction was one of shock and disbelief.[7] Going on with colleagues to form the Child Migrants Trust, Humphreys played a central role in the development of a network of former child migrants and advocates who gave renewed public attention to the history of the schemes through newspaper articles, popular dramas and direct lobbying of migration organizations and politicians. Renewed public awareness of the schemes – now critical of their traumatic effects on children's lives – led, however, to few successful prosecutions of individuals who had been directly involved in the abuse of children.[8] In part this was because the Christian Brothers succeeded in ensuring that a major class action against them was heard in Western Australia where it would be ruled inadmissible because it fell outside of the period of the state's statute of limitations for civil cases.[9] Following this, the plaintiffs in the class action were encouraged by the law firm representing them to accept an out-of-court settlement in which most received a minimum payment of AUD 2000, and a few plaintiffs received settlements amounting to tens of thousands of Australian dollars.[10] In 2014, a critical review of Christian Brothers' institutions in Western Australia by the Royal Commission into Institutional Responses to Child Sexual Abuse led the Christian Brothers to invite plaintiffs to submit requests for these payments to be reviewed, leading to increased compensation payments. A proposed settlement of $24 million Australian dollars has also eventually been reached following a class action for physical and sexual abuse pursued by a group of former residents of the Fairbridge Farm School at Molong, the largest single compensation package for a case of historic institutional child abuse to have been agreed in Australian legal history. While financial redress has been provided in some cases for former child migrants to Australia, these provisions remain dependent on the organization with which a child migrant was placed and which part of Australia a child migrant was sent to. In the absence of a consistent, national redress scheme there remain significant differences in the provision that child migrants have received.

Child migrants sent to the Fairbridge Farm School at Pinjarra, for example, seem unlikely to receive anything like the same degree of financial redress as children sent to Fairbridge Molong, because the statute of limitations in Western Australia will prevent the taking out of any comparable class action there. Given the relative lack of criminal prosecutions and inconsistent system of redress, Margaret Humphreys has commented that many former child migrants are left with a sense of a 'lack of truth, lack of justice'[11] in the public response to their past suffering.

In the absence of effective criminal and civil redress, interventions into public memory of the UK child migration schemes to Australia have taken the form of both government reports and public apologies. Separate reports, published in Britain in 1998 and Australia in 2001, have sought to provide critical narratives of the effects of these schemes while also making some practical policy recommendations as to how former child migrants might be best supported in the future. These were eventually followed by full prime ministerial apologies by Kevin Rudd, in 2009, and Gordon Brown in 2010, endorsed by leaders of opposition parties in both countries. Differing responses to these apologies by former child migrants, however, demonstrate the potential limitations of reliance on such symbolic forms of redress. For some, public apologies constituted a transformative moment of public recognition of their suffering – a symbolic act powerfully counteracting their enduring sense of chronic shame from their childhood. As one former child migrant, Patricia Carlson commented:

> My eldest daughter, when I first started – and I am talking fifteen years ago – she said to me . . . when I said to her, 'I'm going to work really hard and get over all of this,' I – and this is one of the reasons why I became so passionate about doing things about the British child migrants' scheme. She said to me, 'It's going to be a hard road for you, mum. It'll be like a mountain. It will be like you climbing that mountain . . . but when you get to the top, it's easy.' And I've never forgotten that. And that apology, on that day, I got to the top of the mountain.[12]

Symbolic attempts at restitution could, however, also be experienced as empty and meaningless compared to practical support for those still suffering from the effects of the schemes. As another former child migrant, Dilys Budd, put it:

> [Interviewer] What do you think of the British Government's apology?

> [Dilys Budd] Meant nothing to me . . . I thought, well how much longer is this, you know, who's going to apologize next, the Queen? I mean, when does it stop? It's the people who are alive today, it wasn't their fault. They shouldn't be having to apologize every five minutes for something they didn't do.

[Interviewer] What was your reaction to the Catholic Church's apology in 2001 to British child migrants?

[Dilys Budd] They were forced to do it, I think. But unless they improve the system there's no point apologizing . . . But I thought, well, that's the way it was, you know, there's nothing you can do about it. You can help the sick and the lonely now, but that, that's the apology. Put your money where your mouth is, you know, that's all.[13]

Apologies do not necessarily lead to support for civil justice from those making them either. Despite Kevin Rudd's prime ministerial apology in 2009, the Australian Commonwealth government subsequently decided not to set up a redress scheme to alleviate the need for the class action by former residents of the Fairbridge Farm School at Molong, New South Wales to go to court.[14] While a settlement was eventually reached, after six years, some of the elderly plaintiffs had died before being able to benefit from it.

Attempts to heighten public sympathy for victims' suffering through apologies and reports can also constitute a challenge for historical memory. As Ronald Niezen has noted, in the context of the Canadian Truth and Reconciliation Commission into residential schools for indigenous children, the conscious attempt to raise public awareness of historic suffering has in some respects had the effect of fixing certain critical images of past at the expense of more complex historical evidence.[15] Similar difficulties with making generalizations about trauma can also be seen in the case of the British child migration. When Gordon Brown made his prime ministerial apology for the schemes on 24 February 2010, he noted that child migrants were sent mainly without parental consent, that they were lied to about being orphans when their parents were in fact still alive and that children's names and birthdays were deliberately changed to prevent them re-uniting with their families. While there were cases in which each of these things happened, they were not typical of all (or even the majority) of British child migrants sent after 1869 to whom Brown was addressing this apology. The particular traumas of many child migrants to Australia were therefore generalized across the whole of this wider history.

To recognize this is not to suggest that symbolic attempts at restitution for historic trauma lack value. Given that part of many child migrants' trauma was a strong sense of shame and exclusion from society, public acts of recognition can be experienced as deeply significant. Problems arise, though, if it is assumed that the humanitarian shaping of public memory in sympathetic identification with others' historic suffering renders either criminal or civil justice, or more complex understandings of the past, unnecessary.[16] The assumption that public apologies constitute some kind of closure for historic trauma fails to recognize the ways in which the effects of that trauma continue in the lives of those who experienced it and their own families.[17] As one former child migrant has put it: 'My abusive upbringing had a devastating effect on my ability to show love and affection and it is still a problem today. The pain and isolation of my childhood goes on and affects the next generation.'[18]

The enduring influence of humanitarian piety can also be detected in the ways that some organizations involved in child migration work negotiate this legacy. Given that the majority of these are still involved either in the provision of direct services to children or other forms of welfare activity, this historic involvement in child migration work is often perceived as a potential threat to public support for their work today. While none would now attempt to defend child migration as a form of welfare intervention, and some have been more willing than others to acknowledge openly the historic suffering of children in their care,[19] others have adopted various approaches to avoid this legacy from tainting their current humanitarian work. Their involvement in child migration is positioned as being in a distant past – the product of a time in which less enlightened standards of child-care prevailed. To argue that the conditions of late Victorian Britain and America posed very different, and in certain respects more desperate, social challenges compared to contemporary society is obviously not unreasonable. But the notion of the 'distant' past is also sometimes applied to postwar child migration work as well. As one newsletter of C-BERS Services, set up by the Christian Brothers, put it in relation to the residential institutions run by the order in the past – 'by today's standards, the conditions would be considered harsh'.[20] Similarly, the schemes are defended as having been conventional wisdom or accepted policy at the time of their operation. As a representative of the Sisters of Nazareth order commented to the Historical Institutional Abuse Inquiry in Northern Ireland:

> I think we have to acknowledge – that's the government, the British government, the Australian government, the churches, the congregations, the institutes – we all have to put our hands up and acknowledge that maybe it wasn't the right thing to do, even though it was done in the best interests of the child at the time.[21]

The difficult past of child migration is further separated from the present in cases where this legacy is described in sanitized terms – such as cases where the beating of a child is described in softer terms as a 'hiding'.[22] On the Wikipedia entry for the 'Fairbridge charity' – now part of the Prince's Trust in Britain – Kingsley Fairbridge is described as having been so 'moved by levels of deprivation he saw in inner-city areas of England' that he 'established a charity to offer opportunities and education abroad to young people from broken homes'.[23] Fairbridge is thus reclaimed as a humanitarian worker whose motivations were consonant with the charity's contemporary aims. No mention is made of the imperial framing of his mission, his emphasis on it as a form of 'practical eugenics', the role of local agents in Britain in persuading parents to send their children overseas, Fairbridge's resistance to parents attempting to have their children returned from Australia or criticisms of the standards in the Fairbridge farm schools. While some organizations involved in child migration work – such as Barnardo's, the Together Trust and the New York Children's Aid Society – have provided substantial access to archival records of the schemes, some others have been less willing to give comparable access. When the Children's Society, formerly the Church of England Society for Providing Homes for Waifs and Strays, digitized its annual reports and magazines for the period 1882–1920 for public online access any mention of its child migration work to Canada was redacted.

Public memories of child migration work do need to understand it in its historical context. The humanitarian belief in the potential value of child migration in the late Victorian period, for example, should reasonably be seen against the background of a public welfare system that many regarded as failing the needs of the poor. For some children, in that context, migration may have offered better opportunities if they were fortunate enough to be received into a caring and supportive environment than if they had remained in Britain. Understanding child migration in this historical context should not mean, however, situating it entirely in a morally distant past in which its practices are understood to have been widely accepted. To think of child migration as the product of less enlightened times – as simply what was done 'back then' – can reinforce contemporary assumptions that people today are more morally insightful and that the history of modern child-care is a progressive movement towards ever better practice. Neither assumption is correct. The claim, in the C-BERS newsletter, that conditions in Christian Brothers' institutions would be considered harsh 'by today's standards' suggests a rougher past in which hard knocks were a part of life. The catalogue of criticisms recorded in the confidential appendices to the Ross report, however provide just one example of how child migration schemes were seen as problematic in the past. As has been demonstrated throughout this book, critical judgements of child migration work cannot simply be dismissed as an anachronistic imposition of contemporary standards on to the past, because those critical judgements were made across the whole period in which these schemes operated. The fact that the later British child migration schemes used approaches to institutional care and family separation that would have been considered bad practice by some organizations in the late Victorian period further challenges any belief that organizational child-care practices necessarily improve over time.

Charities and churches previously involved in child migration work have often sought to manage this legacy in order to protect public support for their ongoing humanitarian work. The implication underlying this is that any tainting of their reputation will harm vulnerable people today in need of their intervention, an offence against humanitarian piety. As this book has argued, though, such difficult institutional histories cannot simply be contained in a hermetically sealed past whose moral failings are kept at a remove from their work today. Similarly public apologies can be problematic if they create a false sense of distance between past and present, if the emotion of regret creates a false sense of moral resolution and displaces the need for continued critical reflection about what can be learned from that past. Remembering child migration today involves not only finding ways of keeping in mind the experiences of former child migrants but asking more broadly how moral cultures enable those with power and resources to act in ways that harm people who lack them. That is not a question whose relevance lies simply in the past. By remembering how child migration work persisted despite the criticisms raised against it, we may gain more insight into how the humanitarian desire to relieve the suffering of others can continue to give rise to further wounds today.

NOTES

Introduction

1 Astrid Lindgren, *Pippi Longstocking* (Oxford: Oxford University Press, 2007), pp. 42–53.

2 On the use of physical force by adults on children across different cultural contexts, see, for example, Heather Montgomery, *An Introduction to Childhood: Anthropological Perspectives on Children's Lives* (Chichester: Wiley-Blackwell, 2009); also Helen Kavapalu, 'Dealing with the Dark Side in the Ethnography of Childhood: Child Punishment in Tonga', *Oceania*, 63 (1993): 313–29.

3 See Karen Wells, *Childhood in a Global Context* (Cambridge: Polity, 2009), p. 2, on the significance of this dependence as a cross-cultural facet of childhood.

4 Henry Jenkins, *The Children's Culture Reader* (New York: New York University Press, 1998), p. 2. There can be scope for children to resist these projects. As the coming chapters of this book will demonstrate, though, this capacity for resistance varies depending on the kind of discipline and force to which children are subjected, the accountability of adult authorities and the degree to which children are dependent on particular adults (e.g. because of living in isolation from wider social networks).

5 By child migration, in this context, I mean the commonly used definition of schemes that sent children under school-leaving age overseas. In Britain, schemes specifically for children over school-leaving age ('juvenile emigrants') did not develop until the 1920s (see Marjory Harper, *Emigration from Scotland Between the Wars* (Manchester: Manchester University Press, 1998), pp. 157–94, for a discussion of many of these juvenile migration schemes).

6 Although 42.3 per cent of those sent out by the New York Children's Aid Society were also only placed as far as within New York State (Miriam Langsam, *Children West* (Madison: University of Wisconsin Press, 1964), p. 25).

7 See, for example, the strongly critical government reports on child migration schemes in the United Kingdom (*Health Select Committee Third Report* (London: HMSO, 1998)) and Australia (*Lost Innocents: Righting the Record* (Senate Community Affairs Committee, Canberra, Commonwealth of Australia, 2001)).

8 *Health Select Committee Third Report*, Introduction, p. 1. Staff working for charities previously involved in child migration work in Britain would not necessarily express their criticisms of it today in such stark terms as this, though.

9 For a critical analysis of the transnational adoption movement, see Laura Briggs, *Somebody's Children: The Politics of Transracial and Transnational Adoption* (Durham, NC: Duke University Press, 2012).

10 A figure suggested by Mervyn Humphreys based on numbers of former child migrants with whom the Child Migrants Trust has contact.

11 Johanna Sköld, 'Historical Abuse: A Contemporary Issue – Compiling Inquiries into Abuse and Neglect of Children in Out-of-Home Care Worldwide', *Journal of Scandinavian Studies in Criminology and Crime Prevention,* 14.1 (2013): s. 5–23; see also Brian Corby, Alan Doig and Vicki Roberts, *Public Inquiries into Abuse of Children in Residential Care* (London: Jessica Kingsley, 2001).

12 Such as, for example, the Royal Commission into Institutional Responses to Child Sexual Abuse in Australia, inquiries into the sexual abuse of children in the Catholic (archdioceses) of Dublin, Ferns and Cloyne and the ongoing Independent Panel Inquiry into Child Sexual Abuse in the United Kingdom.

13 I have also discussed this issue in the context of a wider range of modern child welfare interventions in Gordon Lynch, 'Saving the Child for the Sake of the Nation: Moral Framing and the Civic, Moral and Religious Redemption of Children', *American Journal of Cultural Sociology,* 2.2 (2014): 165–96.

14 This phrase was used in the context of post-war UK child migration schemes to Australia (see Stephen Constantine, 'The British Government, Child Welfare and Child Migration to Australia after 1945', *Journal of Imperial and Commonwealth History,* 30.1 (2002): 99). It captures well a broader concept of the environments from which child migration believed themselves to be rescuing children, devoid of what was judged to be the necessary social, material and moral conditions of familial domesticity either because of poverty, abandonment, family illness, single parenthood or parental moral failings. This judgement was rarely made with a strong appreciation of the affectional bonds that did exist between children and parents undergoing difficult circumstances.

15 Joy Parr, *Labouring Children: British Immigrant Apprentices to Canada, 1869–1924,* 2nd ed. (Toronto: University of Toronto Press, 1994).

16 See, for example, Anthony Platt, *The Child Savers: The Invention of Delinquency,* 2nd ed. (Chicago: University of Chicago Press, 1977), pp. xi–xxix, for an interpretation of the wider child-rescue movement in terms of political economy. I do not intend to contest that this was an aim, but the deferential productive worker was not simply seen as an economic good by these child migration organizations, but a moral good as well.

17 Andrew Doyle's report to the Local Government Board on the child migration work undertaken by Maria Rye and Annie Macpherson estimated that they made a profit of around £5 per child migrated to Canada. He acknowledged though that this estimate was made without access to, or detailed scrutiny of, their accounts (*A Report to the Right Honourable the President of the Local Government Board by Andrew Doyle, Esq., Local Government Inspector, as to the Emigration of Pauper Children to Canada* (Doyle report, House of Commons, London, 1875), pp. 33–4). Prior to this, the Local Government Board had also noted substantial differences between the significantly higher

charge that Rye made for her migration work of children from Poor Law
Unions compared to the charges levied by Annie Macpherson (Roy Parker,
Uprooted: The Shipment of Poor Children to Canada, 1867–1917 (Bristol:
Policy Press, 2010), p. 45). On the lack of evidence about Rye's accounts, see
Marion Diamond, *Emigration and Empire: The Life of Maria S. Rye* (New
York: Garland Publishing, 1999), pp. 171–2, though one emigration official
wrote of her that 'she is not a philanthropist but she is a passenger agent of
the sharpest description' (p. 185). The Australian Parliamentary inquiry into
child migration questioned whether some organizations, notably Catholic
religious orders, used recurrent government maintenance funding for child
migrants to cross-subsidize their other activities (*Lost Innocents: Righting
the Record,* (Senate Community Affairs Committee, Canberra, 2001),
pp. 5.15–21). Similar questions were raised about the work of religious
orders, including the Irish Christian Brothers who played a leading role in
Catholic child migration to Australia, in the public inquiry into the abuse and
neglect of children within the residential school system in Ireland (*Report
of the Commission to Inquire into Child Abuse (Ryan Commission Report,*
Dublin, 2009), vol. I, 6.42; vol. IV, 2.137, 147–9, 181, 197–8, 202–11 (see
also Interview with Bob Taylor, *Former Child Migrants Oral History Project*
(National Library of Australia, 2011), session 2, 00:17:25–00:19:27). There
were also individual cases of embezzlement of organizational funds that had
an effect on the resources available to support the care of child migrants;
David Hill, *The Forgotten Children: Fairbridge Farm School and Its Betrayal
of Britain's Child Migrants to Australia* (North Sydney: William Heinemann,
2008), pp. 128–30.

18   An account of a funding crisis in Dr Barnardo's Homes is given in *Night
and Day*, December 1893, p. 35 (B), although this does need to be read in
the context of the aim of eliciting funds from supporters. In her testimony to
a select committee in the Canadian Parliament following the Doyle report,
Annie Macpherson presented accounts showing that her child migration work
did little more than break even (Kenneth Bagnell, *The Little Immigrants: The
Orphans Who Came to Canada* (Toronto: Dundurn Group, 2001), kindle
edition loc.558). The Crusade of Rescue's migration work ran at a deficit for
the much of its operation, with it failing to keep up payments to the Catholic
Emigration Association for its administrative management of the emigration
process (Letter from Fr George Hudson to Archbishop of Birmingham,
5 May 1913, (BA)). The Catholic Emigration Association itself later
underwent a serious financial crisis in the 1930s as a result of the cessation
of the migration of children under school-age to Canada, a crisis which
threatened its ability to honour its financial obligations to child migrants to
pay wages it was holding in trust for them (Letter from Revd William Bunce
to the Archbishop of Birmingham, 21 June, 1935 (BA)). At the same time the
Church of England Council for Empire Settlement suffered from significantly
reduced government funding as the numbers of migrants significantly
decreased, mainly due to the effects of the global economic depression. Its
failure to recoup the costs of its fund-raising activities further contributed
to its need to reduce the scope of its work through the 1930s (see, e.g. *Sixth
Annual Report of the Church of England Council for Empire Settlement,*

1931, p. 9 (CE); *Ninth Annual Report of the Church of England Council for Empire Settlement*, 1934, pp. 9–11). Churches and charities undertaking child migration operated in a competitive market of philanthropic and missionary organizations appealing for public donations, and in which the religious imperative of philanthropic activity at home might seem less pressing to donors than the demand to bring the Gospel to mission fields overseas (see, e.g. *The Little Wanderers Advocate*, January 1879, CC6_F04, pp. 2–3 (SC); Shurlee Swain and Margaret Hillel, *Child, Nation, Race and Empire: Child Rescue Discourse, England, Canada and Australia, 1850–1915* (Manchester: Manchester University Press, 2010), pp. 79–84). This is reflected in frequent references to the value and legitimacy of child migration work more generally, as well as its value directly in comparison with overseas missionary work, in organizational annual reports and periodicals.

19 See, for example, Arthur Kleinman, *What Really Matters: Living a Moral Life Amidst Uncertainty and Danger* (New York: Oxford University Press, 2007), pp. 1–3.

20 This can be true of more popular histories in which individual pioneers provide a clear historical focus for constructing a narrative about the development of migration schemes (see, e.g., Annette Fry, *The Orphan Trains* (New York: New Discovery Books, 1994), pp. 11–22) as well as academic histories which discuss child rescue work in terms of the beliefs and ideas of its pioneers (see, e.g. Thomas Bender, *Toward an Urban Vision: Ideas and Institutions in Nineteenth Century America* (Baltimore, MD: Johns Hopkins University Press, 1975), pp. 134–57).

21 See, for example, Webb Keane, 'Minds, Surfaces and Reasons in the Anthropology of Ethics', in M. Lambek (ed.), *Ordinary Ethics: Anthropology, Language and Action* (New York: Fordham University Press, 2010), pp. 64–83.

22 There are two important bodies of literature on the social and cultural analysis of moral communication that informs the approach taken within this book and provides a broader context in thinking about the social uses of the moral to which this book seeks to contribute. One is work within cultural sociology, particularly associated with the 'strong program' developed by Jeffrey Alexander, which focuses on the role that moral meanings play in modern societies, particularly meanings structured around the profound moral distinction between the sacred and profane, see, for example, Jeffrey Alexander, *The Meanings of Social Life: A Cultural Sociology* (New York: Oxford University Press, 2006); Jeffrey Alexander, *The Civil Sphere* (New York: Oxford University Press, 2008); Gordon Lynch, *The Sacred in the Modern World: A Cultural Sociological Approach* (Oxford: Oxford University Press, 2012). The second is work within the field of the anthropology of ethics which examines the social and cultural role of practices of moral communication and reflection, see, for example, Michael Lambek, *Ordinary Ethics: Anthropology, Language and Action* (New York: Fordham University Press, 2010); James D. Faubion, *An Anthropology of Ethics* (Cambridge: Cambridge University Press, 2011); James D. Laidlaw, *The Subject of Virtue: An Anthropology of Ethics and Freedom* (Cambridge: Cambridge University Press, 2013); Didier Fassin and Samuel Leze, *Moral Anthropology: A Critical*

Reader (London: Routledge, 2014). A central concern across this work is how we might understand the relationships between moral meanings, social practice and human experience.

23 Former child migrants' own reflections on their experiences could also be shaped by the desire to present a narrative of trauma or resilience, or in some cases to minimize, deny or rationalize traumatic experiences. One former orphan train rider from New York, Helen Eastin, for example, recalled her indentured childhood in Louisiana in terms of a close new friendship with a neighbour, summer picnics and the chance to take leading roles in school plays. Her eldest daughter, however, recalled that her mother was remembered as a sad and lonely child, mocked as a 'New Yorker' by other children, and who never opened herself up to her own family (see Mary Ellen Johnson, *Orphan Train Riders Stories, volume 1* (Baltimore, MD: Gateway Press, 1992), pp. 127–35).

24 This issue is addressed well in the documentary *The Long Journey Home*, dir. Emily Booker, 2010, in which former child migrants who attended the Fairbridge Farm School in Molong, New South Wales, reflect on their experiences of the long-serving school principal, Frederick Woods. Memories of him ranged more positive accounts of him as an authoritative leader for a group of sometimes difficult children and a caring presence, particularly for younger children, to recollections of his violent temper and aggressive and sometimes uncontrolled use of physical punishment. See also Hill, *The Forgotten Australians*, pp. 109–32.

25 Parker, Uprooted, pp. 277–82 gives a helpful summary of some evaluative studies of child migration schemes to Canada, although the size and scope of these was limited. Alan Gill (*Orphans of the Empire: The Shocking Story of Child Migration to Australia* (London: Vintage, 1997)) estimates that around half of the former child migrants he interviewed for his book had positive recollections of the migration schemes. Understanding the relative benefits and harm caused by a welfare intervention requires more complex analysis than assessing the relative number of positive or negative accounts that people give of it, however. The content of oral history interviews needs to be understood critically in the light of the context in which it takes place, the ways in which the interviewee consciously seeks to present themselves and the unconscious defences through which an interviewee may deny or rationalize traumatic aspects of their experience too difficult to represent fully in awareness. For useful discussions of this see, for example, Michael Jackson, *The Politics of Story-Telling: Violence, Transgression and Intersubjectivity* (Copenhagen: Museum Tusculanum Press, 2002); Mark Klempner, 'Navigating Life Review Interviews with Survivors of Trauma', in R. Perks and A. Thomson (eds), *The Oral History Reader*, 2nd ed. (London: Routledge, 2006), pp. 198–210.

26 Discussed further in Chapter 4.

27 Swain and Hillel, *Child, Nation, Race and Empire* provides an excellent analysis of the moral discourses of the wider child rescue movement. My aim in this book is to shift the focus from the content of moral discourses itself, to how the content and uses of moral cultures relate to social practices and experiences that arise in relation to those.

Chapter 1

1   The phrase, the 'humane remedy' is taken from Charles Loring Brace's
    description of the New York Children's Aid Society's emigration programme in
    Charles Loring Brace, The Dangerous Classes of New York and Twenty Years'
    Work Among Them, 3rd ed. (New York: Wynkoop & Hallenbeck, 1880),
    p. 235.
2   Gillian Wagner, Children of the Empire (London: Weidenfeld & Nicholson,
    1982), p. 3.
3   Peter Williamson, The Life and Curious Adventures of Peter Williamson Who
    Was Carried Off from Aberdeen and Sold as a Slave, 20th ed. (Aberdeen:
    James Daniel & Son, 1878).
4   While some of these initiatives appear to have developed in isolation from
    each other, there was also a clear international flow of ideas between those
    interested in developing new forms of welfare intervention for children.
    Charles Loring Brace, secretary of the New York Children's Aid Society, was
    influenced by his experiences of visiting the Rauhe Haus and the Ragged
    Schools during a trip to Europe in 1850 (Miriam Langsam, Children West
    (Madison: University of Wisconsin Press, 1964), p. 6). Maria Rye and
    Annie Macpherson, who pioneered larger-scale child migration schemes
    from the United Kingdom from 1869, similarly drew on their experiences
    of seeing 'orphan train' schemes in operation during separate visits to New
    York (Roy Parker, Uprooted: The Shipment of Poor Children to Canada,
    1867–1917 (Bristol: Policy Press, 2010), p. 20). Shortly after beginning his
    own child migration work, Thomas Barnardo visited New York in 1884, and
    although unable to meet Charles Loring Brace, met other officers of the New
    York Children's Aid Society, thirty years after their own child emigration
    programme had begun (Night and Day, November, 1884, p. 120 (B)).
5   I am grateful to Johanna Sköld for drawing this history to my attention.
6   See Geoff Blackburn, The Children's Friend Society: Juvenile Emigrants to
    Western Australia, South Africa and Canada, 1834–1842 (Northbridge:
    Access Press, 1993).
7   Parker, Uprooted, p. 3.
8   The term 'orphan trains' was never used by any of the American child
    migration organizations themselves, but was a name popularized by a novel
    that was subsequently made into a television film (James Magnuson and
    Dorothea Petrie, Orphan Train (London: Melbourne House, 1978). The
    term was something of a misnomer as the majority of children sent out
    through the American railroad emigration programmes still had at least
    one surviving parent. The New York Children's Aid Society, Forty-Fifth
    Annual Report, 1897, Series III.1 (NY), p. 13, for example, states that of
    the 93,050 children it had sent West since 1853, only 42,888 were thought
    to be full orphans. The term continues to be used as the most common
    label for these programmes with the Orphan Train Complex in Kansas, the
    main museum for the programmes and fictional and historical work also
    continuing to use it (e.g. Christina Baker Kline, Orphan Train (New York:
    HarperCollins, 2013)).
9   Wagner, Children of the Empire, p. xii.

10 The United Kingdom was only not entirely unique in establishing government-funded international child migration schemes. In the 1960s and 1970s, more than 1,000 indigenous children from the French colony of Réunion were sent to rural areas of France on the basis of relieving overpopulation in Réunion and providing the children with better future work opportunities.

11 See, for example, Marilyn Holt, *The Orphan Trains: Placing out in America* (Lincoln, NE: University of Nebraska Press, 1992), loc.1529.

12 Parker, *Uprooted*, p. 46. Dr Barnardo's Homes similarly expressed concern at the possibility of emigrants to Canada being tempted across the border to better prospects in the United States, seeing this as a serious threat to the project of building Canada up as a viable British dominion (*Night and Day*, May, 1888, p.51 (B)).

13 Ellen Boucher, *Empire's Children: Child Emigration, Welfare, and the Decline of the British World, 1869–1967* (Cambridge: Cambridge University Press, 2014), pp. 5–8.

14 Lord Brabazon, 'State-Directed Emigration: Its Necessity', *Night and Day*, December, 1884, p. 178.

15 This system operated from the 1850s with the practice continuing in some cases into the late 1970s.

16 See, for example, Hugh Cunningham, *Children and Childhood in Western Society since 1500*, 2nd ed. (London: Routledge, 2005); Steven Mintz, *Huck's Raft: A History of American Childhood* (Cambridge, MA: Harvard University Press, 2006).

17 Vivianna Zelizer, *Pricing the Priceless Child: The Changing Social Value of Children* (Princeton, NJ: Princeton University Press, 1994); Harry Hendrick, *Children, Childhood and English Society, 1880–1990* (Cambridge: Cambridge University Press, 1997).

18 Boucher's, *Empire's Children*.

19 Although later annual reports of the New York Children's Aid Society talk in terms of older children being found work placements for pay in rural areas, the placement terms for many of the children sent out through its emigration programme were that wages were not usually expected to be paid before the age of 18. By contrast, Dr Barnardo's Homes, operated a similar placing out scheme during the same period but worked with the strong expectation that child migrants over 14 would receive some form of wage, usually held in trust for them (see, Joy Parr, *Labouring Children: British Immigrant Apprentices to Canada, 1869–1924*, 2nd ed. (Toronto: University of Toronto Press, 1994).

20 New York Children's Aid Society, *First Annual Report, 1854*, Series III.1 (NY), p. 4; Stephen O'Connor, *Orphan Trains: The Story of Charles Loring Brace and the Children He Saved and Failed* (Chicago: University of Chicago Press, 2001), p. 38; Mary Ellen Johnson, *Waifs, Foundlings and Half-Oprhans: Searching for America's Orphan Train Riders* (Westminster, MD: Heritage Books, 2007), p. 13.

21 See also Julie Miller, *Abandoned: Foundlings in Nineteenth-Century New York City* (New York: New York University Press, 2004), pp. 94–8.

22 Holt, *Orphan Trains*, loc.35, 335, 830.

23 In 1850, there were 9,021 miles of railway track in the United States, 74,096
    miles in 1857 and 192,556 miles by 1900 (Holt, *Orphan Trains*, loc.423).
    Seven separate railroads (from Tory and Albany in the East to Buffalo and
    Niagra Falls in the West) began to be integrated into New York Central
    Railroad from 1853 (Johnson, *Waifs, Foundlings and Half-Orphans*, p. 16).
    Having made this investment in the railroad system, railroad companies
    were keen to see increased population in developing States and gave reduced
    fares to placing out organizations, see Peter C. Halloran, *Boston's Wayward
    Children: Social Services for Homeless Children, 1830–1930* (Boston, MA:
    Northeastern University Press, 1994), p. 47.
24 See, for example, New York Children's Aid Society, *First Annual Report,
    1854*, Series III.1 (NY), p. 4; *Second Annual Report, 1855*, Series III.1
    (NY), p. 5. This notion of the greater moral rectitude of rural communities
    persisted late into the nineteenth century. The *Forty-Sixth Annual Report,
    1898*, Series III.1 (NY), pp. 9–10, commends the rural areas in the mid-West
    to which the Society's placed out children were sent for their commitment
    to religious training through Sunday schools and for their strong culture of
    temperance.
25 O'Connor, *Orphan Trains*, pp. 41–2, 166–7.
26 Holloran, *Boston's Wayward Children*, pp. 44–50.
27 Holloran, *Boston's Wayward Children*, p. 98.
28 The Home's original intended name was the Union Mission and Home
    for Little Wanderers. Failure to obtain Legislature approval of the name
    'Union Mission' led to this name being quickly changed to the Baldwin
    Place Home for Little Wanderers (*The Little Wanderers Advocate*, 1865,
    p. 39, CC6_F01 (SC)).
29 The first edition of *The Little Wanderers' Advocate* declared that 'the children
    of those noble men who have fallen during this unholy rebellion shall be
    objects of peculiar care. They shall be doubly welcome. We owe them a debt
    that the kindest treatment can never pay. They are not in the strict sense of
    the word objects of charity, but they have claims upon the public that demand
    our noblest response.' *The Little Wanderers Advocate*, 1865, p. 7, CC6_F01
    (SC), see also p. 38.
30 *The Little Wanderers Advocate*, 1865, p. 9, CC6_F01 (SC).
31 Formal adoption does not appear to have been the norm, though. Most
    placements operated more on fostering terms in which the New England
    Home reserved the right to remove a child from a placement if the child had
    been shown to have been abused there, *An Historical Account of the Origin,
    Plan and Success of the Baldwin Place Home for Little Wanderers, for Seven
    Years*, 1872, p. 13, CC6_F23 (SC). See also *Fourteenth Annual Report of the
    Baldwin Place Home for Little Wanderers*, 1879, p. 37, CC6_F19 (SC).
32 See *The Little Wanderers Advocate*, January 1879, p. 4, CC6_F04, (SC).
33 'It requires time to eradicate the influence of such vile associations and
    implant seeds of truth and principles of manhood, before the child is prepared
    for a home.' *An Historical Account*, p. 5, CC6_F23 (SC).
34 *An Historical Account*, p. 3, CC6_F23 (SC).
35 *An Historical Account*, p. 6, CC6_F23 (SC).
36 *An Historical Account*, p. 10, CC6_F23 (SC). The organization's constitution
    (article 2) stated that it would undertake to save children 'from want and

shame' by placing them in Christian homes, 'with the consent of their parents or legal guardians' (ibid., p. 22).

37 *An Historical Account*, pp. 11–13, CC6_F23 (SC).

38 *13th Annual Report of the Baldwin Place Home for Little Wanderers*, 1878, p. 6, CC6_F18 (SC). See also *14th Annual Report of the Baldwin Place Home for Little Wanderers*, 1879, p. 37, CC6_F19 (SC); Holloran, *Boston's Wayward Children*, pp. 124–5.

39 See, for example, Lydia Murdoch, *Imagined Orphans: Poor Families, Child Welfare and Contested Citizenship in London* (New Brunswick, NJ: Rutgers University Press, 2006), on the ways in which poor parents would try to manage the limited range of welfare support available to them.

40 *An Historical Account*, p. 24, CC6_F01 (SC).

41 *Fourteenth Annual Report of the Baldwin Place Home for Little Wanderers*, 1879, p. 37, CC6_F19 (SC).

42 Brace, *The Dangerous Classes*, pp. 74–96; O'Connor, *Orphan Trains*, pp. 39–82.

43 See New York Children's Aid Society, *First Annual Report, 1854*, Series III.1 (NY), pp. 6–7.

44 New York Children's Aid Society, *Forty-Second Annual Report*, 1894, Series III.1 (NY), pp. 9–10.

45 The New York Children's Aid Society, *Eighth Annual Report*, 1861, Series III.1 (NY), gives an estimate of 1,000 children attending its industrial and training schools in that year, with 804 children sent out through its emigration programme. By contrast, the Society's *Forty-Ninth Annual Report, 1901*, reports 15,671 enrolments at its industrial schools with only 407 children placed out through its emigration programme.

46 O'Connor, *Orphan Trains*, pp. 101–3.

47 Almost all States in the United States received children sent out by the New York Children's Aid Society, of which Illinois, Indiana, Iowa, Kansas, Michigan, Minnesota, Missouri, Nebraska, Ohio and Wisconsin each received at least two or three thousand children each (see New York Children's Aid Society, *Forty-First Annual Report, 1893*, Series III.1 (NY), p. 10).

48 On Brace's arguments against the large congregate institutions of his time, see O'Connor, *Orphan Trains*, pp. 158–61;

49 Holt, *The Orphan Trains*, loc.1615; Parker, *Uprooted*, p. 46.

50 Recollections of the experience of these distributions are given by several former orphan-train riders in *The Orphan Trains*, dir. Janet and Edward Grey (PBS documentary, 1995).

51 Holt, *The Orphan Trains*, loc.1332.

52 Leroy Ashby, *Endangered Children: Dependency, Neglect and Abuse in American History* (New York: Twayne, 1997), p. 49.

53 Holt, *Orphan Trains*, loc.1641.

54 Johnson, *Waifs, Foundlings and Half-Orphans*, p. 48. While the newspaper account is clearly intending to exploit humanitarian identification with the suffering of the children to enable their placement, the empathy for their suffering is also notable.

55 Poster Advertising Distribution Meeting, no date, Series XI.1 (NY). The wording on these publicity posters varied over time, with posters in the early twentieth century using a simpler formula that the children were expected to

be raised within the family and properly boarded, clothed and schooled until the age of 18 when it would be hoped that some other arrangement could be reached in which the child could continue to remain with the family.

56 See Langsam, *Children West*, pp. 18–19; O'Connor, *Orphan Trains*, pp. 96–7.
57 Formal adoption of children placed out by the New York Children's Aid Society was very rare for the majority of those sent out through its emigration programme, although more reference is made to this by the start of the twentieth century (see, e.g. New York Children's Aid Society, *Fifty-First Annual Report, 1903*, Series III.1 (NY), p. 20).
58 Although one of the largest schemes to apply this principle, it was not the only child-saving organization to do so. For example, the New England Home for Little Wanderers justified the out-of-State placement of its children partly on the grounds that certain family environments constituted a moral threat to the child. 'If children are given up who have had or still have relatives whose character and habits are immoral, they cannot be located within their reach and influence without danger' (*An Historical Account*, p. 6, CC6_F23 (SC)).
59 The New York Juvenile Asylum, founded in 1851, was one of the first public institutions in the United States to operate with a legal right to remove children from family homes deemed unfit (see Matthew A. Crenson, *Building the Invisible Orphanage: A Prehistory of the American Welfare System* (Cambridge, MA: Harvard University Press, 1998), pp. 61–5); Johnson, *Waifs, Foundlings and Half-Orphans*, pp. 36–8). See also George Behlmer, *Child Abuse and Moral Reform in England, 1870–1908* (Stanford, CA: Stanford University Press, 1982), pp. 6–7; Lela Costin, Howard Karger and David Stoesz, *The Politics of Child Abuse in America* (New York: Oxford University Press, 1996), p. 51.
60 Seth Koven, *Slumming: Sexual and Social Politics in Victorian London* (Princeton, NJ: Princeton University Press, 2004), pp. 98–103; Shurlee Swain and Margaret Hillel, *Child, Nation, Race and Empire: Child Rescue Discourse, England, Canada and Australia, 1850–1915* (Manchester: Manchester University Press, 2010), pp. 11, 30.
61 Behlmer, *Child Abuse and Moral Reform*, pp. 50–73; Costin, Karger and David Stoesz, *The Politics of Child Abuse*, pp. 59–67.
62 Bruce Bellingham, 'Waifs and Strays: Child Abandonment, Foster Care, and Families in Mid-Nineteenth-Century New York', in *The Uses of Charity: The Poor on Relief in the Nineteenth-Century Metropolis*, ed. Peter Mandler (Philadelphia: University of Pennsylvania Press, 1990), p. 151. Brace's view was to become more widespread among those overseeing child welfare provision. In 1877, the Secretary of the Massachusetts Board of Charities asked 'whether there is not among our people too much of a sentimental feeling about the sacredness of the family relation' and 'whether the highest good of all does not require that some families be broken up beyond all possibility of re-union', Crenson, Building the Invisible Orphanage, p. 68. In 1883, the secretary of the Ohio Board of Charities, A. G. Byers similarly advocated the removal of children from homes characterized by 'vice, and intemperate or otherwise criminal parentage' into public county homes for children (Crenson, p. 66, loc.846).
63 Crenson, *Building the Invisible Orphanage*, p. 209.

64 Johnson, *Waifs, Foundlings and Half-Orphans*, p. 24.

65 As with the later UK child migration programmes, it is not clear how much children's decisions to be placed out-of-state were influenced by tantalizing accounts of what their new lives might be like. In one case, a placed-out child recalled that he had enthusiastically taken up a place in the emigration programme because of the prospect of getting to see cowboys, Indians and buffalos (Holt, *Orphan Trains*, loc.735).

66 Holt, *Orphan Trains*, loc.718, 735. Already, by 1859, more than a quarter of the children (222 out of a total of 914) placed out by the CAS that year had been taken from the Randall's Island nursery (Johnson, *Waifs, Foundlings and Half*-Orphans, p. 24). Placing out became an increasingly useful option for public institutions in New York State after the passing of the State's Children's Law of 1875, enacted following a series of critical reports on conditions in State almshouses by William Letchworth, which required children above the age of two to be removed from any parents residing in poor houses and almshouses (Holt, *Orphan Trains*, loc.1671; Crenson, *Building the Invisible Orphanage*, pp. 76–7, Johnson, *Waifs, Foundlings and Half-Orphans*, p. 52).

67 Holt, *Orphan Trains*, loc.1446. CAS annual reports did sometimes note cases where parents in New York had tried to reclaim their placed out children, but did this in the context of stories where children refused to return in order to demonstrate how happy they were in their new placements (ibid., 1455).

68 Something that had a much longer history in both Britain and the colonial-era America, Carol Singley, *Adopting America: Childhood, Kinship and National Identity in Literature* (New York: Oxford University Press, 2011), pp. 27–30.

69 Bellingham's study has been widely cited in subsequent literature on the orphan trains, but his primary data (on the placing out of children by the New York Children's Aid Society in 1853/54) actually precedes the first emigration plan party sent out to Dowagiac, Michigan.

70 O'Connor, *Orphan Trains*, pp. 103–4; The New York Children's Aid Society, *Thirtieth Annual Report, 1882*, Series III.1, p. 13, for example, also gives a detailed breakdown of the annual cost per child of its services, arguing that these were less than 40 per cent of the costs of the New York Catholic Protectory or public jails.

71 *The Little Wanderers Advocate*, 1865, p. 24, (SC) CC06_F01.

72 Paul Boyer, *Urban Masses and Moral Order in America, 1820–1920* (Cambridge, MA: Harvard University Press, 1992), p. 104; O'Connor, *Orphan Trains*, p. 72. On the wider stream of liberal Protestant moral imagination on childhood and family that Brace exemplifies, see, for example, Singley, *Adopting America*, pp. 99–116.

73 Charles Loring Brace, *Short Sermons to News Boys, with a History of the Formation of the News Boys' Lodging House* (New York: Charles Scribner, 1866), pp. 5–11

74 Crenson, *Building the Invisible Orphanage*, pp. 61–3; Brace, *Dangerous Classes*, pp. 44–5, 48. In relation to one poor family, Brace even observed that the best hope for the children was that their mother would die in order to free them for a new life, Ashby, *Endangered Children*, p. 46.

75 O'Connor, *Orphan Trains*, p. 88.
76 O'Connor, *Orphan Trains*, p. 91.
77 Brace, *Short Sermons*, introduction. Similar approaches to incentivizing
    children into moral behaviour were evident in other schemes in that period.
    For example, in its day industrial school in New York, which opened in
    1854, the American Female Guardian Society gave merit tokens to children
    attending the schools (worth between one and ten cents each), which were
    collected at the end of each week and could then be used to redeem clothing
    for themselves and their families which had been made at the school.
78 Johnson, *Waifs, Foundlings and Half-Orphans*, p. 20.
79 See, for example, New York Children's Aid Society, *Second Annual Report*,
    1855, Series III.1, p. 10; also O'Connor, *Orphan Trains*, pp. 216–21.
80 Holt, *The Orphan Trains*, loc.491.
81 See, for example, his enthusiasm for the home as a locus for the moral
    cultivation of society in *Home Life in Germany*.
82 Holt, *The Orphan Trains*, loc.211.
83 See the newspaper article by V. A Cooper, Superintendent of the Home for
    Little Wanderers on the proper moral ethos of the relationship between adult
    and placed child, which emphasizes teaching the child obedience, gratitude,
    service to the family to reciprocate for the care they receive, avoidance of bad
    influences outside of the home, and avoiding pitying or petting them 'until
    they begin to get the upper-hand of you' (Johnson, *Waifs, Foundlings and
    Half-Orphans*, p. 49).
84 *The Little Wanderers Advocate*, (SC), 1865, p. 5: 'To care for homeless
    children requires no creed or denominational peculiarity . . . We shall
    receive children from parents of all creeds, and invite Christians from all
    denominations to receive them into their homes, and give them intellectual,
    moral and religious instruction, and thus prepare the child for usefulness and
    heaven.'
85 Accounts of the non-sectarian nature of their work by Protestant
    organizations themselves also sometimes suggest that their liberal assumption
    that true Christian faith could be found across many denominations
    underpinned their assimilation of Catholic children. '[A boy] who was
    brought in by his mother who had trained him up in the Catholic Church,
    when first handed a Bible, threw it across the room, exclaiming he would not
    read a heretic book. He is now a member of a Christian church, and a noble,
    exemplary boy' (*An Historical Account*, p. 11, CC6_F23 (SC)). While trying
    not to engage in open conflict with the New England Home, the Catholic
    Home for Destitute Children in Boston would at times intervene directly to
    prevent the admission, or remove, Catholic children who had been received
    by the New England Home, see Crenson, *Building the Invisible Orphanage*,
    pp. 84–5.
86 Crenson, *Building the Invisible Orphanage*, pp. 70–9.
87 This is striking because other sympathetic accounts of selection meetings with
    other agencies did not fail to note the distress involved for children. 'After
    the religious service the work of assigning them [children from the Home of
    Little Wanderers] began. It was an affecting scene as the little children parted
    companionship and tore asunder the ties that had linked them in child-like
    affection, the purest, the truest the most lasting on earth. Their eyes silvered

with tears as they separated to enter the attachments of their new homes and hundreds looked sympathetically on, deeply touched by the affecting scene.' Johnson, *Waifs, Foundlings and Half-Orphans*, p. 47, citation of newspaper account of Little Home of Wanderers selection meeting in Kokomo, Indiana in 1889.

88 *The Crusade for Children: A Review of Child Life in New York During 75 Years, 1853–1928, Children's Aid Society of the City of New York, 1928*, Series III.1 (NY), p. 12; O'Connor, *Orphan Trains*, p. 110.

89 See, for example, a letter from a family that had received a child from the New England Home for Little Wanderers in which their delight in their child John (whom they have renamed 'Frankie') is premised partly on the fact that 'he is easily governed, tries to do what we wish him to in every respect' (*An Historical Account*, CC6_F23, p. 15).

90 Holt, *The Orphan Trains*, loc.530 notes the recollection of a former orphan train rider that he took the unusual step of refusing to go out on the first two placements that he was chosen for, and was seen as behaving badly by holding out for something that he felt happier with. Similar stories are told by former orphan train riders in *The Orphan Trains*, dir. Janet and Edward Grey (PBS documentary, 1995).

91 The New York Children's Aid Society's published statistics on children sent out through its emigration programme show that around 50 per cent of its child migrants were not American born (see, e.g. New York Children's Aid Society, *Thirtieth Annual Report*, 1882, p. 30). On the threat of a disaffected, foreign underclass as a distinct, unassimilated social group, see New York Children's Aid Society, *Second Annual Report, 1855*, Series III.1 (NY), p. 3. Brace also saw part of the risk of the Dangerous Classes of New York in terms of the frustration of their inherently American self-motivation and drive by their experience of exclusion from the fruits of wage labour (*Dangerous Classes*, chapter 2); their inherent racial traits were therefore being thwarted by their social environment. On Brace on less civilized races, see Ashby, *Endangered Children*, p. 46, also Holt, *Orphan Trains*, loc.775. Holt also situates Brace's racial evaluation of immigrants in the context of wider post-bellum concern about the effects of immigration on American society, exemplified by Josiah Strong's widely discussed book of 1885, *Our Country: Its Possible Future and the Present Crisis* (New York: Baker & Taylor).

92 Ashby, *Endangered Children*, p. 48.

93 Holt, *The Orphan Trains*, loc.1431. The New York Children's Aid Society, *Twentieth Annual Report, 1872*, Series III.1 (NY), p. 9 complained that the organization's emigration work had been 'seriously hampered by a bigoted opposition among the poor'.

94 See, for example, O'Connor, *Orphan Trains*, p. 161.

95 The Society's rather informal approach to placement agreements and monitoring meant that it lost track of where some of its placed children went if they moved from their initial placement. By 1893, for example, just under 10 per cent of the children it had placed in Kansas were recorded as 'whereabouts unknown' (Holt, *The Orphan Trains*, loc.572). The Society began to make wider use of follow-up visits to placements in the later years of the scheme, but this still did not operate in a comprehensive or systematic way (ibid., loc.636). Records of the total number of supervision visits received

by its placed out children begin to feature in the Society's annual reports from
its *Forty-Ninth Annual Report, 1901*, Series III.1, p. 15, onwards, although
the minimum frequency of supervision visits for an individual child is not
stated.

96 O'Connor, *Orphan Trains*, pp. 111–12.

97 Crenson, *Building the Invisible Orphanage*, pp. 206–7.

98 O'Connor, *The Orphan Trains*, p. 290. Crenson, *Building the Invisible
     Orphanage*, pp. 210–11.

99 Crenson, *Building the Invisible Orphanage*, p. 215. The notion that the
     placed out child might be seen primarily as a source of labour than a member
     of the family also circulated in the popular mid-nineteenth-century genre of
     adoption literature, for example, in Sarah Baker's novel, *Bound Out, or Abby
     at the Farm*, in which in the eponymous lead character is initially treated
     merely as domestic labour but eventually wins over her family and becomes
     fully accepted by them (Singley, *Adopting America*, p. 91).

100 Crenson, *Building the Invisible Orphanage*, p. 212.

101 Crenson, *Building the Invisible Orphanage*, p. 82.

102 Crenson, *Building the Invisible Orphanage*, p. 222; Holt, *The Orphan Trains*,
     loc.1488.

103 Holt, *The Orphan Trains*, loc.1123. It is clear, though, that abolitionists
     would have been very uncomfortable with any attempt to use children as
     direct replacements for slave labour. Proposals, for example, to set up colonies
     of child workers to replace slave holdings in Missouri were, for example,
     never taken up by placing out organizations (ibid., loc.923).

104 See Holt, *The Orphan Trains*, loc.1360; also Parker, *Uprooted*, p. 166–7;
     Gillian Wagner, *Barnardo* (London: Weidenfeld & Nicolson, 1979), p.246.

105 In its public presentation of its work, the Society also began to down-play
     somewhat the extent of its emigration programme. In its *Fifty-First Annual
     Report, 1903*, its emigration work is subsumed under the heading of the
     'Placing Out Department' and it is claimed that since 1853, the Society has
     placed out 23,061 orphans or abandoned children as well as 25,200 older
     boys and girls 'provided with situations in the country' (p. 21) for wages.
     This is far less than the actual total of 95,823 children placed out through its
     emigration programme by that year. Its annual reports stop providing detailed
     statistical tables for its emigration programme after 1897, and its official
     review of the history of its work, *The Crusade for Children: A Review of
     Child Life in New York During 75 Years, 1853–1928, Children's Aid Society
     of the City of New York, 1928*, Series III.1 (NY) gives no total figure for the
     number of child migrants sent out through its work.

106 See Holt, *The Orphan Trains*, loc.1842; Ashby, *Endangered Children*,
     pp. 95–6. As Ashby notes, a parent could be seen as 'morally unfit' for reasons
     ranging from demonstrating too much affection or attachment to a child
     ('spoiling them'), using tobacco, not keep a clean home, drinking alcohol or
     failing to attend church.

107 Langsam, *Orphans West* was the first academic history of the schemes
     published in 1964. Since the publication of the Magnuson and Petrie's,
     Orphan Train novel in 1978, and linked television film in 1979, there has
     been a slow but steady growth in fictional and documentary treatments of
     this history. Public interest in the schemes continues with Christina Baker

Klein's *Orphan Train: A Novel* (New York: HarperCollins, 2013), reaching the *New York Times*' bestseller list and a new documentary, *West by Orphan Train* (dir. Colleen Bradford Krantz) being released in 2014. *Orphan Train: The Musical* was written and performed for the centenary celebrations of the Grand Central Terminal in New York in 2013. An annual reunion network developed among some former orphan train riders, growing out of an informal meeting in 1961.

Chapter 2

1 The line 'In the children's land of promise' is taken from a poem published in *Night and Day*, December, 1883, p. 136 which extols the value of migration to Canada. 'Yet smiles through our tears are dawning/When we think of the hope that lies/In the children's land of promise/'Neath the clear Canadian skies./Tho' the frost is thick on the windows/Tho' the roof with snow is white/We know our Canadian children/Are safe and warm tonight./Come help us, answer the summons/Pealing across the seas/"A home and hearty welcome/To hundreds such as these./It comes from Nova Scotia/And from wide Ontario's shore"/ We have loved and sheltered your gathered waifs/ There is room for thousands more.'

2 Gillian Wagner, *Children of the Empire* (London: Weidenfeld & Nicholson, 1982), pp. 36–7; see also Marion Diamond, *Emigration and Empire: The Life of Maria S. Rye* (New York: Garland Publishing, 1999), p. 212; Roy Parker, *Uprooted: The Shipment of Poor Children to Canada, 1867–1917* (Bristol: Policy Press, 2010), pp. 10–22; Roger Kershaw and Janet Sacks, *New Lives for Old: The Story of Britain's Child Migrants* (Kew: The National Archives, 2008), p. 23.

3 George Bogue Smart, *Juvenile Immigration 1924–25* (Department of Immigration and Colonization, Dominion of Canada, Ottawa), p. 6 (MCA) gives a total of 82,026 children having migrated from the United Kingdom to Canada between 1868 to 1925. This total, however, is less than the complete total of UK child migrants to Canada, however, because the date ranges during which data is presented for child migration organizations does not include the full period in which these organizations were involved in child migration work. The report, for example, gives a figure of 4,183 children sent to Canada by Quarriers Homes between 1890 and 1925, but Quarriers sent their first party of child migrants to Canada in 1872, and their own annual report in 1914 stated that they had already sent out 6,039 children by then. Similarly Catholic Children's Society (Westminster) has a total of 10,107 case files relating to individual children sent to Canada from the United Kingdom by Catholic migration agencies. *Juvenile Immigration* only records 8,036 children as being sent out from the major Catholic agencies. Figures for Annie Macpherson's migration parties are also only given from 1886, despite her having sent out parties of child migrants from 1869. No comprehensive figure is possible, partly because of incomplete or lost record-keeping, and the degree of undercounting of child migrants in *Juvenile Immigration* suggests that an estimate of around 90,000 child migrants to Canada between 1869

and 1925 would be reasonable. It has been suggested that the total numbers could be lower than this if there was some double-counting of individual child migrants through administrative error, but I have seen no evidence of this in researching this book.

4 See Marjory Harper and Stephen Constantine, *Migration and Empire* (Oxford: Oxford University Press, 2010), p. 2. Departure records for the first half of the nineteenth century do not distinguish between British citizens and other nationals travelling out from the United Kingdom. As a consequence the numbers of British nationals travelling to outside of Europe before 1853 would actually have averaged less than 91,000 per year. On the comparatively low levels of emigration from the United Kingdom in the late eighteenth and early nineteenth centuries, see also Hugh Johnston, *British Emigration Policy 1815–1830: Shovelling Out Paupers* (Oxford: Clarendon Press, 1972), pp. 6–7.

5 Harper and Constantine, *Migration and Empire*, p. 3.

6 Johnston, *British Emigration Policy*, p. 5; see also Sarah Wise, *The Blackest Streets* (London: Vintage, 2009); Anna Davin, *Growing Up Poor: Home, School and Street in London 1870–1914* (London: Rivers Oram Press, 1996). Poverty also remained widespread in rural areas as well, though did not tend to attract so much of the attention of the urban-based child-saving and philanthropic organizations.

7 David Englander, *Poverty and Poor Law Reform in 19th Century Britain, 1834–1914: From Chadwick to Booth* (London: Longman, 1998); F. David Roberts, *The Social Conscience of the Early Victorians* (Stanford: Stanford University Press, 2002); Seth Koven, *Slumming: Sexual and Social Politics in Victorian London* (Princeton, NJ: Princeton University Press, 2004); also Ellen Boucher, *Empire's Children: Child Emigration, Welfare, and the Decline of the British World, 1869–1967* (Cambridge: Cambridge University Press, 2014), pp. 29–31, on public responses to poverty and emerging discourse of imperial colonies as offering new opportunities.

8 See Johnston, *British Emigration Policy*, pp. 18, 36–7.

9 Johnston, *British Emigration Policy*, pp. 69–90.

10 Johnston, *British Emigration Policy*, pp. 105–6.

11 Harper and Constantine, *Migration and Empire*, pp. 20–1; John Crowley, William J. Smyth and Mike Murphy (eds), *Atlas of the Great Irish Famine* (Cork: Cork University Press, 2012).

12 Harper and Constantine, *Migration and Empire*, p. 28; also Marjory Harper, *Emigration from Scotland Between the Wars* (Manchester: Manchester University Press, 1998), p. 72.

13 Ivy Pinchebeck and Margaret Hewitt, *Children in English Society, Vol.II, from the Eighteenth-Century to the Children Act 1948* (London: Routledge & Kegan Paul, 1973), pp. 554–62.

14 Diamond, *Emigration and Empire*, pp. 65–155.

15 Diamond, *Emigration and Empire*, pp. 169–71.

16 Diamond, *Emigration and Empire*, pp. 181–8.

17 Diamond, *Emigration and Empire*, pp. 200–201.

18 Parker, *Uprooted*, p. 19; Diamond, *Migration and Empire*, pp. 230–1.

19 Englander, *Poverty and Poor Law Reform*, pp. 105–8; see also pp. 29, 44, 47, 51 on regional variations in the provision of outdoor relief.

20 William Quarrier, *A Narrative of Facts Relative to Work Done for Christ in Connection with the Orphan and Destitute Children's Emigration Homes* (Scotland: Glasgow, 1872), pp. 10–17.

21 In the case of early Catholic child migration in London, it appears that reducing the costs of long-term institutional care for children in Catholic institutions was also a consideration in some cases, see Jim Hyland, *Changing Times, Changing Needs: A History of the Catholic Children's Society (Westminster)* (London: CCS Westminster, 2009), p. 40.

22 The principle of desertion applied to a much wider range of cases than parents who have given over their child into the care of a Poor Law institution without any intention of remaining in contact with them. Many children placed in the care of Poor Law schools had widowed or unmarried mothers who were unable to maintain regular contact with them either because they had other children to care for or they had to maintain full-time work to survive. Children were therefore given up through pressures of poverty rather than abandoned because a parent had no emotional attachment to them (Parker, *Uprooted*, pp. 39–41). The principle that child migrants did not have viable family relationships to provide them with care and support at home in Britain was a claim made more generally about the admission criteria for child migration schemes. As Dr Barnardo's Homes put it, 'We never receive boys who have fathers able to work, or mothers capable of supporting their children' (*Night and Day*, June, 1884, p. 48). Quarriers similarly stated that admission to their emigration homes was aimed first at orphans and street children, then children of widows and finally children of dissolute parents who were willing to give them up (Quarrier, *Narrative of Facts*, 1872, p. 30). Subsequent case studies and reports in later editions of Quarriers' *Narrative of Facts*, however, suggests that children were also admitted from parents who were unable to offer care not because of 'dissolution' but poverty or chronic ill-health (see, e.g. Quarrier, *Narrative of Facts*, 1873, p. 13).

23 Parker, *Uprooted*, p. 46.

24 Parker, *Uprooted*, p. 49.

25 Andrew Doyle, *Copy of a Report to the Right Honourable the President of the Local Government Board, by Andrew Doyle, Esquire, Local Government Inspector, as to the Emigration of Pauper Children to Canada* (London: House of Commons, 1875), p. 16.

26 Ironically, some years later, Barnardo's criticized Poor Law institutions precisely for sending pauper children to Canada without having given them appropriate training in advance, with this carelessness doing damage to responsible child migration work being undertaken by their organization (*Night and Day*, May, 1888, pp. 49–50 (B)).

27 Doyle, *Report*, p. 16, see also p. 36.

28 Doyle, *Report*, p. 7. Children who migrated overseas from Poor Law institutions were required to give their consent to this in front of a magistrate (Parker, *Uprooted*, pp. 40–2). There was no such requirement for children sent directly by voluntary organizations.

29 Doyle, *Report*, p. 15.

30 Doyle, *Report*, p. 19.

31 Doyle, *Report*, p. 24.
32 Doyle, *Report*, p. 12. Doyle estimated that no more than 10 per cent of
    households requesting children wanted them for the 'highest motives' of
    charitable concern. Nearly fifty years later, the British Overseas Settlement
    Delegation to Canada, *Report to the Secretary of State for the Colonies,
    President of the Oversea Settlement Committee, from the Delegation
    Appointed to Obtain Information Regarding the System of Child Migration
    and Settlement in Canada* (Bondfield Report) (London: HMSO, 1924),
    confirmed this pattern. The Bondfield report (p. 7) noted that only a small
    proportion of child migrants were taken by families wishing to take them into
    their household as a member of the family (with even less formally adopted).
    Most applications for child migrants were from households wanting them 'in
    a capacity of a help' (see also Joy Parr, *Labouring Children: British Immigrant
    Apprentices to Canada, 1869–1924*, 2nd ed. (Toronto: University of Toronto
    Press, 1994), pp. 82–98).
33 Doyle, *Report*, p. 36.
34 Doyle, *Report*, pp. 13, 31.
35 Doyle, *Report*, pp. 16, 20, 36. A high level of demand for UK child migrants
    to Canada remained a feature of the system under it largely ended in the
    1920s. Smart, *Juvenile Immigration*, p. 5, records that there were in total
    13,971 applications for the 2000 UK child migrants who came to Canada
    in 1924/25. The highest level of demand, at that point, was for children sent
    out by Dr Barnardo's Homes, for whom 6,676 applications were received for
    268 child migrants.
36 Doyle, *Report*, pp. 10, 20.
37 Doyle, *Report*, pp. 12, 27.
38 Doyle, *Report*, p. 21.
39 Doyle, *Report*, pp. 14, 29.
40 Doyle, *Report*, pp. 22, 25, 27.
41 Doyle, *Report*, pp. 22, 28.
42 Doyle, *Report*, p. 30.
43 Doyle, *Report*, p. 36.
44 Kenneth Bagnell, *The Little Immigrants: The Orphans Who Came to Canada*
    (Toronto: Dundurn Group, 2001), loc.553–603; Kershaw and Sacks, *New
    Lives for Old*, pp. 39–43; Marjorie Kohli, *The Golden Bridge: Young
    Immigrants to Canada, 1833–1939* (Toronto: Natural Heritage Books, 2003),
    pp. 22–8. Problems identified by Doyle persisted, however, with one child
    migrant sent to Canada with Rye in 1888, for example, recalling having no
    supervision visits after being placed out (see Phyllis Harrison (ed.), *The Home
    Children: Their Personal Stories* (Winnipeg: Gordon Shillingford Publishing,
    2003), p. 32).
45 Parker, *Uprooted*, pp. 53–4.
46 In practice, though, when publicly funded child migration Canada did
    resume, the inspection process did take place under the auspices of the
    Department of Immigration (or later, the Department of Agriculture; see
    Pinchbeck and Hewitt, *Children in English* Society, p. 574) and did, generally,
    produce very positive accounts of the effects of the work (see, e.g. Secretary's
    Report of Visit to Canada, Jan 1919 to the Committee of the Catholic
    Emigration Association, p. 1 (AB)).

47 Bondfield report, pp. 10–11; on lack of detailed supervision reports, see also Pinchbeck and Hewitt, *Children in English Society*, p. 575.

48 It became an explicit requirement of 1888 regulations agreed between the Canadian Government and the Local Government Board that children should receive six months' instruction in a workhouse school, or other institutions run by local Boards of Guardians, or at a local elementary school for which the local Board would pay the fees (Pinchbeck and Hewitt, *Children in English Society*, p. 574).

49 Expectations about the terms under which children of different ages were to be placed varied among the different placement agencies. In the case of Dr Barnardo's Homes, children up to the age of 8 or 10 were either placed with families for adoption or on the basis of boarding out payments paid by the migration organization. From then, up until the age of around 14, children would be expected to contribute to household work on the basis of receiving board, lodging, schooling and, occasionally, pocket money. From the age of 14, children would expect to contribute fully to the labour of the household or farm and would receive a wage for this, usually held in trust by the child migration organization and payable to the child when they reached the age of 18. See Parr, *Labouring Children*, pp. 85–6. In Dr Barnardo's Homes' supervision books the terms on which each child was placed were a key piece of information recorded in the notes.

50 See, for example, case record for H.C. (78) in Marchmont Records Book, LON, 1902–1903 (B), in which staff at Marchmont contact H. C.'s employers to remind them that he is eligible to receive wages under the terms of their contract. 'I explained that as he had such a good home that we had not referred to terms before but that as he was 16 we thought something should [now] be done for him.'

51 See Parr, *Labouring Children*, pp. 94–6. Parr notes that some child migrants actively resisted attempts to move them or to pressure their employers to pay higher wages, either because the child wanted to preserve the sense of enjoying some measure of privileges as being a member of the household family or because they were reluctant to see their household placed under financial pressure.

52 For histories of Dr Barnardo's Homes' child migration work to Canada see June Rose, *For the Sake of the Children: Inside Barnardos 120 Years of Caring for Children* (London: Hodder & Stoughton, 1987) pp. 82–111; Gillian Wagner, *Barnardo* (London: Weidenfeld & Nicolson, 1979); Parr, *Labouring Children*; see also the celebratory account given in Mrs Barnardo and James Marchant, *Memoirs of the Late Dr Barnardo* (London: Hodder & Stoughton, 1907), pp. 154–84.

53 See *Night and Day*, October, 1883, pp. 83–4. Barnardo also established a training farm in Manitoba, along the lines of a vocational training centre encouraged by the Doyle report, for juvenile migrants over the age of 16 (*Night and Day*, May, 1888, pp. 56–8). By 1892, Dr Barnardo's Homes had included a 'Canada clause' in the written agreements for all children admitted in their homes in Britain, giving Dr Barnardo's Homes the authority to send children overseas without any further consent required from their parent or guardian (see Gail Corbett, *Nation Builders: Barnardo Children in Canada* (Toronto: Dundurn Press, 1997), p. 31).

54 Originally run by Annie Macpherson, Marchmont had subsequently been transferred to Quarriers. When Quarriers acquired another distribution home they handed Marchmont over to Ellen Wallace (nee Bilborough), one of Macpherson's original assistants who ran Marchmont as an independent home financed by British organizations who used its services, particularly the Manchester and Salford Boys' and Girls' Refuges and Homes. It was subsequently sold to the Liverpool Sheltering Homes and then, eventually in 1920, absorbed into Dr Barnardo's Homes.

55 See General William Booth, *In Darkest England and The Way Out* (London: International Headquarters of the Salvation Army, 1890). Lack of surviving records of the Salvation Army's migration work with unaccompanied children makes it difficult to establish when the first party of child migrants were actually sent out.

56 Bogue Smart, *Juvenile Immigration*, p. 10. For accounts of the range of organizations involved in child migration work to Canada see particularly Parker, *Uprooted*, also Kohli, *The Golden Bridge*.

57 Together Trust case records show that a total of 2,045 children were sent to Canada by the Manchester and Salford Boys' and Girls' Refuges and Homes.

58 As noted above, the Catholic Emigration Association was formally created in 1904, but diocesan rescue organizations had been operating prior to this.

59 In addition to the larger schemes run by larger voluntary organizations and churches, a significant number of child migrants to Canada were sent by schemes run by individuals or informal networks (see Parker, *Uprooted*, pp. 111–28).

60 This humanitarian emphasis was also evident in the American child emigration programmes. In his introduction to *Short Sermons to News Boys, with a History of the Formation of the News Boys' Lodging House* (New York: Charles Scribner, 1866), p. 10, Charles Loring Brace observes that some critics regarded such humanitarianism with suspicion as influenced by 'European socialism' and lack of fidelity to a spiritual message of salvation.

61 *Night and Day*, August, 1887, pp. 62–3 (B). Mrs Barnardo and James Marchant, *Memoirs of the Late Dr Barnardo*, p. 184 offers an interesting concluding reflection on his emigration work to Canada. While arguing that it was done primarily for humanitarian reasons for the best interests of the individual child, it reflects the increasing imperialist emphasis of early twentieth-century Britain by noting that this humanitarian initiative also benefitted nation and race through supporting Britain's imperial mission.

62 See Shurlee Swain and Margaret Hillel, *Child, Nation, Race and Empire: Child Rescue Discourse, England, Canada and Australia, 1850–1915* (Manchester: Manchester University Press, 2010); Gordon Lynch, 'Saving the Child for the Sake of the Nation: Moral Framing and the Civic, Moral and Religious Redemption of Children', *American Journal of Cultural Sociology*, 2.2 (2014), pp. 165–96.

63 Lydia Murdoch, *Imagined Orphans: Poor Families, Child Welfare and Contested Citizenship in London* (New Brunswick, NJ: Rutgers University Press, 2006).

64 Charles Loring Brace, *The Dangerous Classes of New York and Twenty Years' Work Among Them*, 3rd ed. (New York: Wynkoop & Hallenbeck, 1880), p. ii.

65 Wagner, *Children of the Empire*, p. 113. While these views reflect political judgements about the future consequences of a socially disaffected underclass, it is possible to some degree to see in the anxiety about poor children a wider Victorian interest in the principle that childhood experiences formed adult traits (see Sally Shuttleworth, *The Mind of the Child: Child Development in Literature, Science and Medicine, 1840–1900* (Oxford: Oxford University Press, 2010), pp. 1–12).

66 See, for example, *Annual Report of the East End Juvenile Mission, 'Dr Barnardo's Homes', 1881–1882*, p. 6 (B).

67 *Night and Day*, December, 1888, p. 145 (B); see also Mrs Barnardo and James Marchant, *Memoirs of the Late Dr Barnardo*, p. 154.

68 *Night and Day*, December 1884, p. 180. The argument that child migration was a valuable mechanism not simply for improving children's prospects, but also for reducing the burden of welfare spending on the public purse continued to be made, in relation to child migration work to Australia, in the twentieth century. In a letter to *The Times*, 8 November 1927, p. 10, for example, Ellen McDougall observed that 'every year at least 60,000 children leave our Poor Law and other institutions to swell the labour market and to intensify the struggle for work. Each of these children has cost the ratepayers from £35 to £45 a year from infancy up to the age of 14 or 15, and then is launched into the community to compete with the children of hardworking families, who themselves have a difficulty in retaining their work and yet have to support, through the rates, these poor children, who eventually become the competitors of their own children for such jobs as are to be had.'

69 *Narrative of Facts*, 1873, p. 6.

70 William Bramwell Booth, *The Darkest England Scheme: Notes on the Work in 1896 with Review* (London: Salvation Army, 1896), p. 12 (SA).

71 'Who Is to blame?', *Night and Day*, 1882, vol. 6, pp. 96–9 (B).

72 Booth, *Darkest England Scheme 1896*, p. 14 (SA).

73 *The Surplus, Being a Restatement of the Emigration Policy and Methods of the Salvation Army*, (London; Salvation Army International Emigration Office, 1909), p. 4 (SA).

74 *The Surplus*, p. 14.

75 While including direct competition between different Protestant and Catholic groups, this should also be understood in terms of competing religious understandings of the spiritual heart of the project of building a Greater Britain, see Hilary M. Carey, *God's Empire: Religion and Colonialism in the British World, c.1801–1908* (Cambridge: Cambridge University Press, 2011), pp. 3–39.

76 Parker, *Uprooted*, p. 92.

77 One example of this was the national Prayer Book controversy of 1927/8 in which a proposed revision of the 1662 Prayer Book for the Church of England was voted down by Parliament, with anti-Catholic arguments playing an important place in Parliamentary debates and strong associations being made between Protestantism and national loyalty (see John Maiden, *National Religion and the Prayer Book Controversy, 1927/8*, Studies in Modern British Religious History (Woodbridge: Boydell Press, 2009)).

78 Even by the postwar period, Catholic child-care administrators and senior clergy were still expressing strong reservations about the capacity and willingness of public child-care institutions to provide appropriate religious

training for Catholic children (see, e.g. Comments of Canons Bennett, Flint and Flood and Father Arbuthnott on the Home Secretary's Letter of 12th March on Roman Catholic Voluntary Homes, CR2/64 (W)).

79 See, for example, an allegation of a Catholic organization abducting a child from one of the Manchester and Salford Boys' and Girls' Refuges and Homes before being required to return him by the child's brother (Letter from JF to Leonard Shaw, 19 July 1897, (case file for TF), M189/7/5/1 (TT)). 'The Barnardo Judgment', *The Tablet*, 8 November 1890, p. 745–7, also provides a detailed account of a court ruling that Dr Barnardo's Homes would have to return a 12-year-old child placed in its care by his mother, who subsequently wanted to remove him from Dr Barnardo's in order to have him placed in a Catholic institution. The case is remarkable for the degree of antipathy involved, with associates of Dr Barnardo's secretly compiling a record of the mother's activities over a number of months in order to present this as evidence of her unsuitability to make decisions about her son's future. See also 'Truth on Dr Barnardo's Methods', *The Tablet*, 19 May 1894. In an article 'Dr Barnardo in Liverpool – Opposition to His Intrusion', *The Tablet*, 2 April 1892, pp. 539–40, Dr Barnardo is contrasted very unfavourably with other Protestant philanthropists such as Samuel Smith MP, Louisa Birt and William Quarrier who are claimed to be far more supportive of the principle of not trying to proselytize Catholic children. An accommodation between Thomas Barnardo and the Catholic hierarchy was eventually reached after 1899, however, in which Barnardo agreed to pass on Catholic children recently received into his homes on to appropriate Catholic homes (see Hyland, *Changing Times, Changing Needs*, p. 26). Tensions also existed between Protestant organizations with, for example, William Rudolf, the founder of the Church of England Waifs and Strays Society expressing strong concern that while Dr Barnardo's Homes provided Protestant formation for its children, this was insufficiently Anglican and children passing through their care may well be lost to the Church of England (Parker, *Uprooted*, pp. 83–4).

80 In Letter from Marcella Swan, Nazareth House Nursery, Hammersmith to Crusade of Rescue, 20 April 1954, CR2/64 (W), an incident is reported in which a local authority children's officer removed a child from the care of the Sisters of Nazareth for him to be fostered out and refused to give his new address 'on the grounds that she could not trust the Nazareth Sisters'. The Sisters of Nazareth in turn questioned whether the boy was genuinely going to be placed out with a Catholic family. The response by the Crusade of Rescue is interesting in playing down any attempt to protest to the local authority at this interaction and reflects a concern with not trying to alienate local authority workers.

81 See, for example, Minutes of meeting at the Home Office with Roman Catholic Diocesan administrators, 22 March 1955, CR2/64 (W) which note criticisms made by John Ross that Catholic residential homes for children were lagging behind other voluntary organizations in terms of their standards of care and that the slow take up of appropriate professional child-care training by Catholic organizations was hampering the policy of fostering children out now being encouraged by central Government. Ross was also critical, more generally, of the fact that Catholic organizations more generally

did not seem to fully support the more widely accepted principle that foster-care in a family environment was preferable to residential care. The Home Office was also very critical of the standards in some Catholic residential homes and threatened, for example, to de-register St Charles, Brentwood, run by the Christian Brothers, in 1954 (see Letter from Miss D. M. Rosling, Home Office to Canon Flood, 1 March 1954, CR2/64 (W)). This was only averted by the decision to close the school by the Archbishop of Westminster. Reservations about standards of care and training in Catholic religious orders were also privately shared among some senior Catholic clergy and administrators as well (see, e.g. Comments of Canons Bennett). See also Letter from Mrs Murtagh to Archbishop of Birmingham, 3 March 1949, (AB) which recognizes the value of new training programmes for residential child-care workers being taken up by some members of female religious orders and concurs with the Home Office in deploring the standards of care in Christian Brothers' home. Helen Murtagh's criticisms were grounded both in her long-standing experience as a health-visitor and a member of the Curtis Committee, nominated by the Archbishop of Westminster (see Hyland, *Changing Times, Changing Needs*, pp. 58–62).

82 *The Policy of the Rescue Society, Presented to His Grace, the Reverend Thomas L. Williams, MA, Archbishop of Birmingham*, 1932, pp. 4–7 (BA). For other examples of this emphasis on safeguarding faith, see also *Address of His Eminence Cardinal Griffin at the Annual General Meeting of the Crusade of Rescue*, 28 October 1954, CR2/64 (W): 'Unable to fend for itself in this world it [the child] needs direction in its efforts to know the truth about the next world. We all share in the teaching mission of the Church and it is our duty to make every effort to save the faith of these children who are deprived of a normal home life.'

83 *Secretary's Report on Visit to Canada*, p. 5 (AB).

84 See, for example, 'Crusade of Rescue', *3rd Annual Report*, pp. 11–12 (CCS); also Parker, *Uprooted*, p. 94. As Roy Parker has pointed out to me, as well, child migrants sent by Catholic organizations were more likely to be placed in small communities rather than very isolated farms to ensure greater access to a priest.

85 The placement of children in non-English-speaking households in communities at best ambivalent to British rule suggests that the child migration scheme cannot be understood straightforwardly as an exercise in the consolidation of the Empire and the formation of children as imperial citizens (contra Boucher, *Empire's Children*). French-speaking Catholic communities in Quebec had been accepted as full members of the British dominion following the Catholic Bishop of Quebec's support for Britain in the 1812 war against the United States (Carey, *God's Empire*, p. 66). Their somewhat liminal status in relation to the ideal of the Anglo-Saxon Greater Britain, however, suggests that Catholic networks placed the eternal fate of child migrants above their status as imperial citizens and imagined them more within the trans-national Catholic community of faith.

86 Quarriers and the Manchester and Salford Boys' and Girls' Refuges and Homes had ended their child migration work to Canada by then. The latter decided not to re-start child migration to Canada after the work was interrupted during World War I, although they did send a handful of children

to Australia in the 1920s via the Fairbridge Society. Quarriers stopped
sending children to Canada in 1897, upset that the passing of an Act by the
Ontario state legislature 'to regulate the immigration into Ontario of certain
classes of children' constituted an unwarranted intrusion into 'Christian
work' (*Narrative of Facts*, 1897, p. 48).

87   See Parr, *Labouring Children*, p. 152.
88   Wagner, *Children of the Empire*, p. 275.
89   Boucher, *Empire's Children*, pp. 80–5.
90   See David Goutor, *Guarding the Gates: The Canadian Labour Movement and
     Immigration, 1872–1934* (Vancouver: University of British Columbia Press,
     2007); also Geoffrey Sherrington and Chris Jeffery, *Fairbridge: Empire and
     Child Migration* (London: Woburn Press, 1998), kindle edition, loc.1237.
91   See Wagner, *Children of the Empire*, pp. 225–8, and Boucher, *Empire's
     Children*, pp. 85–9, on the context and recommendations of the Bondfield
     report.
92   Bondfield report, pp. 8–10.
93   Bondfield report, pp. 12–13.
94   Bondfield report, p. 13.
95   Wagner, *Children of the Empire*, pp. 242–5. See also a family account of a
     child sent to the Duncan school, Patricia Skidmore, *Marjorie, Too Afraid to
     Cry* (Toronto: Dundurn, 2012).

Chapter 3

1   UK child migrants were also sent to South Africa, but prior to the
    development of the mass schemes to Canada after 1869. As noted in
    Chapter 1, the Children's Friend Society had sent 1,300 young apprentices
    to the Cape before its work was publicly discredited. A later offer of land in
    South Africa to Thomas Barnardo, in 1902, to establish a training home for
    child migrants did not lead to further children being sent there, however, after
    a scoping visit by Barnardo's eldest son indicated that the social and political
    conditions were far less promising for child migration than in Canada (see
    Ellen Boucher, *Empire's Children: Child Emigration, Welfare, and the Decline
    of the British World, 1869–1967* (Cambridge: Cambridge University Press,
    2014), pp. 43–50).
2   The Rhodesian scheme was therefore very different in intent to the Canadian
    and Australian schemes which place a stronger emphasis on vocational
    training for manual labour, and ran as a separate initiative to the Fairbridge
    Society's main emigration work (Boucher, *Empire's Children*, p. 151). In
    practice, though, poor after-care for children after they'd left the school
    meant that few went on to higher education or to adopt elite roles within
    Rhodesian society (Philip Bean and Joy Melville, *Lost Children of the Empire:
    The Untold Story of Britain's Child Migrants* (London; Unwin Hyman,
    1989) pp. 106–7).
3   See UK Parliamentary Health Select Committee, Third Report, paras 27–38.
4   Boucher, *Empire's Children*, pp. 164–5.
5   Bean and Melville, *Lost Children of the Empire*, p. 98.

6 Such an inquiry in New Zealand was specifically recommended in the 1998
   UK Parliamentary Health Select Committee report on child migration (see
   UK Parliamentary Select Committee on Heath Third Report 1998 (London:
   House of Commons, Recommendations, 1998), p. 115.
7 There is no single authoritative figure on the number of UK child migrants
   to Australia. For a range of figures on the possible number of child migrants
   sent, see *Lost Innocents: Righting the Record on Child Migration Report*
   (Canberra: Parliament of Australia Senate, 2001), pp. 263–5. A good
   indication of the numbers of children sent after the Second World War are the
   numbers of children sent to Australia by British government subsidy, which
   Constantine, 'British Government', has calculated to be 3,170. That is not
   likely to be a comprehensive figure as it only relates to children for whom
   government funding was sought, and some children may have been sent
   without this.
8 The lack of clarity about these exact figures is indicated by the *Lost Innocents*
   report (pp. 264–5) which gives ranges of numbers for these organizations
   based on different date ranges and sources of data. The numbers given here
   are therefore intended to be illustrative of the relative proportion of child
   migrants sent out by each organization.
9 Commonwealth Relations Office, *Child Migration to Australia: Report
   of a Fact-Finding Mission,* (Ross Report), 1955, DO35/6381 (NA), p. 14.
   The fact that the Federal Catholic Immigration Committee of Australia's
   receipt of government-assisted child migrants ended, with the exception of
   a handful of children, by 1957 meant that by 1965, the Fairbridge Society
   had sent and received slightly more postwar child migrants than this – 997
   children compared to the Catholic agency's eventual 946 (see Stephen
   Constantine, 'The British Government, Child Welfare and Child Migration to
   Australia after 1945'. *Journal of Imperial and Commonwealth History*, 30 (1)
   (2002), pp. 99–132).
10 Alan Gill, *Orphans of the Empire: The Shocking Story of Child Migration
   to Australia* (London: Vintage, 1998), kindle edition, loc.951, states that
   the Children's Friend Society sent seventy-one children aged under 16 to
   Australia, but doesn't give the source for this.
11 See *Ragged School Union Magazine*, 1849, p. 41; 1850, pp. 5–7; 1857, p. 83;
   1864, p. 26. I am grateful to Laura Mair for drawing my attention to this
   material.
12 See Marjory Harper and Stephen Constantine, *Migration and Empire*
   (Oxford: Oxford University Press, 2010), pp. 56–7.
13 See Andrew Thompson, *Imperial Britain: The Empire in British Politics,
   c.1880–1932* (London: Pearson International, 2000), pp. 46–9.
14 Andrew Thompson, *The Empire Strikes Back? The Impact of Imperialism on
   Britain from the Mid-Nineteenth Century* (Harlow: Pearson, 2005), pp. 9–38.
   The aristocratic support on which the Fairbridge Society was able to draw
   reflected a longer-standing involvement of the aristocracy in managing the
   Empire. As Thompson (p. 15) notes, between 1885 and 1914, sixty-five peers
   held imperial office as either governors or ministers.
15 The 'White Australia' policy was initially given a legal framework through
   the Immigration Restriction Act of 1901, which gave immigration officers
   powers to deny migrants entry to Australia which were primarily used along

racial lines. The 'White Australia' principle also found wider public support as a central element of Australian national identity. Opposing the conscription of Australian soldiers during the First World War, on the grounds that this would encourage an influx of cheap, non-white workers to fill gaps in the labour market, the Catholic Archbishop of Melbourne, Daniel Mannix, declared that 'we, a handful of whites in a huge continent, insist on White Australia policy. Our coloured fellow-citizens of the Empire ask for entry. But no, not even for Empire's sake do we lift the embargo. Australia is first and the Empire, with its coloured people, and its allies, has to fall into second place' (Eric Richards, *Destination Australia* (Sydney: University of New South Wales Press, 2008), p. 68. On child migration on the context of Australian immigration policies, see also Boucher, *Empire's Children*, pp. 92–106.

16 *Australia's Offer to British Boys*, 1924, M189/7/6/3 (MCA), pp. 2–3.
17 This experience was commemorated later in the Kingsley Fairbridge Memorial at Umtali, Rhodesia, unveiled by Queen Elizabeth the Queen Mother on 8 July 1953 (see *The Times*, 9 July 1953, p. 7).
18 Geoffrey Sherrington and Chris Jeffery, *Fairbridge: Empire and Child Migration* (London: Woburn Press, 1998), loc.491.
19 Letter from Kingsley Fairbridge to Earl Grey, 5 August 1908, D296/A1/1 (L). Earl Grey was already well known to the Fairbridge family, and the letter appears to have been an attempt if not to solicit funding from Earl Grey for this initiative, then at least to enlist his support as 'one of half a dozen, prominent influential men' who would actively support it.
20 Kingsley Fairbridge, *The Emigration of Poor Children to the Colonies: Speech Read before the Colonial Club at Oxford,* 19 October 1909, D292/A2 (L).
21 Sherrington and Jeffrey, *Fairbridge: Empire and Child Migration*, loc.624.
22 Sherrington and Jeffrey, *Fairbridge: Empire and Child Migration*, loc.754.
23 This level of funding was still less than the farm school required to cover its running costs, making the sale of produce from the farm school, grown by the children, a source of funds on which the farm school was economically reliant (Sherrington and Jeffrey, *Fairbridge: Empire and Child Migration*, loc.1972).
24 Some Fairbridge children were also sent to the Hagley Farm School in Tasmania, which was run by the Tasmanian Educational Department. The Fairbridge Society also acted as the recruitment agent for children sent to the Northcote Farm School at Bacchus Marsh, near Melbourne.
25 Barnardo's subsequently set up three institutions to receive British child migrants, all in New South Wales, at a farm school in Picton (1929), a training home and hostel in Burwood (1938) and a residential home in Normanhurst (1954). The Manchester and Salford Boys' and Girls' Refuges and Homes also sent a handful of children to Australia in the 1920s through the Fairbridge Society (see *The Children's Haven*, 1920–1928, M189/8/2/9–14 (MCA)).
26 See, for example, Andrew Thompson, *The Empire Strikes Back? The Impact of Imperialism on Britain from the Mid-Nineteenth Century* (London: Routledge, 2005); also Sherrington and Jeffrey, *Fairbridge: Empire and Child Migration*, loc.807. Note also that the Bondfield report supported the continuation of juvenile migration, for example, and recognized the value of migration schemes as a necessary means of supporting British dominions.

27 *Daily Mail*, 17 June 1914. See also Sherrington and Jeffrey, *Fairbridge: Empire and Child Migration*, loc.838.
28 *Night and Day*, November 1884 (B), p. 124; see also Annual Report of the East End Juvenile Mission, 'Dr Barnardo's Homes', 1884–1885 (B), p. 15.
29 Boucher, *Empire's Children*, pp. 126–40.
30 *Report to the Secretary of State for the Colonies, President of the Oversea Settlement Committee, from the Delegation Appointed to Obtain Information Regarding the System of Child Migration and Settlement in Canada* (Bondfield Report) (London: HMSO, 1924), p. 7; Boucher, *Empire's Children*, pp. 128–9.
31 Data taken from *Lost Innocents*, pp. 259–60. Many of these institutions also received children born in Australia.
32 Annual Report of the Church of England Council of Empire Settlement, 1925, CECES-2, (CE), p. 3.
33 See *Seventh Annual Report of the Church of England Council of Empire Settlement*, 1932 (CE).
34 *Report of the Advisory Council of the Church of England Advisory Council of Empire Settlement for the Year 1st January to 31st December 1948*, CECES-2-CA935, (CE), p. 3.
35 *Church Assembly: Report of the Empire Settlement Commission*, 1954, CECES-2-CA1100, p. 9. The 1956 Ross Report (pp. 4–5) noted that receiving institutions for child migrants during this period did have around 700 unfilled places and that there was an 'erroneous' view on the part of receiving institutions that there was a large supply of children suitable for migration from the United Kingdom if only there was sufficient will to facilitate this in Britain.
36 Immediately prior to its launch, the Overseas Settlement Department of the British government's Dominions Office, wrote to the secretary of the Catholic Emigration Society to welcome the launch of the organization but also to say that its request for core funding for its administrative costs would not be forthcoming from the government until the Society had established a clear track record of facilitating migrations. Letter from J. F Plant to the Secretary of the Catholic Emigration Society, 27 January 1927 (BA).
37 Of particular concern to the Catholic hierarchy was the migration work of organizations such as the Church of England, including through the Church Army, and the Salvation Army, see Circular Letter to Catholic Clergy from Francis Ross, member of the General Committee of the Catholic Emigration Society, 9 December 1927 (BA).
38 Catholic Emigration Society Pamphlet, 28 January 1927 (BA).
39 Letter from George Craven, Administrator, Crusade of Rescue to William Bunce, Secretary, Father Hudson's Homes, 14 October 1935 (BA); Letter from Bernard Griffin, Secretary of the Catholic Emigration Association to the Archbishop of Birmingham, 6 January 1939 (BA).
40 *Lost Innocents*, p. 42; see also Health Select Committee Third Report, *Document Three, Historical Background to Child Migration;* Jim Hyland, *Changing Times, Changing Needs: A History of the Catholic Children's Society (Westminster)* (London: CCS Westminster, 2009), pp. 74–6.
41 Conlon had previously managed to arrange the migration of 100 children to Christian Brothers' institutions and then returned select a further 400

children for possible migration to Australia in 1947, in the context of renewed Catholic plans to encourage mass migration to postwar Australia; Health Select Committee Third Report, *Document Three, Historical Background to Child Migration*.

42 *Church Assembly: Report of the Empire Settlement Commission*, p. 5.

43 *Church Assembly: The Church of England Council for Commonwealth and Empire Settlement*, Report for the fifteen months, 1 January 1955 to the 31 March 1956, CECES-2-CA1176 (CE), p. 4; on Anglican anxiety about Catholic child migration, see also *Lost Innocents*, p. 34.

44 Wagner, *Children of the Empire*, pp. 231–2.

45 The Child Emigration Society, Appeal Letter, January 1914, D296.F1.1 (L).

46 *The Times*, 3 February 1926, p. 11.

47 *The Times*, 29 March 1928, p. 9.

48 The Duke of York's public pledge of 1,000 pounds to Fairbridge in 1934 formed a central part of a major fund-raising campaign launched by the Society to extend its work, see *The Times*, 21 June 1934, p. 32.

49 *The Times*, 15 November 1927, p. 20. Amery himself had close personal links to Kingsley Fairbridge (see Sherrington and Jeffrey, *Fairbridge: Empire and Child Migration*, loc.1652) and wrote the preface to Fairbridge's posthumous autobiography.

50 Bondfield report, pp. 9, 12.

51 *Report of the Care of Children Committee (Curtis Committee Report)*, September 1946 (London: HMSO), p. 5. On the countervailing demand in Australia for renewed immigration after 1945, see Richards, *Destination Australia*, pp. 167–203.

52 Curtis Committee Report, p. 148.

53 Curtis Committee Report, p. 152.

54 Curtis Committee Report, p. 160.

55 Curtis Committee Report, p. 177.

56 Growing criticism, and fears of increasing government restriction, of child migration led to the formation of the Council of Voluntary Organisations for Child Emigration in 1951, a collaborative initiative between fifteen different organizations to promote child migration work (see Kathleen Paul, 'Changing Childhoods: Child Migration Since 1945', in Jon Lawrence and Pat Starkey (eds), *Child Welfare and Social Action in the Nineteenth and Twentieth Centuries: International Perspectives* (Liverpool: Liverpool University Press, 2001), pp. 125–9). The Council's claims about the careful management of the schemes and the quality of staffing and provision gave a very different image of the work compared to the account provided in the Ross report.

57 See Constantine, 'Child Migration to Australia after 1945' for a fuller discussion of these various initiatives by the Home Office. This was not the first time that critical views about child migration had been expressed within the British government. During the Second World War, two separate UK High Commissioners in Canberra had offered critical assessments of wider aspects of child migration work as well as problems with specific institutions, such as those run by the Christian Brothers in Western Australia (see Roger Kershaw and Janet Sacks, *New Lives for Old: The Story of Britain's Child Migrants* (Kew: The National Archives, 2008), pp. 215–19).

58 John Moss, *Child Migration to Australia* (London: HMSO, 1953).

59 Meeting at the Home Office on 22 March 1955, with Roman Catholic Diocesan Administrators, Note by the Home Office, G2/64 (W).

60 Ross report, p. 6.

61 The Home Office, by 22 June 1956 had drawn up its own evaluation of institutions based on the Ross team's confidential reports (Letter from Whittick to Shannon, 22 June 1956, BN29/1325 (NA)). Ten institutions were placed in 'Category A' (not fit to receive further child migrants): St Joseph's Orphanage, Lane Cove; Dhurringile Rural Training Farm; St Joseph's, Neerkol; Salvation Army Training Farm; Methodist Home, Magill; St Vincent's Orphanage, Castledare; St Joseph's Farm School, Bindoon; St John Bosco's Boys' Town; Fairbridge Farm School, Pinjarra; Fairbridge Farm School, Molong. Eight institutions were placed in 'Category B': Melrose, Pendle Hill; Murray Dwyer, Orphanage, Mayfield; Goodwood Orphanage, Adelaide; Clontarf Boys' Town, Perth; St Joseph's, Leederville (Subiaco); Methodist Home, Victoria Park; Swan Homes, Midland Junction; Nazareth House, East Camberwell. Eight institutions were considered to 'pass muster' (although Ross had noted significant criticisms even of some of these): Dr Barnardo's Homes, Burwood; Dr Barnardo's Homes, Normanhurst; Northcote School, Bacchus Marsh; St John's Church of England Home, Canterbury; Burton Hall Farm School; Methodist Home, Burwood; Clarendon Church of England Home, Kingston Park; Hagley Area Farm School, Tasmania.

62 Fact-Finding Mission to Australia, Confidential Appendix, BN29/1325 (NA), reports on Fairbridge Molong; Riverview Training Farm; Methodist Home, Magill; Dhurringile Training Farm; St Vincent's, Castedare; and St Joseph's, Bindoon.

63 Confidential Appendix, individual reports on Melrose Home (U.P.A.); Fairbridge Pinjarra; St Joseph's, Bindoon; Methodist Home, Victoria Park; St John Bosco Boys' Town; Riverview Training Farm; Dhurringile Training Farm; St Joseph's, Neerkol; St Vincent's, Castledare; Clontarf Boys' Town.

64 Confidential Appendix, Dhurringile Training Farm.

65 Confidential Appendix, St Joseph's, Leederville (Subiaco). The transfer of children within and between institutions was also noted in a number of the other reports including for St Vincent's Castledare (in relation to children transferred from there to Clontarf Boys' Town) and the Methodist Home, Victoria Park.

66 Confidential Appendix, Fairbridge Pinjarra. See also, for example, the report on St Joseph's, Leederville (Subiaco).

67 Confidential Appendix, report on Clontarf Boys' Town.

68 In the Confidential Appendix, report on St John Bosco Boys' Town, the principal was reported as saying that he found it difficult that he did not have the option of expelling child migrants from his school, and noted one such difficult child who had merited such an intervention was one who was 'enuretic and abnormally timid'.

69 Confidential Appendix, report on St Vincent's, Castledare.

70 See Confidential Appendix, Melrose Home (U.P.A.); Dr Barnardo's Home at Normanhurst; the Clarendon Home; Murray Dwyer Boys' Orphanage; St John's House, Canterbury; and Nazareth House, East Camberwell.

71 The geographical remoteness of institutions was particularly noted in the Confidential Appendix reports on Fairbridge Molong; Fairbridge Pinjarra; St Joseph's, Lane Cove; St Joseph's, Bindoon; the Northcote Training Farm; Dhurringile Training Farm; and St Joseph's, Neerkol.

72 Confidential Appendix reports on St Joseph's, Lane Cove; St Joseph's, Neerkol; the Murray Dwyer Boys' Orphanage; St John's Bosco Boys' Town; St Joseph's, Bindoon; St Joseph's, Leederville (Subiaco); St Vincent's, Castledare; Clontarf Boys' Town; and St Vincent de Paul's Orphanage, Goodwood.

73 Confidential Appendix, report on St Joseph's, Neerkol.

74 Confidential Appendix, report on Nazareth House, East Camberwell.

75 See Confidential Appendix reports on Methodist Home, Victoria Park; Fairbridge Pinjarra; Clontarf Boys' Town; Nazareth House, East Camberwell; St Joseph's, Bindoon; St Joseph's, Lane Cove; Dhurringile Training Farm; St Vincent's, Castledare; and St Joseph's, Neerkol.

76 Confidential Appendix, report on St Joseph's, Neerkol.

77 Confidential Appendix, report on Fairbridge Molong.

78 David Hill, *The Forgotten Children: Fairbridge Farm School and Its Betrayal of Britain's Child Migrants to Australia* (North Sydney: William Heinemann, 2008), pp. xi–xiii, 117–20.

79 Such complaints about the poor quality of child migrants were made in the Confidential Appendix reports for Fairbridge Molong; Fairbridge Pinjarra; St Joseph's, Lane Cove; St Vincent de Paul Orphanage, Goodwood; the Murray Dwyer Orphanage; Dhurringile Training Farm; Nazareth House, East Camberwell; St John Bosco Boys' Town (whose principal claimed that sending agencies were dumping problem children from their own residential homes in Britain on Australia); St Joseph's, Neerkol; and St Joseph's, Bindoon, where one staff member blamed the low quality of the child migrants they were working with on their 'poor heredity'.

80 See, for example, Confidential Appendix reports on Hagley Training Farm; Methodist Home, Burwood.

81 Letter from John Ross to Secretary of State for Commonwealth Relations, 28 March 1956, DO35/6381 (NA).

82 Letter from Whittick to Shannon, 22 June 1956, BN29/1325 (NA).

83 Letter from the Office of the High Commissioner for the United Kingdom, Canberra, to the Commonwealth Relations Office, 12 April 1956, DO35/6381 (NA).

84 The Ross mission was made up of three members – Ross himself, Miss C. M. Wanborough-Jones, the Children's Officer for Essex County Council, who had already been a leading spokesperson for criticisms of child migration from local authority welfare officers in the United Kingdom, and William Garnett, a former deputy high commissioner to Australia. Garnett's membership of the team was proposed by the Commonwealth Relations Office to act against Ross and Wanborough-Jones's critical stance that was more typical of the Home Office's view of the child migration schemes.

85 Internal Minute within the Commonwealth Relations Office, Noble to Secretary of State, 19 April 1956, BN29/1325.

86 Internal communications within the Commonwealth Relations Office also show that there was also concern about the reaction of Australian public

opinion to the Ross report: 'Australian public opinion, which specially resents criticism from the United Kingdom, is likely to be irritated, with consequent strain on relations only a few months before the Prime Minister's visit' (Memo from Shannon to Sir Saville Garner, 29 May 1956, DO35/1381).

87 Minute of Meeting on 27 April 1956 to discuss the Report of the Fact-Finding Mission on Child Migration to Australia, BN29/1325 (NA). Initially, it was decided to release only copies of the main report to the Australian authorities. As the Commonwealth Relations Office formulated plans over the next few weeks to liaise with Australian authorities to begin a process that made it appear that concerns in the report were being addressed, it was then decided to release the report's appendices to them as well on a confidential basis to guide this process. These appendices were not to be shared directly with the relevant voluntary organizations, however (Telegram from Commonwealth Relations Office to Office of the UK High Commissioner in Australia, 25 June 1956, DO35/1381 (NA)).

88 Letter from Cherns, HMSO, to Johnston, Commonwealth Relations Office, 12 July 1956, DO35/1381 (NA).

89 At an early stage, the Office of the UK High Commissioner had recognized the political sensitivities around the findings of the Ross report and had liaised directly with the Prime Minister's Department in Canberra on how to respond to this (see Letter from Fraser, Office of the UK High Commissioner, to Johnson, Commonwealth Relations Officer, 20 September 1956, BN29/1325 (NA)).

90 Telegram Commonwealth Relations Office to Office of the UK High Commissioner, Canberra, 25 May 1956, DO35/1381.

91 Memo from Ewans to Costley-White, 10 May 1956, DO35/1381 (NA). See also Extract from the County Council Association's Official Gazette, October 1956, DO35/1381 (NA) for an account of the Board's later criticisms of the Ross report in terms of the 'halcyon expectations of experts', which needed to be replaced with a 'more realistic view'. This article, published for local authority staff, made the interesting point that while the Fact-Finding Mission may well have been justified in its criticisms of standards in Australia, standards in Britain itself were still far from ideal with over 12,000 children still resident in large children's institutions. 'It is probable that conditions in a large number of voluntary Homes in this country vary very little from those described in Australia.' The chairman of the Board, Commander Allan Noble, one of the leading spokesmen for its criticisms of the Ross report, was also a Conservative member of the government, MP for Chelsea and Parliamentary Under-Secretary for Commonwealth Relations.

92 Telegram Commonwealth Relations Office to Office of the UK High Commissioner, Canberra, 6 June 1956, DO35/1381.

93 This point had recently been made to the Commonwealth Relations Office by the chair of the Overseas Migration Board who noted their disappointment that the report would fail to achieve what they hoped it would in terms of easing the doubts of local authorities in the United Kingdom 'as to whether they would be morally justified' in allowing children in their care to be migrated to Australia. The Board's plan of weakening its recommendations by 'finding as much fault with the report as possible, so as to provide a sort of counter-irritant' was risky though given their self-acknowledged lack

of understanding of current child-care standards and direct evidence of provision in Australian (Letter from Commander Noble, Chairman of the Overseas Migration Board to Commonwealth Relations Office, 4 June 1956, DO35/1381 (NA)).

94 Confidential internal notes attached to draft telegram from the Commonwealth Relations Office to Office of the UK High Commissioner, Canberra, 6 June 1956, DO35/1381.

95 Memo from Shannon to Sir Saville Garner, 9 June 1956, DO35/1381.

96 Memo from Shannon to Smedley, 11 June 1956, DO35/1381.

97 Telegram from Commonwealth Relations Office to Office of the UK High Commissioner in Australia, 12 June 1956, DO35/1381.

98 Memo Joyce to Cockram, 27 July 1956, DO35/1381. Particular concern was raised that press interest might expose differences in opinion on the report between the Home Office and Commonwealth Relations Office.

99 Letter from Ross to Shannon, 5 July 1956, BN29/1325.

100 Letter from Costley-White to Whittick, 9 June 1956, DO35/1381 (NA).

101 Letter from Whittick to Costley-White, 15 June 1956, DO35/1381 (NA).

102 Home Office staff had been optimistic in late June that the Commonwealth Relations Office would indeed opt for a temporary suspension of approval of child migration applications (Memo from Whittick to Munro, 23 June 1956, BN29/1325). This possibility had also been encouraged by the willingness of the Australian authorities to contemplate a short-term, informal suspension (caused by 'administrative' delays in the approval process) to give them enough time to be seen to be doing something in response to the content of the Ross report (Telegram from Office of the UK High Commissioner, Canberra to Commonwealth Relations Office, 25 June 1956, BN29/1325 (NA)).

103 Letter from Ross to Shannon, 28 June 1956, BN29/1325.

104 Telegram from Office of the UK High Commissioner, Canberra to Commonwealth Relations Office, 5 July 1956.

105 The Commonwealth Relations Office had again been urging the UK High Commissioner's Office to press the Australian government to take some initiative on the residential institutions, just two days before the Australian government proposed its own review (Telegram from the Commonwealth Relations Office to the UK High Commissioner's Office, Canberra, 3 July 1956, BN29/1325 (NA)).

106 Telegram from Commonwealth Relations Office to the Office of the UK High Commissioner, Canberra, 6 July 1956, BN29/1325.

107 Telegram from Commonwealth Relations Office to the Office of the UK High Commissioner, Canberra, 13 July 1956, BN29/1325.

108 Letter from Gwynn to Shannon, 12 July 1956, BN29/1325 (NA); see also Home Office minute 10 July 1956, BN29/1325 (NA).

109 Permission had already been given to another child migrant, WL, to be sent to Dhurringile even though it been one of the institutions put up for blacklisting by Ross. This was done on the flimsy grounds that despite the problems at Dhurringile, which it was hoped would be rectified at some point, it was better for WL to be placed there with other children sharing his national and religious background than at another institution where he wouldn't have this in common with others (Letter from Munro to Costley-White, 22 June 1956, BN29/1325 (NA)).

110 Dodds-Parker's wife, Lady Aileen, would later become chairman of the Fairbridge Society.

111 It is not clear how quickly and how much information about the Fact-Finding Mission's report had been passed on to the Fairbridge Society, though it is striking in this context that the Society had already made numerous enquiries about its content by mid-April. Lady Bessborough, a member of the Overseas Migration Board, who had personal links to a child migration organization had also unsuccessfully requested in May that detailed information (i.e. the confidential appendices) be provided to the Board about criticisms made of specific schools (Memo from CRW to Shannon, 25 May 1956, DO35/1381).

112 Note from A. D. Dodds-Parker MP to Home Secretary, no date, DO35/1381 (NA).

113 Private, brief typed notes from Rouse on each institution are recorded in BN29/1325 (NA).

114 Rouse, note on Fairbridge Farm School, Pinjarra, visited 20 July 1956, BN29/1325 (NA).

115 Rouse, note on Clontarf Boys' Town, Perth, visited 20 July 1956, BN29/1325 (NA).

116 Rouse note on Clontarf.

117 Letter from Bunting, Prime Minister's Department, Canberra to Tory, Office of the UK High Commissioner, 10 September 1956, BN29/1325 (NA).

118 Report by R. H. Wheeler, Assistant Secretary, Department of Immigration, Canberra, and G. C. Smith, Director of Social Services Department, Tasmania, on St John Bosco Boys' Town, BN29/1325 (NA).

119 Report by R. H. Wheeler, Assistant Secretary, Department of Immigration, Canberra, and J. V. Wilson, Director, Children's Services Department, Victoria on Dhurringile Rural Training Farm, BN29/1325 (NA).

120 Report by R. H. Wheeler, Assistant Secretary, Department of Immigration, Canberra, and J. McCall, Director, Child Welfare Department, Western Australia, BN29/1325 (NA).

121 Rouse report on Dhurringile Rural Training Farm, BN29/1325 (NA).

122 Rouse report on St John Bosco Boys' Town, Hobart, BN29/1325 (NA).

123 Rouse report on St Joseph's Farm School, Bindoon, Western Australia, BN29/1325 (NA).

124 Letter from Bunting, Prime Minister's Department, Canberra to Tory, Office of the UK High Commissioner, 10 September 1956, BN29/1325 (NA).

125 Letter from Fraser, Office of the UK High Commissioner, to Johnson, Commonwealth Relations Officer, 20 September 1956, BN29/1325 (NA).

126 Letter from Gibson to Whittick, 23 November 1956, BN29/1325 (NA).

127 Draft letter from Whittick to Gibson, unsent, BN29/1325 (NA).

128 Home Office minutes, 27 November and 5 December 1956, BN29/1325.

129 Home Office minutes, 5 December.

130 See Paul, 'Changing Childhoods', pp. 134–6.

131 Fairbridge Society brochure, D296/F1 (L); Hill, *Forgotten Children*, pp. 283–4.

132 It is not clear whether this policy was followed consistently by child migration organizations in subsequent years. No other child migration organization mentioned this policy in their records at this point.

133 *Church of England Council for Commonwealth and Empire Settlement Report for the 12 Months*, from 1 April 1957 to 31 March 1958, CECES-2-CA1250 (CE), p. 4.

134 There were also some instances of children being placed out through public selection meetings at Canadian distribution homes, see Phyllis Harrison (ed.), *The Home Children: Their Personal Stories* (Winnipeg: Gordon Shillingford Publishing, 2003), p. 34.

135 See, for example, Miriam Langsam, *Children West* (Madison: University of Wisconsin Press, 1964), p. 25. On the very limited role of the federal government in relation to child-care policies into the early twentieth century, see Michael Katz, *In the Shadow of the Poor House: A Social History of Welfare in America* (New York: Basic Books, 1996), p. 124.

136 Former child migrants who provided witness statements to module 2 of the Historical Institutional Abuse Inquiry in Northern Ireland frequently noted the lack of individual supervision meetings with welfare officials from the Australian states formally responsible for their care. Such meetings, they recalled, only took place at the point where they left institutional care or they ceased to be wards of the state. The witness statement and evidence relating to HIA358 is unusual in providing a case where there were active attempts to monitor his individual progress from Britain after he was sent to Dhurringile. This was because he was sent by a local authority in Northern Ireland who took a far more pro-active approach than did the voluntary organizations reviewed by the inquiry in checking individual children's welfare after migration.

137 See, for example, Interview with Len Magee, Forgotten Australians and Former Child Migrants Oral History Project, National Library of Australia, 2012, 1:38:00–1:46:01, on the contrasting perspectives of different 'generations' of child migrants to the Fairbridge Farm School at Molong.

138 Strikingly, again, though, this principle of using local residential care rather than child migration schemes for Catholic children in New York did not carry over to Boston, where the Home for Destitute Catholic Children ran its own emigration programme.

Chapter 4

1 'Mrs Chapman Has Asked the Queen for Help', *Evening News*, 14 March 1951; 'All in Village Aid a Child', *Evening Standard*, 16 March 1951; 'Girl Pined for Home', *The Star*, 15 March 1951.

2 See, for example, Letter to Mrs Bayliff, displayed in *On Their Own* exhibition curated by Australian National Maritime Museum and V&A Museum of Childhood, London, October 2015.

3 'The Drama of a Child – the Queen Intervenes', *Melbourne Argus*, 10 March 1951, p. 1.

4 'I Love Both My Mummies, Says Marcelle', *Melbourne Argus,* 12 March 1951, p. 1.

5 www.smh.com.au/national/i-can-still-hear-the-kids-screams-20110611–1fyap. html.

6 See, for example, Gail Corbett, *Nation Builders: Barnardo Children in Canada* (Toronto: Dundurn Press, 1997), pp. 99–105.

7 See *A Report to the Right Honourable the President of the Local Government Board by Andrew Doyle, Esq., Local Government Inspector, as to the Emigration of Pauper Children to Canada* (Doyle report, House of Commons, London, 1875), p. 11; *Report to the Secretary of State for the Colonies, President of the Oversea Settlement Committee, from the Delegation Appointed to Obtain Information Regarding the System of Child Migration and Settlement in Canada* (Bondfield Report) (London: HMSO, 1924), p. 4

8 See, for example, positive recollections of child migrants of placements with families in Canada in Phyllis Harrison (ed.), *The Home Children: Their Personal Stories* (Winnipeg: Gordon Shillingford, 2003), pp. 35, 79–83, 87, 98, 106, 110, 118, 130, 131, 145, 152, 172, 178. The precarious nature of placements, however, meant that these positive experiences could be shortlived if the placement family experienced ill-health, death, financial misfortune or moved away to a different region.

9 See report on E. T., June 1894, M189/7/4/2/92 (TT); see also report on F. V., May 1894, M189/7/4/2/95 (TT).

10 *The Orphan Trains*, dir. Janet Graham and Edward Gray, 1995.

11 See, for example, David Hill, *The Forgotten Children: Fairbridge Farm School and Its Betrayal of Britain's Child Migrants to Australia* (North Sydney: William Heinemann, 2008), pp. 297–8.

12 See, for example, Jacob Riis, *How the Other Half Lives* (New York: Charles Scribner & Sons, 1890); Joy Parr, *Labouring Children: British Immigrant Apprentices to Canada, 1869–1924*, 2nd ed. (Toronto: University of Toronto Press, 1994), pp. 14–26; Anna Davin, *Growing Up Poor: Home, School and Street in London, 1870–1914* (London: Rivers Oram Press, 1996), pp. 21–6; Lydia Murdoch, *Imagined Orphans: Poor Families, Child Welfare and Contested Citizenship in London* (New Brunswick, NJ: Rutgers University Press, 2006), pp. 67–91; Sarah Wise, *The Blackest Streets: The Life and Death of a Victorian Slum* (London: Vintage, 2009).

13 See, for example, Murdoch, *Imagined Orphans*, pp. 92–119, on ways in which parents from low-income families sought to stay actively involved in the lives of children whom they had had to give over into institutional care.

14 William Quarrier, *A Narrative of Facts Relative to Work Done for Christ in Connection with the Orphan and Destitute Children's Emigration Homes* (Scotland: Glasgow, 1873), p. 13.

15 See, for example, Hill, *Forgotten Children*, pp. 1–16.

16 An important but relatively under-studied part of the history of these child migration schemes is the active role played by local agents of child migration organizations in persuading parents struggling with poverty to give over their children to migration schemes. The fact that some migration schemes recruited children from particular local areas in which agents were particularly active, such as Cheltenham or Newcastle in the United Kingdom, indicates the importance of such influence. I am grateful to both Ian Thwaites and Roy Parker for pointing these patterns out to me.

17 See, for example, John Lane, *Fairbridge Kid* (South Fremantle: Fremantle Arts Centre Press, 1990), in which he describes his experience of being happily placed with foster carers by Barnardo's but then subsequently removed from them to be sent to Fairbridge, Pinjarra. See also witness statements HIA358 and HIA326, Historical Institutional Abuse Inquiry, Northern Ireland.

18 See, for example, the one- and two-parent schemes introduced by the
    Fairbridge Society (see, e.g., the Fairbridge Society, publicity brochure, no
    date, D296.F1 (L)).
19 Unclear memories of early, disrupted childhood are illustrated in a letter
    sent by a former child migrant to the Manchester and Salford Boys'
    and Girls' Refuges and Homes asking for them to help him trace family
    members back in the United Kingdom, which they did (see letter from A.
    V., M189/7/5/1 (TT)). In the letter, he writes 'my dear mother I don't know
    her name any more than mother but I love her all the same and would like
    to see her again'. His mother had in fact died in his early infancy before he
    entered the children's home in Manchester, and the person he may have been
    remembering as his mother was in fact an unrelated couple with whom he
    and his siblings lodged for a period of time.
20 See, for example, Peter Harding, *Apology Accepted: A 1950s Kid from
    Fairbridge* (Big Thumb Publishing, Kindle Edition, 2014) in which the main
    reprieve from institutional life, and the abuse of his cottage mother, was a
    fortnight's holiday camp at a seaside resort away from Fairbridge, Pinjarra.
21 Parr's (*Labouring Children*, p. 131) analysis of her sample of children sent
    to Canada by Dr Barnardo's Homes indicated that only 15.8 per cent of
    the boys went on to own their own farmland by their mid-thirties or 4.1
    per cent had entered professional jobs by the same age. On cases of former
    child migrants to Canada being able to buy their own land, see, for example,
    Harrison, *Home Children*, pp. 28, 37.
22 On both variations in understandings of well-being and more fundamental,
    existential aspects of well-being see Michael Jackson, *Life within Limits:
    Well-Being in a World of Want* (Durham, NC: Duke University Press, 2011),
    and Michael Jackson, *The Politics of Story-Telling: Variations on a Theme
    by Hannah Arendt*, 2nd ed. (Copenhagen: Museum Musculunam Press,
    2013).
23 See also Daniel Miller, *Material Culture and Mass Consumption* (Oxford:
    Blackwell, 1987), on the ways in which the experience of human subjectivity,
    possibilities and desire is always framed in relation to shifting material
    cultures.
24 See Johanna Sköld, 'Historical Abuse: A Contemporary Issue – Compiling
    Inquiries into Abuse and Neglect of Children in Out-of-Home Care
    Worldwide', *Journal of Scandinavian Studies in Criminology and Crime
    Prevention*, 14.1 (2013).
25 For examples of child migrants' memories of treatment that showed no
    insight into their emotional lives, see, for example, Harrison, *Home Children*,
    pp. 77, 105, 133; also Philip Bean and Joy Melville, *Lost Children of the
    Empire* (London: Unwin Hyman, 1989), pp. 15, 121.
26 Letter from L. R. to Mrs Wallace; see also letter from employer re L. R.,
    M189/7/4/3/68 (TT). On other examples of child migrants' loneliness, see,
    for example, Harrison, *Home Children*, pp. 90, 153, 169, 181; also Bean and
    Melville, *Lost Children*, pp. 23, 122.
27 Letter from S. S., M189/7/4/3/77 (TT). Such letters contrast with those
    who were placed closed to family members, and who expressed gratitude
    for this (see, e.g. letter from J. N. to Mrs Shaw, M189/7/2/4/103, (TT)).
    Plaintive requests to see family members did also sometimes translate

into opportunities to visit them, see Letter from S. W. to Mrs Wallace, M189/7/4/3/97 (TT) in which S. W. makes an emotional request to see her sister, with a meeting between them then recorded in her sister's case file (M189/7/4/3/96, (TT)).

28 Letter from R. W., M189/7/4/2/99 (TT); see also, for example, letter from S. S. to Mrs Shaw, in which S. S. expresses her distress and anger at Mrs Shaw not having replied to one of her previous letters, M189/7/4/3/83 (TT).

29 See, for example, O'Connor, *Orphan Trains*, p. 144.

30 HIA273 witness statement, Historical Institutional Abuse Inquiry, Northern Ireland. On memories of separation from siblings on migration to Canada, see, for example, Harrison, *Home Children*, p. 35, 56, 92.

31 Lee Nailing, *The Orphan Trains*, PBS documentary, dir. Janet Graham and Edward Gray, 1995, 0:18:45–0:19:59.

32 Len Magee in *The Long Journey Home,* dir. Emily Booker, prod. Emily Booker and David Hill, 2009.

33 Matthew A. Crenson, *Building the Invisible Orphanage: A Prehistory of the American Welfare System* (Cambridge, MA: Harvard University Press, 1998), p. 221. See similar accounts of lack of emotional warmth in some child migrants' placements in Harrison, *Home Children*, pp. 18, 70.

34 *Report to the Secretary of State for the Colonies, President of the Oversea Settlement Committee, from the Delegation Appointed to Obtain Information Regarding the System of Child Migration and Settlement in Canada* (Bondfield Report) (London: HMSO, 1924), p. 12. Similar stories of social or symbolic exclusion within placements are also given in Corbett, *Nation Builders*, p. 90, Harrison, *Home Children*, pp. 58, 66, 95, 159, and Bean and Melville, *Lost Children*, pp. 3, 129.

35 Parr, *Labouring Children* (p. 104), notes that children who repeatedly wet their beds were over-represented among those returned by employers within her sample of children placed out in Canada by Dr Barnardo's Homes. Relatively happy placements could also break down for unexpected reasons as well. In the case of 'Dot' noted earlier, her placement with an affectionate couple broke down when their house burnt down and the couple returned her to the distribution home because they did not believe they could continue to offer suitable care in their straightened circumstances (M189/7/4/2/92, (TT)). See also letter from employer re W. U. where W. U. was returned because of illness in the employing household, M189/7/5/1 (TT).

36 Letter from employer to Mrs Wallace re S. W., M189/7/4/2/100 (TT).

37 Harrison, *The Home Children*, pp. 20, 35, 58, 91, 95, 103, 106, 108–9, 169; Bean and Melville, *Lost Children*, pp. 15, 117, 125, 129; also Anna Magnusson, *The Quarriers Story* (Edinburgh: Birlinn, 2006), p. 89. On failure to make agreed or reasonable pay on placements, see, for example, Harrison, pp. 59, 144, 152, 157, 171. Some children recalled everyday items given to them by employers – even a pair of socks given as a Christmas present – subsequently being deducted from their wages (Harrison, *Home Children*, p. 59).

38 Corbett, *Nation Builders*, p. 97.

39 Again this contrasts with cases where children were successfully able to learn the work expected of them, (see, e.g. Letter from S. S. to Mrs Shaw, M189/7/4/3/83, (TT)).

40 Letter from employer re A. S., M189/7/4/2/88. See also an employer complaint about E. B. being 'too young and small', Dr Barnardo's Homes register, E1897/98, p. 32 (B); Harrison, *Home Children*, p. 158.

41 Employers were not therefore always sympathetic to the fact that children had already had disrupted early lives which might be demonstrated in challenging behaviour. As one wrote of a girl placed with her, 'she persists in habits and actions that might be excused in a small child' (report on E.W., M189/7/4/2/105 (TT)). See also Harrison, *Home Children*, p. 37.

42 J. C. (born 29 January 1892), Marchmont LON record book, 1902/03 (B).

43 Letter from employer re A. V., M189/7/5/1 (TT).

44 See Parr, *Labouring Children*, pp. 94–6.

45 'Farmer Censured – Harsh and Cowardly Treatment of Immigrant Boy', *Evening Telegraph*, St John's Newfoundland, 10 January 1924.

46 See 'A Barnardo Boy – Investigation into the Cause of His Death', *Daily Mail and Empire*, 21 November 1895; 'The Barnardo Boy – Miss Findlay Sent for Trial for Manslaughter', *Daily Mail and Empire*, 22 November 1895.

47 Kenneth Bagnell, *The Little Immigrants: The Orphans Who Came to Canada* (Toronto: Dundurn Group, 2001), loc.738–818. This followed a wider pattern of criminal cases of abuse and neglect of child migrants to Canada generally not resulting in convictions, see Roy Parker, *Uprooted: The Shipment of Poor Children to Canada, 1867–1917* (Bristol: Policy Press, 2010), pp. 221–7.

48 Not all cases of abuse known to organizations received wider media attention. Ellen Boucher (*Empire's Children: Child Emigration, Welfare, and the Decline of the British World, 1869–1967* (Cambridge: Cambridge University Press, 2014), pp. 23–4) notes the case of a boy returned from Canada to Britain by Dr Barnardo's Homes who had run away from his placement because of ill-treatment and hidden under a barn on the farm over-night where he contracted frost-bite. The boys' legs subsequently had to be amputated and he returned to Britain for further medical treatment. This case was not formally discussed in any management meeting at Dr Barnardo's Homes and was not covered by any newspaper.

49 See, for example, Harding, *Apology Accepted*; HIA295 witness statement, Historical Institutional Abuse Inquiry, Northern Ireland.

50 Parr, *Labouring Children*, pp. 108, 152. Suicides among child migrants were not limited to cases of abuse, however, but were also symptomatic of more general distress. On the crippling effects of sustained physical abuse of an 'orphan train rider', see the account by Elliott Hoffman Bobo of the case of an abused child migrant in his local community, *The Orphan Trains*, PBS documentary, dir. Janet Graham and Edward Gray, 1995, 0:33:25–0:34:41.

51 Doyle report, p. 30.

52 See, for example, C. M. who was removed from her placement by Dr Barnardo's Homes after she was found to have two black eyes from her employer, see C. M., Dr Barnardo's Homes records book, E1897/98 (B), p. 128; Parr, *Labouring Children* (pp. 105–6), notes that there was evidence of excessive punishment of 9 per cent of boys and 15 per cent of girls in the sample of child migrants in her study, and suggests that actual prevalence was likely to be higher than this. For a useful discussion of the complexities of judgements about what constituted appropriate physical punishment in the

late nineteenth and early twentieth centuries, see Anna Davin, *Growing Up Poor*, pp. 129–31.

53 J. S., Dr Barnardo's Homes record book, E1897/98 (B), p. 160.

54 On failures in the removal of children from placements in which they were at risk, see Parker, *Uprooted*, pp. 221–7.

55 E. A., Dr Barnardo's Homes record book, E1897/98 (B), p. 219. On child migrants' recollections of harsh beatings, exceeding normal standards of corporal punishment, see Harrison, *Home Children*, pp. 55, 58, 92, 94, 99–100, 109, 122, 158, 169; Corbett, *Nation Builders*, pp. 88, 98–9; Magnusson, *The Quarriers' Story*, p. 96; Bean and Melville, pp. 3, 11, 22–3, 116–18, 120, 122–4.

56 For example, HIA318's witness statement (Historical Institutional Abuse Inquiry, Northern Ireland) recalls an aggressive member of staff at Bindoon, in fear of whom children would wet themselves. Cultures of violence in residential institutions also involved violence between children. As HIA354's witness statement recalled, at Dhurringile 'older boys also beat us . . . but that is what the older boys did to the younger ones. I think it was part of growing up'. Child migrants at some residential institutions recalled that staff made their own physical implements for beating children, sometimes reinforced with metal (e.g. Bean and Melville, *Lost Children*, pp. 20–1). In a number of cases children were left with physical injuries, some persisting into adulthood such as children suffering hearing loss as a result of being beaten around the head.

57 HIA279 witness statement, Historical Institutional Abuse Inquiry, Northern Ireland.

58 Testimony from Ian Bayliff, *The Long Journey Home*, ABC documentary, dir. Emily Booker and David Hill, 2009.

59 HIA310 witness statement, Historical Institutional Abuse Inquiry, Northern Ireland.

60 HIA392 witness statement, Historical Institutional Abuse Inquiry, Northern Ireland. While experiences such as these are often publicly associated with institutions run by the Christian Brothers, they were not unique to them. See, for example, Ken Pound's recollection of physical and sexual abuse at the Church of England Padbury Boys' Farm, Forgotten Australians and Former Child Migrants oral history project interview, National Library of Australia.

61 HIA308 witness statement, Historical Institutional Abuse Inquiry, Northern Ireland.

62 See, for example, UK Parliamentary Health Select Committee, *Third Report*, para 51. See also Harrison, *Home Children*, pp. 92–3; Bean and Melville, pp. 21, 23–4, 118, 130–1, 146.

63 See Royal Commission into Institutional Responses to Child Sexual Abuse, Public Hearing – Case Study 11 (Day WA13).

64 See Submission to the Historical Institutional Abuse Inquiry by Dr Margaret Humphreys, 1 September 2014, 3.9.

65 See, for example, report on E. W., M189/7/4/2/105 (TT). On sexual abuse and rape in relation to child migrants to Canada, see also Parker, *Uprooted*, pp. 227–30; Parr, *Labouring Children*, pp. 115–17.

66 HIA333 witness statement, Historical Institutional Abuse Inquiry, Northern Ireland.

67 HIA288 witness statement, Historical Institutional Abuse Inquiry, Northern Ireland.

68 HIA346 witness statement, Historical Institutional Abuse Inquiry, Northern Ireland.

69 See, for example, Parker, *Uprooted*, pp. 232–3.

70 HIA273 witness statement, Historical Institutional Abuse Inquiry, Northern Ireland. This sense of displacement continued for many former child migrants to Australia who found that when they eventually traced families back in the United Kingdom – including their mothers – their experience of family reunions were difficult and did not repair their sense of loss of family life (see, for example, witness statements HIA285, HIA295, HIA305, HIA306 and HIA308, Historical Institutional Abuse Inquiry, Northern Ireland).

71 Former child migrant, Norman Johnston, cited in UK Parliamentary Health Select Committee, *Third Report*, para 67.

72 See, for example, Stephen Pattison, *Shame: Theory, Therapy, Theology* (Cambridge: Cambridge University Press, 2000).

73 See, for example, Miriam Langsam, *Children West* (Madison: University of Wisconsin Press, 1964), pp. 56–7.

74 See, for example, Corbett, *Nation Builders*, pp. 60, 111; Magnusson, *The Quarriers Story*, p. 100; Harrison, *Home Children*, pp. 38, 51, 67, 123, 134, 161–2. One child migrant sent to a French-speaking community in Canada recalled the shame of being labelled an 'immigré d'Angleterre' (Harrison, *Home Children*, p. 40).

75 See also former child migrants' accounts of feeling stigmatized in local community schools they attended in Hill, *Forgotten Children*, pp. 203–4.

76 HIA303 witness statement, Historical Institutional Abuse Inquiry, Northern Ireland.

77 HIA306 witness statement, Historical Institutional Abuse Inquiry, Northern Ireland.

78 Royal Commission into Institutional Responses to the Sexual Abuse of Children, Case Study 11, Transcript Day WA13, WA1529.

79 HIA303 witness statement, Historical Institutional Abuse Inquiry, Northern Ireland. As the confidential appendix by the Ross Fact-Finding Mission had noted, children who wet the bed at Bindoon were made to sleep separately on a concrete veranda with little effective protection against the weather. Memories of beatings and public humiliation for bed-wetting form many of the main traumatic memories in Peter Harding's memoir, *Apology Accepted*. See also Bean and Melville, *Lost Children*, pp. 122–4.

80 On the shameful experience of eating poor food in the presence of staff eating better meals, see also Royal Commission into Institutional Responses to the Sexual Abuse of Children, Case Study 11, Transcript Day WA13, WA1537.

81 The classed nature of assumptions about children's futures is illustrated by the contrast between the Fairbridge Memorial College in Southern Rhodesia which sought to attract primarily middle-class children for future roles in colonial leadership with the Fairbridge farm schools in Australia and Canada which sought to produce a new generation of 'farmers and farmer's wives'. Some differences are also notable in the United States, where, for example, the New York Children's Aid Society openly celebrated those sent out through its emigration programme who had gone on to have prominent public lives

(see, e.g. the letter from a former orphan train rider, 'On the staff of the Governor', *New York Children's Aid Society Fiftieth Annual Report*, 1902, pp. 132–24; see also Stephen O'Connor, *Orphan Trains: The Story of Charles Loring Brace and the Children He Saved and Failed* (Chicago: University of Chicago Press, 2001), pp. 177–202.

82 See, for example, Harrison, *Home Children*, pp. 19, 29, 67, 74, 77, 92, 103, 109, 117, 122, 131, 139; Bean and Melville, *Lost Children*, pp. 6, 127–8, 150. Concerns about whether British child migrants to Canada received the same degree of schooling as if they had remained in Britain were often voiced while the schemes were in operation (see, e.g. Parr, *Labouring Children*, pp. 108–10). In 1883, an editorial in the Glasgow Herald asked to know 'what is done for the very young children who are sent out – whether they receive the education which they would be compelled to receive in this country if they remained here; whether at the most tender years they are not hired out to struggling farmers; whether they are treated with ordinary fairness, not to speak of ordinary humanity?' (Magnusson, *The Quarriers Story*, p. 97). One British child migrant placed in a French-speaking community recalled that attending school was of no benefit to him because all the lessons were in French (Harrison, *Home Children*, p. 40). For a more detailed analysis of the educational opportunities of children placed in rural areas of Canada, see Parker, *Uprooted*, pp. 143–9.

83 See Hill, *Forgotten Children*, pp. 186–207; as some former Fairbridge residents have noted, there was an irony that they experienced very limited educational opportunities and expectation of them in Australia despite the fact that IQ screening had been used to ensure that only children graded as having average or above average intelligence would be sent to Australia. On other recollections of blocked educational opportunities see also HIA305 witness statement, Historical Institutional Abuse Inquiry, Northern Ireland.

84 Examples of this include one former child migrant to Canada who used his disappointment at the lack of educational opportunities he received to work as an adult to create the first high school in his village (Harrison, *Home Children*, p. 19).

85 See, for example, account by Hazelle Latimer rejecting her placement in *The Orphan Trains*, PBS documentary, dir. Janet Graham and Edward Gray, 1995, 0:27:25–0:29:28.

86 See, for example, employer's letter about M. T., M189/7/4/2/92, (TT); also Harrison, *Home Children*, pp. 22, 27.

87 See, for example, Harrison, *Home Children*, pp. 40, 52.

88 Supervision report on A. W., M189/7/4/2/96 (TT).

89 See, for example, O'Connor, *Orphan Trains*, pp. 216–19

90 In *Apology Accepted*, for example, Peter Harding recalls an occasion in which he and a friend absconded from Fairbridge Pinjarra during a recreation day so that they could visit his friend's girlfriend in another town. Their terror at being caught marked the experience so much that they never attempted it again.

91 Hazelle Latimer, *The Orphan Trains*, dir. Janet Graham and Edward Gray, 1995, 0:14:18–46.

92 HIA278 witness statement, Historical Institutional Abuse Inquiry, Northern Ireland.

93 HIA322 witness statement, Historical Institutional Abuse Inquiry, Northern
    Ireland.
94 See, for example, Humphreys, *Oranges and Sunshine* (London: Corgi, 2011),
    pp. 365–9 for an illustrative case of a parent whose attempts to reclaim
    their child from Australia after the child had been sent there without their
    knowledge were obstructed by the sending organization. The sense of loss
    of agency for former child migrants who realized that their parents had
    given little or no consent to them being sent to Australia contrasts strongly
    with stories of older child migrants who actively chose migration who had a
    greater sense of control over this decision (see, e.g. Harrison, *Home Children*,
    pp. 37, 143).
95 This use of children's labour needs to be understood in the wider social
    context in which the late nineteenth and early twentieth centuries child
    migration schemes operated, where the expectation that children would be
    kept from labour and adult social realities was reserved for the middle and
    upper classes, and working-class children would more commonly be expected
    to make some of kind of contribution to the household economy through
    their own income or other unpaid work for the family (see, e.g. Anna Davin,
    'When Is a Child Not a Child?', in Helen Corr and Lynn Jamieson (eds),
    Politics of Everyday Life: Continuity and Change in Work and the Family
    (Basingstoke: MacMillan, 1990), pp. 37–61; Karin Calvert, *Children in
    the House: The Material Culture of Early Childhood, 1600–1900* (Boston:
    Northeastern University Press, 1992); Parr, *Labouring Children*, pp. 14–26.
96 For accounts by former child migrants to Canada about shortcomings in the
    supervision of their placements, see Harrison, *Home Children*, pp. 55, 124–6,
    133; Bean and Melville, *Lost Children*, pp. 8, 25.
97 See Anthony Rouse, private note on visit to St Joseph's Farm School, Bindoon,
    BN29/1325 (NA). See also the criticism of inadequate supervision structures
    in UK Parliamentary Health Select Committee, Third Report, para 47. In a
    submission to the Australian Royal Commission into Institutional Responses
    to Child Sexual Abuse (Case Study 11, Transcript Day WA13, WA1514), the
    children's services department for the State of Western Australia has argued
    that legislation at that time only allowed the State to undertake discretionary
    rather than mandatory inspections of institutions to which child migrants
    were sent.
98 The emphasis on the inhumanity of childhood suffering and the
    humanitarian injunction to intervene to relieve this was pervasive, even
    across organizations that had specific religious rationales for their work,
    such as safeguarding Catholic faith. In a Lenten pastoral letter of 1899, for
    example, the Archbishop of Westminster, Cardinal Vaughan, wrote that 'a
    vigorous expansion must be given to the rescue branch of our work. Only
    thus can pastor and people escape the guilt of the inhumanity and impiety
    of allowing thousands of orphans and destitute children, either to be
    robbed of the priceless treasure of their Faith, or to be accounted as human
    refuse' (Jim Hyland, *Changing Times, Changing Needs: A History of the
    Catholic Children's Society (Westminster)* (London: CCS Westminster,
    2009), p. 24).
99 See, for example, Didier Fassin, *Humanitarian Reason* (Berkeley: University
    of California Press, 2012).

100 New York Children's Aid Society, *The Crusade for Children*, p. 4.

101 John Urquhart, *The Life Story of William Quarrier: A Boy's Resolve and What Became of It* (London: Partridge, 1900). Another biographer wrote of Quarrier: 'His faith removed mountains, and triumphed over obstacles and difficulties which seemed to human eyes insurmountable. The work he initiated is still carried on in the spirit of its founder, and it can only be fully understood in the light of his career' (Alexander Gammie, *A Romance of Faith: The Story of the Orphan Homes of Scotland and the Founder William Quarrier* (London: Pickering & Inglis, 1951), p. 10).

102 From Leo Amery's preface, *The Autobiography of Kingsley Fairbridge* (London: Oxford University Press, 1927), pp. viii–ix.

103 For example, in lists of gifts made by individual donors, examples of which can be found in the *Little Wanderers Advocate*, 1865, p. 128; *Narrative of Facts*, 1890, pp. 3–15;

104 *The Little Wanderers' Advocate*, 1866, pp. 6–7.

105 Crusade of Rescue, *3rd Annual Report*, 1890, p. 13.

106 *The Little Wanderers' Advocate*, 1865, p. 101.

107 *The Little Wanderers' Advocate*, 1865, p. 28.

108 *The Children's Haven*, July 1898, p. 14 (TT).

109 *New York Children's Aid Society 20th Annual Report*, 1872 (NY), p. 10.

110 Crusade of Rescue, *27th Annual Report*, 1914, p. 66.

111 See, for example, colour illustrations passim in *The Young Helpers League Magazine*, 1901 (B).

112 See, for example, *Narrative of Facts*, 1873, p. 2. A variant of this was the use, by the New York Children's Aid Society, of photographs of their most successful cases – boys from the emigration programme who had gone on to reputable careers in the professions or public service (see, e.g. New York Children's Aid Society, *Fiftieth Annual Report*, 1902, p. 133 (NY)). On criticisms of Barnardo's use of highly staged before and after photographs, see Seth Koven, *Slumming: Sexual and Social Politics in Victorian London* (Princeton, NJ: Princeton University Press, 2004), pp. 112–24.

113 On the reverse side of promotional photographs taken for the Fairbridge Society, credit stamps can be seen for commercial photographic agencies based in Fleet Street, in London, who also produced images of parties of child migrants for national newspapers.

114 See, for example, the printing of hymns passim in *The Little Wanderers' Advocate* (SC). An illustration of a party of child migrants performing hymns at Dr Barnardo's Homes' annual public meeting in London in June, 1893, is printed in *Night and Day*, November 1893 (B), p. 43.

115 *Narrative of Facts*, 1873, p. 14. The same hymn is also reproduced in *The Little Wanderers' Advocate*, 1866 (SC), p. 14.

116 Charles Loring Brace, *The Dangerous Classes of New York and Twenty Years' Work Among Them*, 3rd ed. (New York: Wynkoop & Hallenbeck, 1880), p. 442.

117 See Hill, *Forgotten Children*, pp. 194–202.

118 See, for example, brochure from mid-1950s for Fairbridge Farm School, Molong, New South Wales, D296.F1.18 (F).

119 UK Parliamentary Health Select Committee, *Third Report*, paras 61, 62, 73. These claims were treated with considerable scepticism by the committee.

120 Departmental note, Commonwealth Relations Office, 19 April 1956, BN29/1325 (NA).
121 Bagnell, *The Little Immigrants*, loc.628.
122 See, for example, statement by Sr Brenda to Historical Institutional Abuse Inquiry, Northern Ireland, day 49.
123 The history of the Fairbridge Society provides several examples of conflicting opinions between the London office and local management committees in Western Australia and New South Wales. However, despite these differences, for example over matters of staffing, there was sufficient trust that all parties were engaged in beneficial work for children for the organization to operate.
124 B. Coldrey, *The Scheme: The Christian Brothers and Childcare in Western Australia*, ed. O'Connor (Washington,: Argyle Pacific, 1993), p. 242.
125 Quarriers, *Narrative of Facts*, 1872, p. 11.
126 Magnusson, *The Quarriers Story*, p. 85.
127 Making children aware of God's love for them was a central emphasis, for example, in Charles Loring Brace, *Short Sermons to News Boys* (New York: Charles Scribner, 1866). This was not always a consistent emphasis in the faith that child migration organizations sought to cultivate in children.
128 See, for example, notes of sermons preached by Kingsley Fairbridge to early groups of child migrants at Pinjarra, D296.A2 (L).
129 See, for example, in particular, Fassin, *Humanitarian Reason*, pp. 243–57.
130 Koven, *Slumming*.

Chapter 5

1 See Johanna Sköld and Shurlee Swain (eds), *Apologies and the Legacy of Abuse of Children in 'Care'* (Basingstoke: Palgrave MacMillan, 2015).
2 See, for example, Dominic LaCapra, *Writing History, Writing Trauma* (Baltimore, MD: Johns Hopkins University Press, 2001); Didier Fassin and Richard Rechtman, *The Empire of Trauma: An Inquiry into the Condition of Victimhood* (Princeton, NJ: Princeton University Press, 2009).
3 For a discussion of child abuse inquiries, redress schemes and apologies in the context of notions of transitional justice, see Johanna Sköld, 'Apology Politics: Transnational Features', in Sköld and Swain (eds), *Apologies and the Legacy of Abuse of Children in 'Care'*, pp. 13–26.
4 See, for example, *Lost Innocents: Righting the Record on Child Migration Report* (Canberra: Parliament of Australia Senate, 2001), pp. 217–26.
5 See, for example, Melissa Nobles, *The Politics of Official Apologies* (Cambridge: Cambridge University Press, 2008); Danielle Celemajer, *Sins of the Fathers and the Ritual of Apologies* (Cambridge: Cambridge University Press, 2009).
6 This raises wider questions about why far fewer public apologies have been performed in the United States compared, for example, to Australia or Ireland. In addition to broader political, legal and cultural factors, more benign memories of the American 'orphan trains' may, in part, reflect the particular ways in which memories of the American schemes have been transmitted. The major collection of life-stories of former American 'orphan

train riders' (Mary Ellen Johnson (ed.), *Orphan Train Riders: Their Own Stories*, vols. 1–4 (Baltimore, MD: Gateway Press, 1997) contain relatively few accounts of traumatic experiences for children, but are produced primarily from material provided by children or other relatives of those migrated through these schemes. By contrast, Phyllis Harrison (ed.), *The Home Children: Their Personal Stories* (Winnipeg: Gordon Shillingford, 2003), which uses letters from former child migrants to Canada (who were likely to have experienced similar conditions to child migrants in the United States) contain far more accounts of neglect, exploitation and mistreatment. As contributors to Harrison's book themselves acknowledge, former child migrants were often unlikely to tell their spouses or children about traumatic experiences in childhood and often only spoke about these as stories of abuse became more publicly discussed.

7   Margaret Humphreys, *Empty Cradles* (London: Doubleday, 1994), pp. 32–7.
8   In its submission to the Historical Institutional Abuse Inquiry in Northern Ireland, the Child Migrants Trust noted that it had records of only one case in which an individual had received a custodial sentence for the abuse of child migrants (Historical Institutional Abuse Inquiry, module 2, transcript for Day 42, p. 130).
9   *Lost Innocents*, p. 221.
10 Royal Commission into Institutional Responses to Child Sexual Abuse, Public Hearing – Case Study 11, (Day WA13), WA1521.
11 Historical Institutional Abuse Inquiry, transcript for day 42, p. 130.
12 Patricia Carlson, oral history interview for Forgotten Australians and Former Child Migrants Oral History project, National Library of Australia, session 3, 01:21:30–01:22:40.
13 Dilys Budd, oral history interview for Forgotten Australians and Former Child Migrants Oral History project, National Library of Australia, session 4, 01:08:54–01:11;47.
14 Submission to the Royal Commission into Institutional Responses to Child Sex Abuse, Issues Paper no. 5 Civil Litigation, from David Hill, April 2014.
15 Ronald Niezen, *Truth and Indignation: Canada's Truth and Reconciliation Commission on Indian Residential Schools* (Toronto: University of Toronto Press, 2013). A specific example of this is the broad perception of the schools as places in which indigenous languages were forbidden, contradicted by some schools in which staff sought to use indigenous languages in their work with children.
16 As Danielle Celemajer observes, in *The Sins of the Nation and the Ritual of Apologies* (Cambridge: Cambridge University Press, 2009), symbolic acts of restitution are likely to be perceived as lacking legitimacy if they displace criminal or civil redress before those options have been exhausted or if victims of abuse have a strong sense of injustice about the harm committed by an individual perpetrator who has gone unpunished.
17 See, for example, Nell Musgrove, 'The Role and Importance of History', in Sköld and Swain (eds), *Apologies and the Legacy of Abuse of Children in 'Care'*, pp. 147–58.
18 Witness statement HIA333, Historical Insitutional Abuse Inquiry, Northern Ireland.

19 See, for example, the acknowledgement of historic suffering on Barnardo's website – http://www.barnardos.org.uk/what_we_do/our_history/working_with_former_barnardos_children-2013/child_migration.htm, downloaded 22 June 2015.
20 C-BERS Services ex-press newsletter, vol.1:1, December 1997.
21 Statement by Sr Brenda, Historical Institutional Abuse Inquiry, Northern Ireland, day 49.
22 See, for example, C-BERS Services ex-press newsletter, vol.1:1, December 1997.
23 https://en.wikipedia.org/wiki/Fairbridge_(charity) downloaded on 22 June 2015.

INDEX